Real Life in China at the Height of Empire

To Mike and Joyce
Something off the beaten track
David
December 2014

Real Life in China at the Height of Empire
Revealed by the Ghosts of Ji Xiaolan

Edited and Translated by
David E. Pollard

The Chinese University Press

Real Life in China at the Height of Empire:
Revealed by the Ghosts of Ji Xiaolan
    Edited and Translated by David E. Pollard

© The Chinese University of Hong Kong 2014

All rights reserved. No part of this publication may
be reproduced or transmitted in any form or by any
means, electronic or mechanical, including photocopying,
recording, or any information storage and retrieval
system, without permission in writing from
The Chinese University of Hong Kong.

ISBN: 978-962-996-601-0

The Chinese University Press
The Chinese University of Hong Kong
Sha Tin, N.T., Hong Kong
Fax: +852 2603 7355
E-mail: cup@cuhk.edu.hk
Website: www.chineseupress.com

Printed in Hong Kong

I will a round unvarnished tale deliver.

William Shakespeare

When I write of other people's affairs, I always set down what is told to me; whether it is false, factual, or less than the whole story, others are in a position to know, but I am not....

However, since I do endeavour to give a full and fair rendering, and try to impart some kind of positive moral—not, as so many similar works of the past, standing facts on their head, paying off personal scores, romancing about fine dandies and fair ladies, or catering to prurient interests—I hope that gentlemen of discernment will not think my work beneath their notice.

Ji Xiaolan

The stories the old folks in my village told were mysterious and scary, but quite spellbinding. In those stories there was no clear dividing line between living and dead people, neither was there one between animals and plants; even various objects like a broom, a human hair, or a tooth that had fallen out could, when the time was ripe, acquire supernatural powers.

Mo Yan, Nobel laureate in literature

Skeleton Chronology

Western Zhou dynasty	circa 11th century BC–771 BC
Eastern Zhou dynasty	770 BC–221 BC
Qin dynasty	221 BC–206 BC
Western Han dynasty	206 BC–AD 25
Eastern Han dynasty	25–220
Three Kingdoms (Wei, Shu and Wu)	220–280
Western Jin dynasty	265–316
Eastern Jin dynasty	317–420
Southern and Northern Dynasties	420–589
Sui dynasty	581–618
Tang dynasty	618–907
Five Dynasties	907–960
Northern Song dynasty	960–1127
Southern Song dynasty	1127–1279
Yuan (Mongol) dynasty	1279–1368
Ming dynasty	1368–1644
Qing (Manchu) dynasty	1644–1911

CONTENTS

List of Illustrations		ix
Introduction		xi
Illustrations		xxxiii

Part I: The Supernatural and the Curious

1	Spirits, Spectres and Demons	3
2	Ghosts	20
3	Hauntings	47
4	Foxes	52
5	Fortune-telling	68
6	Beyond Belief	87
7	Reincarnation	100
8	Curiosities	104
9	The Wild West	111

Part II: The Official's Milieu

10	Officialdom	123
11	Legal Dilemmas and Disputes	135
12	Yamen Staff	152
13	Servants	160

Part III: Family and Friends

14	Hearth and Home	175
15	Piety and Paragons	186

16	Love Pledged and Blighted	195
17	Friends and False Friends	210
18	Personal	217

Part IV: A Mirror on Society

19	Dogma and Dogmatists	225
20	Morality	239
21	Pedants	260
22	Women	264
23	Homosexuality	281
24	Impersonation	290
25	Fraud	296
26	Merchants	304
27	Bandits, Brigands and Robbers	309
28	Physical Prowess	320
29	Jesuits in China	325

LIST OF ILLUSTRATIONS

Figure 1.	Ji Xiaolan in official regalia.	xxxiii
Figure 2.	Emblem for Emperor Qianlong's imperial robe.	xxxiv
Figure 3.	Emblem for the court robe of first rank civil officials.	xxxv
Figure 4.	The layout of the imperial garden of Yuanmingyuan.	xxxvi
Figure 5.	A couplet in running hand by Ji Xiaolan.	xxxvii
Figure 6.	Ji Xiaolan's memorial to the throne in regular script.	xxxviii
Figure 7.	Finely crafted purple sand bamboo-shaped wrist rest and chestnut-shaped cup.	xxxix
Figure 8.	Translator tries to be friends with author's ghost in Ji Xiaolan's old Peking residence.	xl
Figure 9.	Luo Pin's big-headed ghost.	43
Figure 10.	Zhong Kui the Ghost Catcher by H. Y. Ting.	46
Figure 11.	Ferdinand Verbiest (1623–1688) and his *Map of the World*.	94
Figure 12.	A hairy savage.	113
Figure 13.	Xing Tian.	115
Figure 14.	Stage performances as depicted by the famous Qing painter Ju Chao.	295
Figure 15.	The Catholic Southern Church in Peking.	330

INTRODUCTION

It might seem perverse to represent a collection of short sketches that relate to the paranormal as revealing the "real life" of an era, as my title claims. The justification for that will gradually emerge. We need first to explain what kind of material we are dealing with, what kind of age gave rise to it, and what sort of a person the author was.

The Medium and Its Messages

The Chinese title of Ji Xiaolan's collection classes it as *biji*. That does not promise very exciting reading, because *biji* means something like "notes and jottings". In its broadest compass, *biji* literature may indeed be nothing more than that, odds and ends—comments on people and places, reflections on things at hand, animadversions on historical and scholarly matters. But more narrowly the reference is to *biji xiaoshuo*, short narratives or sketches centring on occurrences worthy of note. For such occurrences, isolated or linked together, to be worth recording, they must be unusual; in turn the unusual merges into the abnormal, and the abnormal into the paranormal or supernatural. Historically the genre of *biji xiaoshuo* has leaned in the last direction.

The early extant classics in the *biji* genre, written in the Six Dynasties [AD 420–589], included fable, exemplary tales and jokes, but were mostly about miraculous happenings, magical transformations, journeys down into hell and such like; since that was an age of turmoil when Buddhism and Taoism flourished and rationalistic Confucianism waned, nothing very different could be expected. In the succeeding dynasties *biji xiaoshuo* maintained a foothold, but in terms of narrative literature were eclipsed by more sophisticated, appetizing, this-world tales, complete with satisfying plots. Nevertheless *biji xiaoshuo* continued to serve scholarly tastes (they all used the classical language) for matters edifying, quirky, ingenious, erudite or witty.

To drastically curtail its history, *biji* literature saw its last flowering in Ji Xiaolan's lifetime, the eighteenth century. A considerable number of hefty collections by talented writers and eminent scholars were published then. Three authors stand out as having their works still in print, namely Pu Songling, Yuan Mei and Ji Yun, better known as Ji Xiaolan. All three have been translated into European and Asian languages. The first to be translated into English was Pu Songling, whose *Liaozhai zhiyi* was rendered in part by Herbert Giles under the title of *Strange Stories from a Chinese Studio* and first published in 1880, to a warm and lasting welcome. Less attention has been given to Ji Xiaolan's collection, though in China it has always been accorded comparable esteem, on different if no less worthy grounds. Before attempting to say where the difference lies, for convenience we have to give an English title to Ji Xiaolan's collection. It is made up of five separate volumes composed in his old age, between 1789 and 1798, later combined by his student Sheng Shiyan under the general title of *Yuewei caotang biji*. *Yuewei caotang* is simply the name of Ji's study, and so has no direct bearing on the contents, but as *yuewei* suggests the notion of small inklings or perceptions of great truths, we shall call it *Perceptions*.

Typically Pu Songling's narratives are crafted as fully fledged stories, being variously captivating, imaginative, colourful, graphic and sensual. Some recast and amplify old themes, but many are original creations, arising from the author's experience of life and exemplifying good and bad traits of humanity that he has observed. They impress not by their profundity but by their strength of feeling. The most striking tell of encounters with bewitching ghosts or fairy maidens, and given that the recipient of such favours is a poor unsuccessful scholar like the author, it would not be unfair to describe them as wish-fulfilling. Ji Xiaolan classified Pu Songling's style as "literary artistry", in contrast to his own approach which, compliant with the Confucian disdain for fabrication, was that of the scribe or compiler. With that remark we come within sight of his purpose to depict, albeit tangentially, the real life not of himself but of his times. Again by way of contrast, he had no cause to seek wish-fulfilment in his work, because in his case all worldly wishes were fulfilled. His family was wealthy, he rose to the top of the civil service, was laden with honours, enjoyed the emperor's favour, had a long and vigorous sex life (he had six concubines, though not all at the same time), and smoked the biggest pipe in the nation.

The scribal role limits what is recorded to incidents personally witnessed or read about by the author, or attested to by others, the provenance being noted in every case (which is why so many of the pieces translated here start with "So-and-so contributed this"). The key factor is that the entries are not the product of the compiler's imagination, that is, not pure fiction. Of course the compiler has no way of knowing whether or not his informant has made up the story he tells: his job is done if he faithfully records what he hears. At the same time, by putting the stories down he accords them a certain status, and a degree of credibility. Usually an assessment or comment is added at the end.

In all, *Perceptions* includes around 1,200 entries (compared with the 500 of *Strange Stories*). Some go back to things seen and heard in his childhood, others derive from encounters over his long career, but the bulk are contributed by friends and associates. Ji's own excuse for amassing such a huge collection of what are for the most part seemingly trivial items was that it was his habit to write something of his own every day, and in his declining years it was simply an untaxing amusement to fill in leisure time, at least to begin with. But after the interest shown in the first of his five volumes, people in his circle supplied him with more and more material of a similar kind, so the project prolonged itself.

As we have indicated, the choice of subject matter was by no means eccentric: the retailing of what we can broadly call ghost stories was extremely widespread in his time. The contributors Ji names range from the highest intellectuals and statesmen in the land right down to peasants, servants, soldiers and traders. Domestically his grandfather's generation spun ghost stories to him in his childhood, his student circle swapped and debated them, and in mature life his colleagues amused themselves with them. Needless to say, the viewpoint behind these stories varied greatly, from awe and trembling stemming from belief to deliberate exploitation as parables for comment on society. A fuller discussion of belief in the supernatural will come later; as a preliminary we just remind ourselves that the Chinese people in Ji's time regarded the unseen world as part of, not separate from, the natural world. In that they differed only in degree from people in the western hemisphere before the scientific revolution made itself fully felt. For their part, the Chinese had their native cosmology that generously accommodated an unlimited number of unseen higher beings, which accounted for the plethora of idols, shrines and cults outside the recognized religions of Buddhism and Taoism. In the Christian world such manifold objects of worship had long ago been subsumed under the One God, the Holy Family and the Church's saints; the Chinese had many more diverse powers to revere, propitiate and supplicate: at any moment these powers could intervene in their lives, to punish or relieve. In accounting for the business of the spirit world, manifest in uncanny happenings, the minor literature of *biji* performed the legitimate function of broadening knowledge beyond what high literature dealt with, as well as illustrating in ordinary lives the rewards for good conduct and penalties for bad. Both those purposes Ji Xiaolan emphatically endorsed, in theory and in practice. Hardly any of his items do not contain a moral, either self-evident or expressly drawn, unlike Yuan Mei's nearly contemporary *Zi bu yu* (*What the Sage Did Not Speak of*), which disclaims any didactic purpose. We must suppose that there was something about the social climate that made Ji so single-minded.

The Times Are out of Joint

Ji Xiaolan lived in the middle of the Qing dynasty [1644–1911], founded by an alliance of Manchu tribes who ousted the ethnically Han Ming dynasty. His adult life spanned the entire reign of the Qianlong emperor [1736–1795], which aspired to be the most splendid in Chinese history and certainly was the most lavish. The economy was prosperous overall, and the empire was strong. Militarily the main preoccupation was with troublesome but containable insurrections on its Inner Asian borders, which it had largely expanded. The European powers with Britain in the lead had not yet impinged upon the Chinese picture of the world. In brief, the Chinese empire thought of itself as self-sufficient. That was indeed the message bluntly given to the British embassy led by Earl Macartney when it came knocking at the door in 1793 to negotiate terms of trade: You have nothing that we need.

Internally the last major rebellions against alien Manchu rule had been put down in the early 1680s. By the turn of the eighteenth century the Han Chinese, high and low, were not only reconciled to Manchu rule, but took pride in the Great Qing Empire. The educated classes had long since returned to the pursuit of an official career via the state examination system, and the domination of Confucianism in life and thought had been reinforced by fiat of the ruling dynasty.

To return to the person of the Qianlong emperor, he was extremely well favoured by endowment and education. His stern father Yongzheng had relentlessly prosecuted corruption, imposed economies and tightened supervision from the centre, which put the son in a position to spend. And spend he did. Much of the architectural splendour which remains to be admired in China is owed to the building carried out in his reign. Grandeur in all aspects was the keynote of Qianlong's philosophy: grandeur in authority, in display, and crucially to our particular concern, grandeur in the arts. He was something of a culture vulture, and in his own estimation a supreme poet to boot: a total of 41,800 verses are attributed to him, a count that rivalled the

Quan Tang shi (*Complete Tang Poems*) tally of 48,000 (covering 300 years). Perhaps it was the intoxication of power that made his administration in the second half of his sixty-year reign increasingly erratic, swinging from the despotic to the culpably lax. No more certain proof of that was the way an officer in his Manchu guard, Heshen by name, was whisked to prominence at the sole whim of the emperor, bypassing the regular channels. After proving his acumen and efficiency in limited matters, Heshen was promoted in quick succession to control the key instruments of power and decision in the state. His domination lasted from roughly 1775 to 1799, the years when Ji Xiaolan compiled his *Perceptions*.

As the emperor's right-hand man, Heshen's loyalty was to him rather than the state; accordingly he devised irregular means to fill Qianlong's depleted coffers. One of his innovations was to introduce "discretionary fines" as a substitute for demotions or possibly severe punishment for errors and omissions committed by senior bureaucrats, thus effectively undermining the primacy of strict discipline and proper conduct, and monetarizing morality. Some bureaucrats actually pre-empted fines by paying in advance for as yet unknown peccadillos. To placate or buy off Heshen was a protection against incurring the dangerous displeasure of the emperor, hence Heshen's personal wealth came to rival the assets of the central treasury. He was brought down only after Qianlong died, four years into the reign of his successor.

The emperor himself led the way in the taste for luxury and acquisitiveness. In a manner befitting his ambition to be recognized as the greatest ruler in Chinese history he filled his palaces with jewels, works of art and antiques, either bought or presented to him in fealty. Lower down the scale, dignitaries acquired such rare objects by fair means and foul, with a view to possible presentation. An attendant practical question is where the liquid assets came from to facilitate the rapid and easy transfer of wealth needed to support this trade in luxuries: the simple answer is, in the currency of silver. In the eighteenth century China's export of commodities—chiefly teas, silks and ceramics—dwarfed its imports: by this gross imbalance of trade China sucked in a very large proportion of the silver mined in Central and South America, doubling the previous internal supply. Officials at all levels connived to share this form of wealth, and naturally the higher up the ladder the bigger the shares. Greater riches meant more nutriment for venality.

Ji Xiaolan was named by a trained observer, a Korean ambassador to the Qing court, as one of a handful of senior officials not in the pocket of Heshen, and no historical account I have read taints him with any double dealing. At the same time, he lived and breathed at the centre of the bureaucratic web, and must have been very aware of the slide into more than usual corruption; in fact he was once openly suspected by Qianlong of encouraging a junior censor to bring down Heshen by indicting his servant for possessing ill-gotten gains. It is surely no accident that a reading of *Perceptions* leaves the impression that his society was peopled by far more sinners than saints. Unable to name and blame, he might have devoted himself the more assiduously to a literature where justice, not to be expected from the civil authorities on earth, is unerringly delivered from the spirit world.

The Privileges and Perils of Eminence

Let us now look more closely at who our author was and what he did. The Ji clan had emigrated from the Yangtze Valley to Hebei province in the early fifteenth century. They settled in Xian county, Hejian prefecture, which lies to the south of Tianjin. By Ji Xiaolan's grandfather's time they were local magnates, having built up very extensive land holdings. According to county histories they founded and financed charity schools, and opened their granaries to feed the starving when floods occurred. So they enjoyed a good reputation. Several of Ji's ancestors had attempted to climb the examination ladder, but his father Ji Rongshu was the first to get a degree at the provincial level (in 1713), though he failed subsequent attempts at the highest, or metropolitan, level. After a long wait he did get a post in a ministry (1734), and went on from there to serve as a prefect. Considering his own frustration, it is no wonder that when Ji Rongshu's third wife bore him a son who was precociously bright, quick-witted and blessed with a prodigious memory, he made sure the boy would have the best possible education. The home tutors engaged to teach Xiaolan were learned enough, but after his father bought a residence in the capital when Xiaolan was about ten years old, some of the most distinguished scholars of the age agreed to tutor him. The teenager became talked of among the upper crust for his wit and flair. True to promise, he came top in the first-level prefectural examination at the age of twenty (1744). The state examinations were not, however, a test of genius but rather of ability to work to formulas: it took him two attempts to pass the provincial examination, but when he did in 1747 it was with flying colours. Again he failed the top-level metropolitan examination in the following year; then, delayed by going into mourning for his mother, it was not until 1754 that he cleared that final hurdle, with a good enough pass to be admitted to the prestigious Hanlin Academy, which served among other things as the emperor's personal secretariat. Along this testing way Ji formed lasting bonds with batches of fellow examinees and a succession of examiners (examiners and successful candidates assuming a teacher-student relationship). Those two nexuses merged together as support and friendship groups for a scholar-official's lifetime. A further layer was added when the former student became an examiner, as Ji did. The majority of contributors to *Perceptions* belonged to those circles.

The closest of all relationships were those formed by kinship and marriage. Ji was married at the age of sixteen to a daughter of the Ma clan in the neighbouring county of Dongguang, an alliance which brought together two families of comparable wealth and standing. Their marriage lasted, harmoniously it seems, for fifty-six years (she died in 1795). Members of the Ma family also contributed to *Perceptions*.

So at the age of thirty Ji Xiaolan was at last on the starting grid for a launch into an illustrious career, for those admitted to the Hanlin Academy were judged the best and brightest scholars of the empire. One of the duties of a compiler, which was Ji's initial rank, was to record the daily doings of the emperor. On account of his wit Ji soon attracted the personal attention of Qianlong, who as we have noted was addicted to composing verses. As Ji had an extraordinary ability to produce extempore matching verses, he became the emperor's partner in rhyme. A mark of Qianlong's regard was Ji's appointment as chief examiner for the Shanxi provincial examination in 1759, a high honour for one so young. A more substantial posting that followed was to Fujian province in 1762 to act as Director of Education. It was cut short by the death of his father in 1764, when Ji Xiaolan had to follow the rule of suspending his career to observe mourning for three years.

That seemed a temporary intermission in an inexorable rise to eminence. Ji resumed court duties in 1767. The next year he was slated for a post of prefect in Guizhou, but Qianlong ruled that his superior erudition made him better suited to remain at the academy, though with a promotion in rank. Evidently he was still in the emperor's good books. But in the sixth month of 1768 an event occurred that brought his career to a shuddering halt. Without that fall from grace we would probably not have his *Perceptions*, and Ji Xiaolan's name would now be forgotten along with those of his similarly learned contemporaries.

Much discussion and speculation has been devoted to the detail of the incident, but the bare bones can be simply stated. Lu Jianzeng, grandfather of Ji's son-in-law (married to Ji's eldest daughter), was suspected of receiving benefits from the corrupt sale of permits to transport salt (a government monopoly) while he served as Commissioner for the Huai River Valley. But when a raiding party descended on Lu's mansion to confiscate his valuables, it had already been stripped bare. Therefore he must have got wind of the impending raid, and the warning must have come from someone at court. Ji Xiaolan was found guilty of sending a coded message to his son-in-law in time for the valuables to be removed. He was exiled to serve in the garrison of Urumqi, Chinese Turkestan, the far western reach of the Qing empire, and home of the tribes of the steppes. His journey there under escort took four months, over mountain ranges and deserts; one stretch had to be made by camel.

Ji expected conditions in Urumqi would be extremely primitive, but it turned out to be a large and thriving settlement, besides which he was cushioned from hardship by his personal fame. He served as something like office manager or chief clerk to the commanding general, the first of whose succession was an old acquaintance. All the same, the demotion from lord of the manor in his home village and palanquin-borne court official in the capital was precipitous. As a criminal in cotton clothes he was owed no respect by the people he rubbed shoulders with, would have been one of the crowd in the street. Inevitably he was made more sensitive to the privations and hazards and cruelties of life for common folk, and on the other hand appreciated at first hand the achievements of farmers, miners and construction workers; so much can be deduced from the 160 poems written in Urumqi, which also express unbounded admiration for the ingenuity of artisans and talents of street players and entertainers. Further clues to his state of mind can be gained from the letters he sent home to his family, which urged attention to famine relief and charitable works, forbad whipping of maids, cautioned against arrogance and extravagance, and warned against contempt for tenants and farm workers. An admonitory tone would have been conventional for a Confucian head of family, but *Perceptions* confirms that those were genuine abiding concerns: when twenty years later he embarked on that work, his underlying theme was precisely the morality of everyday life. And, incidentally, his time in Urumqi gave him a fund of stories that demanded to be told.

The emperor's own great literary enterprise was waiting in the wings when Ji Xiaolan was suddenly recalled from exile in the twelfth month of 1770. He arrived back in the capital in the sixth month of 1771, and was reappointed to the Hanlin Academy, where the work on assembling the biggest ever library of China's written heritage would be initiated. On the recommendation of a very prominent former examiner of his, Ji was appointed in 1773 to be one of the three chief editors of the *Siku quanshu*, a title translatable as *Compendium of the Four Sets of Books*, all books traditionally being assigned to one of four classes. For our purposes we shall refer to it as *Compendium*. It was designed to outdo the encyclopaedic collections compiled in the Yongle reign of the Ming dynasty and the Kangxi reign of Qianlong's grandfather. Since Ji Xiaolan stayed the course for the whole nineteen years of the *Compendium*'s production, he effectively emerged as *the* chief editor.

To preserve the written heritage through finding and collating various texts to produce the best scholarly editions was of course a laudable aim. Rare books were either solicited or demanded (depending on the owners' willingness to lend) from private collectors to supplement the holdings of imperial libraries, and fair copies made; Ji Xiaolan himself volunteered over a hundred books. Given that China's literary history went back thousands of years, the scale of the project was enormous: once under way, the work of editing and hand copying required a staff of 4,300.

It soon transpired, however, that there was a not so laudable agenda behind this conservation project. Qianlong issued instructions that some books submitted should be destroyed, and offending passages deleted or rewritten, if they were deemed to be heterodox; his next set of instructions were more pointed: editors were to expunge anything defamatory or derogatory of the Manchu people, a ruling later extended to such references to all previous alien dynasties, lest the Manchus be tarred with the same brush. Thus conservation evolved into censorship. The editors had above them a battery of directors of ministerial rank, and Qianlong would also be personally monitoring progress. Understandably the tendency was to err on the side of caution: it is said that more of the acquired books were burned than preserved.

Apart from general duties, Ji Xiaolan was given the special task of editing a general catalogue for the *Compendium*, which took him eight years to complete. It consisted of reviews and synopses of 10,230 works, among which 3,470 were selected for copying, the rest being simply noted. The procedure was for experts in different fields to draft the entries, which were then passed up to

Ji and his co-editor. Their recommendations were submitted to the emperor, and after his approval was given the editors did a thorough revision. It is generally agreed that the finished entries bore the stamp of Ji Xiaolan. They are still recognized to be a monumental work of scholarship and acute judgement. No doubt Qianlong appreciated that, for Ji was given successive promotions as he worked. The more general work of editing the books chosen for copying in full, in contrast, proved to be a poisoned chalice. As we have said, Qianlong took a close and active interest in the emergent volumes, and was untiring in ferreting out textual and ideological errors. Editors and sub-editors were many times penalized for real and supposed dereliction of duty. On the whole the editorial task was both enervating and nerve-racking: editors collapsed from exhaustion or were ruined by bearing the cost of recopying and rebinding. Over the years Ji himself suffered several penalties, including one requiring him to repair complete volumes. In all, seven sets of the *Compendium* were completed, one after another, and distributed to specially built libraries around the empire.

In those last decades of Qianlong's reign (he abdicated in 1795), Ji's attendance on the emperor was closer and more frequent than ever. His editing of the *Compendium* involved him having a workplace in the Yuanmingyuan, the imperial park on the northern outskirts of Peking, and at the Summer Resort in Rehe (Jehol), north of the Great Wall, whither the emperor annually repaired. In this period he was appointed concurrently to ministerial posts in the Board of Rites, the Board of War, and the Censorate. On the face of it, those appointments at last gave him authority over more than academic matters, but the duties were not policy making: at the Board of War, for instance, his responsibility was only for such things as logistics and service conditions, nothing to do with the actual conduct of war. In practice Qianlong continued to regard him as a walking encyclopedia, an intellectual sparring partner, and at times no more than a court jester. He once excused Ji for an oversight in an investigation on the ground that he was a "pedant", so not expected to have practical competence. Indeed, the ministerial appointments were merely a transition from charge of a literary bureaucracy to oversight of a clerical one.

Typecasting

Despite all the pointers we have, it is not at all easy to get under Ji Xiaolan's skin, so to speak. Setting aside the comedic television series which have him engaged in a running battle of wits with Heshen, even recent books about him that purport to be biographical incorporate long passages of purely fabricated dialogue: he has been set in the mould of a paragon of wit and wile, never bested. But these developments only magnify a trend that popular literature inaugurated in his lifetime; fictionalized history already had a prototype for him to conform to. Yet there must have been good reason to select him for that role. In real life he probably did adopt a distinct persona in order to survive at a court where to show independence was to ask for trouble, and the pattern for that persona he set for himself when as a young man he accepted his celebration as a brilliant mind, a sparkling genius, gifted with literary flair and inventiveness. In mental agility and way with words he truly excelled over his contemporaries, but the downside was that more solid and sober members of his fraternity attained to far higher positions of responsibility in the state. Not only that—besides the catalogue to the *Compendium*, he left no writing of any depth and consequence.

The aforementioned Korean ambassador believably summed up Ji Xiaolan as relaxed, suave and sophisticated, but that could not have been all he was. A fox spirit he quotes in one of the sketches that follow made a very telling remark: "Where in the length and breadth of the empire would you find anyone willing to show his true self?" As old age came on, Ji expressed regret that he had done little to discharge the scholar-official's traditional duty to uphold the ethics and institutions of his civilization, the more understandably because they were fast being undermined. He might well have chosen the unimpeachable form of *biji xiaoshuo* as a safe way of pursuing that endeavour. If so, the sting in the tail of his little sketches from humble life and tales of the supernatural would have discreetly suited his purpose. But then the question must be asked, did he really have faith in the agency of the supernatural, or did he not care whether it was real or not, as long as he could use it to make a point?

Superstition Is the Poetry of Life (Goethe)

For a start, Ji Xiaolan certainly would not have questioned the central notion of predestination. The assumption of fatefulness was built into daily life. The very notation of time units to designate years and hours (the Heavenly Stems and Earthly Branches) was derived from astrology, and a whole science was devoted to calculating fortunate and unfortunate days for embarking on various kinds of activity, with the results incorporated in calendars. Allied to that, the personal horoscopes of prospective partners in marriage determined the couple's suitability: an adverse reading of the year, month, day and hour of birth normally debarred a union. A belief in Fate (*ming*) was no doubt a psychological necessity to comfort helpless humanity faced with inexplicable and undeserved catastrophes like flood, famine, plague and personal disasters. To afford some perspective, it was matched in the Christian world by the notion of Divine Providence, the mysterious working of the hand of a stern but loving God. And like Divine Providence, Fate to the Chinese, however cruel, was still thought to be guided by a supreme arbiter, Heaven (*tian*) in their case, who/which was ultimately just and benevolent. As we see in the material that follows, Ji Xiaolan never expresses any doubt that Heaven will come down on the side of the just and the righteous. As far as that goes, neither did the leading lights of the European scientific revolution which developed a mechanistic view of the workings of the universe dismiss the possibility of divine intervention (including striking malefactors dead by lightning), or given the testimony in the Bible to the reality of the Devil, rule out the activity of demonic forces and agents.

As to the chief religions of Buddhism and Taoism, their hierarchy was recognized and honoured and indeed in some cases empowered by the court: Zhang Tianshi, for example, was enthroned as the Taoist Pope by imperial order in the Qing dynasty. When our author ventures onto such hallowed ground, it is only as a social pragmatist assessing the human needs each creed catered for. It is at the grass-roots level of uncanny happenings that questions arise and explanations have to be offered; it is by those explanations that his credulity can be measured.

To look first at the evidence of *Perceptions* alone, we have to bear in mind that the great majority of incidents recorded in *Perceptions* are related by others, and Ji's job as scribe is to faithfully represent them. Furthermore, any comment he might add has to serve a literary as well as philosophical purpose, that of rounding off a story fittingly. Yet he does occasionally propose a puzzle on his own behalf, like where the supply of kitchen gods to reside in millions of household comes from: in those cases his application of logical reasoning leads him into scepticism; and sometimes he exposes apparent demonstrations of uncanny power as fraudulent and pooh-poohs fondly believed legends as nonsense. On the other hand, more often he will abandon rationality altogether, unreservedly endorsing the most improbable outcomes and explanations. So we have a mixture of messages.

However, any doubt about Ji Xiaolan's private belief in the reality of unearthly agents and powers intervening in mundane life is dispelled when his personal letters to his family circle are taken into account, for there the role of entertainer and literary artist does not enter into the equation. Given his confessed lifelong fascination with the deeds of ghosts and goblins, he is often consulted on such matters by his relatives, and he has no hesitation in presenting himself as an authority on the subject. Among other things, he confidently defines the nature and character of various kinds of revenants and demons, explains how masters of the occult and souls of the departed can implant themselves in women's wombs, living persons and dead bodies, and assures his correspondents that fox spirits who occupy empty rooms and houses will cause no disturbance if treated with courtesy, adding that he regrets he has never had the pleasure of their company himself. In one letter to his wife he even urges her to burn all the lifelike human figurines the children play with, because one day they might come to life. In sum, the supernatural is firmly established in his mental perspective, as a kind of fourth dimension. (More on these family letters below.)

So we cannot go along with Ji Xiaolan's modern celebrators who are eager to think of him as an enlightened thinker; on the contrary, he was a man of his times, and conventional in his view of the world, which actually qualifies him for giving a credible overview of his society, through snapshots that can be pieced together. The supernatural does not enter into some of his sketches, and where it does it does not invalidate the truthfulness of the milieu in which it features. Every abnormal happening has to have normality to measure itself against or be embedded in: if it is not tethered in a recognizable setting, it lacks persuasiveness; in other words, the more credible the background, the more credibility the supernatural element can borrow. Not having been around at the time, though, we can only judge the balance between the mundane and the supernatural in each story on whether the mundane aspect "feels right" or "rings true".

Quality

The majority of Ji's 1200-odd items are very short and utterly simplistic demonstrations of the working out of the universal principle of reward and punishment for good and bad deeds, embodied in the kind of yarns passed around in local communities. In that, they do not differ from the standard fare of *biji* collections, and hold no interest for present day readers. The longer stories and discursive pieces which do interest us are, first of all, exceptionally well composed. Syntactically that is more obvious in the Chinese, where one clause can glide smoothly into the next without the litter of connectives that modern European languages are forced to employ. In terms of content there is a great variety of modes and tones. Stories might be deflating or outright comic, eerie or hair-raising, pathetic or even tragic—though our author leaves room for the reader to imagine, rather than spelling things out. In short, nothing in the narrative is laboured. But what makes the material really special are the pieces which are vehicles for satire and for serious discussion. I think uniquely in this type of *biji* literature one has the pleasure of encountering a keen intellect, willing to interrogate and speculate, and to consider both sides of a coin. Not least welcome are the mildly quizzical remarks occasionally appended to items, demonstrating that rare commodity we call humour.

Family Letters

A collection of Ji Xiaolan's letters to his family circle was published in 1937 by the Shanghai Zhongyang Shudian under the title *Ji Xiaolan jiashu* (*Family Letters of Ji Xiaolan*) as one of a series entitled Family Letters of Ten Eminent Persons of the Qing Dynasty. A reprint of the same collection, with some omissions, was published in 2012 by the Beijing Foreign Languages Press under the same title. Large numbers of these letters share anecdotes with *Perceptions*. I have added endnotes to *Perceptions* items where the letters give significant variants or extra details for the same stories. In a few cases I have translated complete letters as addenda to the relevant items in order to give their specific domestic context, and also for the reader to see how Ji refashioned the same material for publication. I have noted the location of the letters by reference to the FLP 2012 edition, that being the more obtainable one.

The Plan of This Book

I chose all the items in this collection solely for the individual insights into social matters and ways of thought they afforded. To prepare a volume for publication, however, they needed to be given some kind of recognizable order, hence they will be found grouped together under topical headings. The problem there is, our author did not set out to compile a social history. At times he does address broad issues, but for the most part his aim is to record particular edifying stories and curious happenings which only incidentally shed light on current life and thought, and do not fit conveniently into any category, so my prefaces intended to provide a general context for the imposed topics may occasionally be disproportionate to the content of the entries. An example is Ji's mention of Jesuits, whose presence in China would be mystifying to readers unfamiliar with the period: to them I hope to have done a service by explaining at some length. Some amplification is also incorporated in the text where that can be done discreetly. My overall intention is to make the matter understandable to all kinds of readers.

In addition there is a table of dynasties, and a survey of contributors, to give an idea of their standing. Those not identified in the text can be assumed to belong to Ji's intimates.

There is a small amount of duplication in the background information provided: that overlap is intended to suit readers who prefer to dip rather than read from end to end, advisable though that may be.

A line gap is left between a contributor's story and Ji Xiaolan's comment, in order to make clear which is which. My own comments are set in italics and graced with asterisks.

For the benefit of sinologists who wish to check my translations, each item is tagged with a note of the collection from which it is taken. Otherwise, sinologists are not catered for, as they will have their own resources. There are no academic footnotes and no bibliography.

Contributors

As a rule our author identifies in his text only story tellers and commentators who would not be known to his immediate readers, his contemporaries: those include members of his extended family, local villagers and estate workers, servants, and suchlike. Out of respect he will also give venerable personages their title. Otherwise he will name a bare name, and not even a formal name but a familiar or "style" name. Who those people were can only be known if as officials, scholars, writers or artists their names appear in historical records; fortunately, given the circles Ji moved in, most do.

Family aside, Ji Xiaolan's first bonding was with his tutors and fellow pupils. In a sense, those communities were like second families to aspiring youths like him, and connections so made could last a lifetime. Home tutors and fellow pupils in childhood feature in *Perceptions* alongside those more distinguished tutors and more privileged fellow pupils with whom he later studied in the capital. For example, one home tutor, Li Ruolang (Li Youdan), held only a provincial degree but his name often crops up in *Perceptions*, and Ji attested that he was "eternally indebted" to him. Among those Ji studied with in the capital, Dong Bangda, who tutored Ji for nine years, was a one-time Minister for Works and famed as a painter and calligrapher; he too remained a firm friend until his death in 1769.

Higher up the academic ladder were examiners for and fellow graduates in the provincial and metropolitan examinations. The former were respected as patrons and the latter accepted as the closest thing to brothers. The relationship with examiners could extend to their sons. Liu Tongxun (1699–1773), for instance, placed Ji first in the provincial exam of 1747. Honoured for dispensing justice without fear or favour, Liu earned a place in the highest councils of state. In 1768 he headed the investigation that found Ji guilty of misconduct in the salt permit case, yet later recommended him to be a chief editor of the *Compendium*, and they remained on very good terms. Liu Tongxun's son, Liu Yong (1719–1804), grew old together with Ji Xiaolan, sharing the same interests and hobbies: among other things, both were big collectors of engraved ink-slabs.

After Ji himself was appointed a chief or co-examiner for the higher examinations, of course he acquired his own "students", as successful candidates were called, and several of those became contributors, too.

Fellow graduates also formed a fraternity. Prominent contributors to *Perceptions* were the Zhu brothers. Zhu Yun (1729–1775) passed the metropolitan examination in the same year as Ji (1754); he similarly was enrolled in the Hanlin Academy, and was a prime mover in the *Compendium* project. Zhu Gui (1735–1806), fellow graduate in the provincial examination of 1747, rose to the dizzy height of Governor-General. He composed Ji Xiaolan's epitaph.

Colleagues in the Hanlin Academy and on the *Compendium* project also contributed in large numbers. Among these, mention must be made of Dai Zhen (1723–1777), who was later regarded as the most original thinker of his age. Dai came to the capital from the central province of Anhui in 1754, armed with a reputation as an independent scholar but with only moderate formal qualifications. Ji soon appointed him as tutor to his children, a post he held for nearly a decade. With Ji's support, Dai was recruited as an editor of the *Compendium*, and in 1774 was appointed Hanlin academician. He was a universal man, versed in philology, astronomy, history, geography and mathematics. Ji wrote in a commemorative poem of him that they "opened their hearts to each other without reserve or misgiving", which bespeaks their intimacy.

The Location of Items

Ji Xiaolan published his "notes" in five successive volumes. These are their titles and dates:

> 1789, *Luanyang xiaoxia lu* 灤陽消夏錄 (*Written to Pass the Season at the Summer Resort*), in six sections, abbreviated as LYXXL.
>
> 1791, *Ru shi wo wen* 如是我聞 (*So Have I Heard*), in four sections, abbreviated as RSWW.
>
> 1792, *Huai xi za zhi* 槐西雜誌 (*Jottings from My Haidian Lodging*), in four sections, abbreviated as HXZZ.
>
> 1793, *Guwang ting zhi* 姑妄聽之 (*No Harm in Listening*), in four sections, abbreviated as GWTZ.
>
> 1798, *Luanyang xu lu* 灤陽續錄 (*More from the Summer Resort*), in six sections, abbreviated as LYXL.

The code for locating the items translated here gives the abbreviated title, followed by the section number (in Roman numerals) and the order in which the item occurs in that section, e.g. LYXXL VI 7.

Debts

The three secondary sources in the English language on which I most relied are:

Leo Tak-hung Chan: *The Discourse on Foxes and Ghosts* (1998)

Tung-tsu Chu: *Local Government in China under the Ch'ing* (1962)

C. K. Yang: *Religion in Chinese Society* (1967)

Secondary sources in Chinese were most helpful for filling in biographical and background details. To give a sample:

張宏傑著。《乾隆皇帝的十張面孔》。臺北：研究出版社，2010

李忠智、馮哲佐著。《真實的紀曉嵐》。北京：社會科學院出版社，2008

韓亞紅、蔣焱蘭著。《紀曉嵐：風流才子的方圓人生》。北京：中國廣播電視出版社，2011

孫建著。《紀曉嵐的老師們》。北京：現代教育出版社，2010

陳錚著。《人間紀曉嵐》。北京：東方出版社，2009

周林華著。《紀曉嵐家族人物》。北京：教育出版社，2010

王鵬凱著。《紀昀研究論述》。臺北：文史哲出版社，2009

I could not have embarked on this project at all without the aid of the three-volume edition of the *Yuewei caotang biji* published by the Sanmin Shuju in Taipei and edited by Yan Wenru (2006): without its extensive annotation and translations into the modern Chinese language I would have been lost.

On a personal level, I am indebted to Eva Hung for her advice, for her all-round technical help, for her sharing of her greatly superior understanding of classical Chinese, and most particularly for her organizing the illustrations, with the generous cooperation of Peter Lam, Lai Suk Yee, Li Chi Kwong and Lee Yun Woon of the Art Museum, The Chinese University of Hong Kong. Alena Chow of the Institute of Chinese Studies helped along the way.

Everyone at The Chinese University Press was very supportive. Special thanks go to Agnes Chan for her editing and K. H. Ma for his production.

ILLUSTRATIONS

Figure 1. Ji Xiaolan in official regalia.

Figure 2. Emblem for Emperor Qianlong's imperial robe. Reproduced by permission of Mr Edwin Mok; image courtesy of the Art Museum of The Chinese University of Hong Kong.

Figure 3. Emblem for the court robe of first rank civil officials. Reproduced by permission of Mr Edwin Mok; image courtesy of the Art Museum of The Chinese University of Hong Kong.

Figure 4. The layout of the imperial garden of Yuanmingyuan where Ji sometime edited the *Compendium*. Photograph by Eva Hung.

Figure 5. A couplet in running hand by Ji Xiaolan, reading: "Failings like autumn grasses, too many to mow out/ Learning like spring ice, never to pile high".

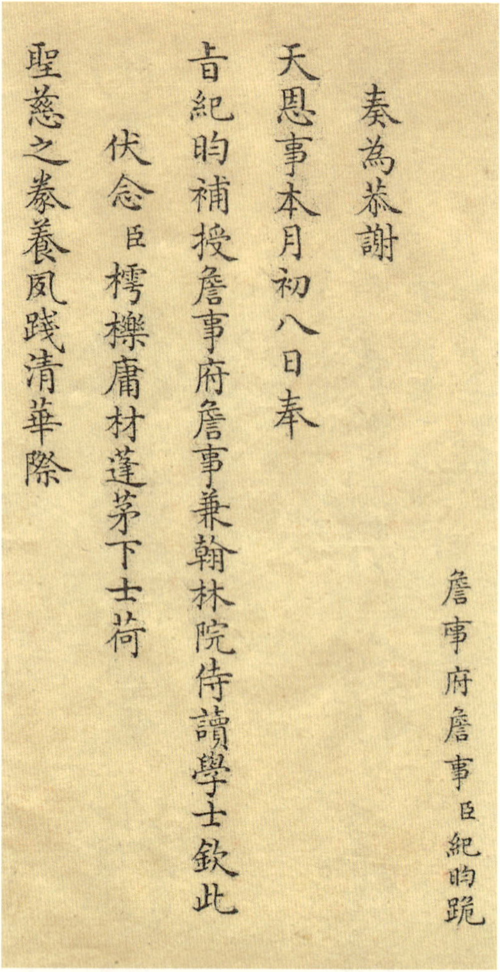

奏為恭謝

天恩事本月初八日奉

旨紀昀補授詹事府詹事兼翰林院侍讀學士欽此

伏念臣樗櫟庸材蓬茅下士荷

聖慈之豢養鳳跱清華際

詹事府詹事臣紀昀跪

Figure 6. Ji Xiaolan's memorial to the throne in regular script, expressing humble thanks for appointment as imperial tutor (1779).

Figure 7. Finely crafted purple sand bamboo-shaped wrist rest and chestnut-shaped cup—a scholar's desk utensils of the kind Ji Xiaolan collected. Reproduced by permission of the Art Museum of The Chinese University of Hong Kong from the collection of the Art Museum of The Chinese University of Hong Kong.

Figure 8. Translator tries to be friends with author's ghost in Ji Xiaolan's old Peking residence. Photograph by Eva Hung.

Part I
The Supernatural and the Curious

1

SPIRITS, SPECTRES AND DEMONS

This section gives a small sample of beliefs current in Ji Xiaolan's time concerning various kinds of beings, spirits and demons that impinge upon human life. An interesting question is their universality, given that at some time in their history most peoples have constructed parallel companies to occupy the dimensions of earth and air. A big difference in the Chinese model is its massive documentation and consequent continuity.

To take the example of long life, a universal human aspiration: the promise of "life everlasting" is given in Christian liturgies, but that is granted only after death. To my knowledge, the Bible instances only one case of fabulously long life on earth, that of Methuselah (969 years), but without explaining the phenomenon. In contrast, the notion of immortality was seized upon in China by Taoists who devised physical regimes to bring it about, besides which "real" immortals proliferated in their writings, so leaving a legacy that buttressed belief in the possibility of immortality (though Ji Xiaolan found aspects of it bemusing).

As regards the guardians of hearth and home, the Israelites had their teraphim, the Romans their lares and penates. The lares protected broad domains that included cities and topographic features along with homes, while penates specifically looked after households and lived in domestic shrines, similar to those still common in Chinese communities. We learn from our author that, consistent with the Chinese fondness for enumeration, household gods there had once numbered five, but actively had been reduced to one, the kitchen god (literally the god of the cooking range). That one was especially important, because it reported annually to the Jade Emperor on the behaviour of the family; prior to its departure, the idol's mouth was routinely smeared with syrup so that it would report favourably. The broader role of the lares was catered for separately in Chinese mythology; at its peak was the ritual worship of the Gods of Earth and Grain, symbolizing the state, conducted at the Altar of Heaven in the capital by none other than the emperor.

Since death comes to us all, the notion of emissaries from the underworld of the dead coming to claim human souls is also common. In Greek mythology Thanatos himself, the personification of death, was the escort to the underworld; he evolved into the Grim Reaper of European paganism. The popular conception in China of these emissaries derived from Buddhism, which inherited it from Hinduism. In Hinduism, Yama, the Lord of Death, sends agents called yamaduts to lead souls to the underworld. In China they took their name wuchang from the Buddhist tenet of impermanence; they were only minor functionaries who occasionally needed help.

Also universal in past times was the worship of ancestors. In other cultures there occurred a transition upward from family to clan to founders of nation, but such has been the continuity of beliefs and reverence for tradition in China that blood lines still come first and foremost.

The explanation of the origin and presence of divine beings given in the item "Primeval Gods" translated here, which does put in a nutshell the traditional Chinese view, has something in common with what in European culture is known as animism, and in particular with the variety called Neoplatonism that swept through Renaissance Europe. Keith Thomas described this Neoplatonism in the following terms: "Instead of being regarded as an inanimate mass, the Earth itself was deemed to be alive. The universe was peopled by a hierarchy of spirits, the cosmos an organic unity in which every part bore a sympathetic relationship to the rest. Even colours, letters and numbers were endowed with magical properties" (Religion and the Decline of Magic, 1971, p. 223). The wilder ranges of such an understanding of phenomena are, however, better matched in the Shan hai jing (The Classic of Mountains and

Seas) *which is of primitive origin, than in the ordered view offered here.*

Otherwise the existence of parochial gods of various hues was made more concrete and present by the erection of shrines and the spectacle of colourful rituals and street processions of their images. To help things along, local gods who had wrought miracles to relieve danger and distress were sanctified by the imperial grant of titles to them.

Kitchen Gods
HXZZ III 5

In ancient times the grand houses sacrificed to five household gods; now commoner households sacrifice only to the kitchen god. As for the other four, namely the gate god, the well god, the privy god and the land god, they might get offerings, or might not. The question is, is there just one kitchen god for the whole empire? One for a whole city or village? Or else one for each household? If there were one kitchen god for the whole empire, like the Fire God, there must be a relevant entry in the canon for ritual sacrifices, but no such entry now exists. If one kitchen god for each city and village, like the City God and God of the Soil, there must be dedicated shrines, but in fact the country is not littered with such shrines. That leaves the possibility of a separate kitchen god for each household.

Now the households of the common people number as many as the grains of sand in the Ganges, so kitchen gods ought to be equally many. Who performs that role? Who appoints them? Would not the number of gods be excessive? Besides, there is no regularity in people's moving house, and no regularity either in a family's rise and decline: what do the kitchen gods do when they are unemployed? When new recruits for kitchen gods are needed, where do they come from? If the paramount deities have to daily appoint and dismiss, redeploy and change these kitchen gods, would it not be a great nuisance? These are truly imponderable matters.

Nevertheless, kitchen gods frequently make themselves felt. When I was small, my maternal grandfather employed an old woman as cook. She was in the habit of emptying refuse into the fire chamber of the kitchen range. One night she dreamed of a man dressed in black berating her and slapping her face. When she awoke her cheeks were swollen, forming a carbuncle; after a few days it had grown to the size of a tea cup. The pus suppurated internally and flowed into the mouth. At every slightest breath the pus got into her throat, making her retch and vomit until she wanted to die. She was cured when she made a vow to pray devoutly to the god. How can that be explained?

A commentator offered this view: "If a shrine is set up in a household, it will surely attract a resident spirit. As long as the shrine exists, the spirit exists. When the shrine is abandoned, the spirit is done with. There is no need for the paramount deity to appoint each and every one."

That might be the answer.

The Worship of Ancestors

HXZZ I 70

Li Wenyuan from Yidu county in Shandong was the younger brother of Li Nanjian, the noted bibliophile. As an antiquarian he was on a par with Nanjian, but in breadth of interest and skill in exposition he was his superior. Sadly he died young. Nanjian asked me to compose his epitaph, but I was too busy to get round to it, and I even lost the biographical material supplied to me. That is a matter of lasting regret.

One day I was discussing ancient ritual with Li Wenyuan in my Gathering Clouds Retreat; in that context he was reminded of the following story.

A certain scholar from Boshan in central Shandong was

taking a walk in the forest one night when he saw a man dressed as a high official sitting under a pine tree. The man called him over. On closer view he recognized the man as an elder on his mother's side of the family, now deceased. The scholar was obliged to go up and salute him. This elder questioned him closely about family affairs, after which the scholar posed this question:

"It has been said since ancient times that the body is buried in the countryside, but the soul attaches itself to the spirit tablet in the place of worship. You, good sir, have a family shrine: why do I find you here?"

"That confusion is due to a narrow interpretation of an ancient text about not sacrificing at graves. Family shrines are the place for making offerings to the dead, the spirit tablets the object of address for prayers: so when the soul descends, that is its destination for those offices. However, if the soul resides permanently in the shrine, attaches itself permanently to its tablet, it is mixed up in a melee of the souls of generations of ancestors and of their living children and grandchildren. Furthermore, family temples and tablets are the preserve of the elite. Now in whole townships and counties, no more than one or two families in ten thousand can build temples, only one or two families in one thousand can afford an ancestral shrine, and only one or two in a hundred can set up spirit tablets. If the soul attaches to the tablet and not the grave, then for countless poor families there would be no resting place for the soul of their ancestors. Does that make sense?

"No one knows the circumstances of ghosts and spirits better than the sages. The ritual of placing funerary artefacts in graves dates back to the Xia dynasty [2070–1600 BC]. Supposing the souls resided in the tablets rather than the graves, the funerary artefacts should be placed in the temples rather than the graves, but in fact they are all buried in the graves. Could the sages have been so irrational as to locate objects dedicated to souls where souls do not go?

"On another point, the practice in the ancient state of Wei of burying husbands and wives in the same tomb but in coffins at some distance from each other represented the customs of the Shang dynasty [1600–1046 BC]; the practice in the state of Lu of the coffins touching one another represented the customs of the Zhou dynasty [first millennium BC]. Confucius approved of the Zhou customs. Now if the souls are not in the tomb, it clearly makes no difference whether the coffins are apart or together, so what is there to approve or disapprove?

"The *Book of Rites* says: 'The reason why one cannot bear to read a father's books after his death is because they carry the imprint of his hands; the reason why one cannot bear to use a mother's cups and bowls after she has passed away is because they carry the imprint of her lips.' Things so small have such great significance. Yet they count a forebear's corpse as nothing, and instead set up a tablet a few inches high and claim 'that is my father or mother's soul'. Isn't that to get things quite out of proportion?

"The temple's dawn bell is about to ring, so I must leave you now. I hope our present encounter will guard you against being led astray by petty pundits."

The scholar hastily stood up. The sky in the east was already lightening. When he looked around, he found he was on the path leading to the elder's grave.

THE GRIM REAPER
RSWW I 55

Gan Bao's *Evidences of the Supernatural* [fourth century AD] tells of the role played by the wife of Ma Shi, née Jiang, a role now known as "Reserve Messenger from the Underworld". In the present day a family named Cao from Wang Qingcha Village in Wuqing county [near Peking] had an old maidservant who performed that task. My late mother once asked her how it was that the courts of the dead lacked their own ghostly agents to claim the souls of the deceased, and had to employ people like her in their stead. Her reply was:

"If people crowd round the sickbed, the yang energy radiates very strongly, and the minions of the underworld are repelled. Alternatively the deceased may have been of true eminence, and his aura is powerful; or a man of rectitude, and his aura is unyielding: those types are particularly hard to approach. Other cases would be an official who oversees executions, with his forbidding air, and violent blackguards, with their murderous air. Only living beings whose dreaming soul is yin but whose vitality is yang are proof against such forces, so must be taken along to act as reserve."

That explanation is very well reasoned, not something a village crone could make up offhand.

Zombies

RSWW IV 53

The Taoists have a technique for sustaining their bodily functions under the ground, and when ready can return to life after having been buried for some hundreds of years. Or so it is said—I have no personal knowledge of such a thing. It is, however, a fact that in ancient times bodies were preserved by being immersed in a coffin filled with mercury. Dong Qujiang gave the following account of life after death.

People posthumously condemned for crimes so heinous that they merited exhuming and their corpse being exposed to public view have been found to be in perfect condition, despite having been buried for many years. Lü Liuliang [who plotted to restore the Ming dynasty] was sentenced to having his bones dug up and burnt; when his coffin was opened, his looks were those of a living man, and blood seeped out when the knife cut into his flesh. It seems that the gods had preserved his body so that it could undergo punishment for his sedition. A certain person (a clansman of Qujiang's whom he named at the time, but I have forgotten what the name was) was serving in Zhejiang at the time, and was ordered to supervise the business: he saw it all with his own eyes. But it is neither these malefactors nor the Taoists who create havoc among the living: that kind are called zombies.

Zombies fall into two types. The first type consists of the newly dead; before they are laid in their coffin they can jerk upright and attack people. The second type consists of those who though long buried have not rotted, but have taken on demonic form. They may come out at night and will grab anyone they meet. Some believe the "drought demon" is of this kind, but that cannot be verified.

Now when a man dies his spirit is parted from his body. Given that detachment, how can he maintain conscious activity? Supposing on the other hand that the spirit is still attached to the body, he is then in a position to return to life: why then does he become a monster instead of a man? Moreover, the newly dead zombie will clutch even his parents and children in an iron grip, digging his fingers into their flesh. If he is not conscious, how can he act with such vigour? If on the other hand he retains awareness, how does he not recognize his nearest and dearest so soon after he has breathed his last? Most likely there is some other unholy force at work here, the corpse being infused with some malevolent energy, and it is not a case of the wandering soul changing of itself into an alien monster.

Our predecessor Yuan Mei has a story in his *What the Sage Did Not Speak of* about the walking corpse of a scholar from Nanchang who met a friend one night. The walking corpse began by begging the friend's favour, went on to express gratitude, fell into melancholy mood—then suddenly took on demonic aspect, attacked and bit his friend. The explanation offered is that men have two souls, the higher soul being sensitive and benign, and the lower soul being dull and brutish. To begin with the higher soul was still in control, and the lower soul was subservient. But towards the end of their encounter the scholar's concerns had been relieved and his higher soul faded away, leaving the lower soul in control. So while the higher soul was present, he behaved like a human being; when it departed he was no longer the same human being. The walking dead are all the creation of the lower soul. Only those who have attained occult powers are able to subdue this soul.

This view is indeed insightful, but from my narrow perspective I suspect there are other causes.

No Fun to Encounter a Zombie
RSWW I 16

Nobody knew where the physician Hu Gongshan came from. Some held that he was originally called Jin, and he had spied for Wu Sangui, the warlord; he changed his name after Wu's rebellion failed. But as there is no evidence to back up that view, the truth of the matter cannot be known. I was about six years old when I saw him, at which time he was over eighty, but he was still as agile as a monkey, and his skill in martial arts was unsurpassed. Once upon a time the boat he was on was boarded at night by a band of robbers. He was unarmed, but he reversed his hold on his tobacco pipe and wielded its long stem like the wind; he felled the seven or eight robbers by thrusting it up their nostrils. Yet he was in terror of spectres, and never dared to sleep on his own.

He told of how in his youth he had encountered a zombie. When he landed blows on it with flailing fists, it was like hitting wood or stone. He very nearly fell into its clutches, but luckily escaped by shinning up a tall tree. The zombie circled the tree in hops and skips all through till dawn, when it wrapped its arms round the tree and stopped moving. Only when he heard the bells of an approaching camel caravan did he dare to look down. The zombie's body was covered with white fur, its eyes were as red as cinnabar, its fingers like hooks, its fangs protruding from its lips like sharp blades. It was so terrifying a sight that Hu almost lost his senses.

On another occasion he stopped overnight in a mountain inn. He was awoken from his sleep by something wriggling under his coverlet: he thought it might be a snake or rodent. Soon the thing straightened and grew like a tree branch, gradually lengthening and expanding. Its head emerged from the coverlet and rested on the pillow alongside his own. It was a naked woman. Her arms tightened around him like the coils of a hawser. When she kissed him her breath was hot, the rank smell of blood clogged his nostrils. He slipped into a coma. The next day he was revived only by having a cordial poured down his throat. Thereafter he lost his courage. After dark he took fright at the sound of the wind and the shadows cast by the moon, and would not venture out.

Drought Demons Et Al.
RSWW I 4

The devastation wreaked by the Drought Demon is alluded to in the *Book of Songs*, which gives it classical status. *The Classic of Mountains and Seas* specifies a female demon, possibly an elaboration in aid of euphony. However that may be, the reference is only to a malicious spirit. Nowadays, in contrast, the Drought Demon is always identified as a zombie; when the said zombie is disinterred and incinerated, that reliably precipitates rain. Now rain is owed to the happy conjunction of heaven and earth: can the puissance of a zombie actually clog up the workings of the universe, frustrating this union? Another explanation for rain is that it is created by dragons. Can the devices of a zombie be so potent as to make a divine being like a dragon cringe and back down before it? What theory could explain it?

On the different matter of fox spirits being able to evade a timed lightning strike, this has been mentioned in many novels and anecdotes from the Song dynasty onwards. Now supposing the fox is guiltless, this would be gratuitous punishment, and the way of Heaven is not like that. Supposing on the other hand that the fox is guilty, it can be struck down at any time: why set a certain hour and day, which will allow it to find out in advance and take refuge? Even if on one occasion the fox were able by chance to escape its fate, why when this appointed time has passed can justice no longer be pursued? That would amount to judicial delinquency, and again the way of Heaven is not like that. So what theory can explain it?

I have picked up the recently published *Nocturnal Discourses* [by He Bang'e, with contents similar to Ji Xiaolan's], and read of one example of a Drought Demon being burned and two examples of foxes escaping execution, so leave the matter open to question, to await detailed analysis by scholars of the science.

THE BOGEY
RSWW I 6

The sha *spirit, here called "bogey", belonged to folklore, and perhaps for that reason had no clear definition. It seems to have been conceived of either as one of a deceased person's several souls, albeit a baleful one, that returns to, or departs from, the coffin some days after death, or a kind of bogey which may accompany a returning soul to the coffin, or most loosely as any kind of baneful spirit.*

* * *

Zhang Du of the Tang dynasty says in his work *The Han Palace*:

"It is popularly believed that some days after a person dies, a bird emerges from the coffin: the bird is given the name '*sha*'. In the Taihe reign of the Wei dynasty [third century AD], a man called Zheng netted a big bird with grey-black plumage which stood some four feet tall. All of a sudden it vanished. He asked the village folk what it could be. The answer came: 'A few days ago someone here died and the diviner foretold that his *sha* would emerge today, so his family gathered round and saw a huge blackish bird come out of his coffin. Would that be what you caught?'"

This is what is now referred to as a "bogey". To quote another source, Xu Xuan [tenth century] says in his *Investigating the Spirit World*:

"Tiger Peng was a big and strong young man who bragged he was not afraid of ghosts. When his mother died, the local shaman warned him: 'On such and such a day the baleful *sha* will return and create mayhem. You would be wise to keep clear of it.' The women and children all left the house and hid, only Tiger stayed behind. That night someone thrust open the door and came in. Tiger was thrown into fear and panic. There being a big vat near at hand, he dived into it and pulled the lid over his head. He felt the presence of his mother above him. A voice asked, 'Is there anybody under the lid?' His mother answered, 'No.'"

This again is what is now called a "bogey".

It is commonly said that if a child dies before it has teeth, it leaves no bogey; if a dead child has teeth, it turns into one, and shamans are able to predict the day it will return. My family bondservants Sun Wenju and Song Wen were both well up in this arcane art. I got hold of their handbooks and found they only contained charts of the sixty-year cycle of year, month and day, nothing more magical or profound than that. As for the claim that at the predicted advent of the malignant bogey certain spells and charms can be used to dispel its power, that is just hocus-pocus to trick people out of their money. It is also said that for those who lived in cramped dwellings which afforded them no room to hide from the bogey, there was still a method to subdue it and prevent its emergence: this was called "slaying the devil", which was even more absurd. All the same, when the wife of my bondservant Song Yu died, he called on a shaman to perform the latter office. To this day there are noises at night in her room, and his young children often see her figure, so it seems bogeys might not all be make-believe.

There is nothing strange under the sun, there is no plumbing the depths of the visible and invisible world. We need not invent tortuous explanations for such things, nor should we go out of our way to controvert such beliefs.

Category Confusion
LYXL II 3

If you maintain that gods and immortals do not exist, some will object that they have encountered them. If you aver they do indeed exist, the objection will be that encounters are few and far between.

Starting with the work of Liu Xiang and going on to those of Ge Hong and Tao Hongjing [second to sixth centuries AD], there have been as many as a hundred books that tell of such beings, and not less than a thousand names are mentioned. However, none of those names recur in later ages, which all have their own roster of gods and immortals. Despite being able to prolong their existence by consolidating their life force, could it be that in the end they still go the way of all flesh? Another problem is, gods and immortals preserve their integrity, while sorcerers effect magical transformations: their paths do not cross. Yet all the books characterize the performers of transformations as gods and immortals, making absolutely no distinction.

Let us turn to Mother Wang, a native of Peking whose home was deep in the hills. She told my late mother of a holy man in those hills whose years had passed the three score. His abode was a small hut, his sustenance wild fruit and spring water, and all his time was spent chanting the scriptures to the beat of a wooden fish. He never visited any home, and if people called on him he did not engage in small talk, neither did he accept any offer of food.

Mother Wang's nephew worked away from home as a labourer. One evening he passed the holy man's hut on his way back to see his mother. The holy man exclaimed in alarm: "A tiger roams these hills at night, you're putting your life at risk! I'll have to go with you."

He led the way, drumming on his wooden fish. They had only gone a few hundred yards before a tiger did spring out in their path. The holy man blocked its way, and the tiger slunk away. The holy man then departed without a word, and was not seen in those parts again. Could he have been an immortal, I wonder?

My paternal uncle Mei'an told me he had seen a man send a boy up to a three-storey high fortified lookout post (in the north these are built on top of houses as a precaution against bandits). At a sign from the man, the boy jumped lightly down, without suffering so much as a scratch. The same man threw a brass ewer into a stream, and at his call the ewer slowly floated to the surface. There we have an example of the proscribed tricks of sorcerers, nothing to do with immortals.

My maternal uncle Zhang Jianting told me of a farmer from the town of Zhuanhe who grazed cattle on common land. One day the whole lot just fell down dead. A sorcerer came by and told the farmer:

"They are not really dead, a demon has just taken possession of their souls. If you hurry up and pour this potion of mine down their throats, you'll be in time to save their vital organs from damage. I'll take it on myself to suppress the demon for you, and restore their souls to the cattle."

The farmer then invited the sorcerer to his house, where he performed a kind of shuffling dance as he cast a spell. In a quarter of an hour the cattle, true to his word, were back on their feet again. Ignoring the farmer's offer of a meal, the sorcerer departed without a backward look.

A person up to the sorcerer's game explained:

"This trick is performed by first mixing a poisonous herb in the cattle's fodder, then administering an antidote, that's all. He refused recompense to show that money was not his object; in fact he was preparing the ground to come back and exploit the locals' gullibility. I saw this fellow pull the same stunt in Shandong."

In the light of this we can see that there are false sorcerers as well as genuine ones: what nonsense to lump them together with gods and immortals!

* * *

Mother Wang's story of the holy man in the hills is by no means unique. There were several local legends about Zen masters (Chanshi) *taming man-eating tigers in the hills.*

Primeval Gods
RSWW I 44

Jiang Boyan [fellow graduate 1754] contributed this.

A certain scholar was walking in the Tongbai Mountains when he came upon a regal cavalcade. From the persons' apparel they seemed to be of the other world. He took cover in the trees, but had already been seen by the dignitary in his carriage, who called on him to come out for a talk. His attitude was remarkably amiable. The scholar respectfully asked the gentleman's title.

"I am the god of these mountains" was his reply.

"In which reign was Your Divinity born? I venture to ask in order to pass on the information to the human world, to the end of improving general knowledge."

"You couch your question in terms of men who have been elevated to gods, whereas I am a primeval god. When Heaven and Earth first separated, ethereal matter coalesced into a myriad forms. On their completion these forms accrued energy, and this energy in turn generated vital essence; the concentration of vital essence bred constitution and character, which when developed ignited the spark of divinity. Hence divine beings were coeval with Heaven and Earth. The sages uniquely perceived the origins of creation, which is why they burned offerings with fragrant kindling wood in worshipping Heaven and buried jade in worshipping Earth, as is recorded in the Six Classics.

"On the advent of storytellers with their trivial tales, vulgarity was begotten. According to them, one god was named Zheng, another named Liu; the ruler of Heaven could be deposed; the River God was named Lü, or maybe Feng, and had a female consort. Confucian theorists took exception to all that. After Zhu Xi rose to prominence in the Song dynasty, they restricted the function of Heaven to the working out of 'principle', or natural law. They dismissed as nonsense the Lord of Heaven giving his mandate to the House of Zhou, as is described in the *Book of Songs*. Furthermore, they ascribed the powers of gods and spirits to the expansion and contraction of the forces of yin and yang.

"In fact, even the vital spark of wood and stone can engender the genii of forest and hills, as can rain and soil give birth to monsters. Given the revolutions of Heaven and Earth and the pervasiveness of primordial ethereal matter, you must surely accept that it is possible to make the ascent to a being who holds sovereign dominion!

"Now I suppose from your dress that you are an educated man. Please spread my word, and make those Confucianists understand why the sages made sacrifices in gratitude for Heaven's benisons."

The scholar bowed and withdrew. But whenever he passed on this message he was suspected of spreading fallacies.

In my opinion, this discourse on the basis and beginnings of spirits and divinities may be very lucid, but it is only Boyan's own ideas, put in the mouth of a god. Why would a high and mighty god bother to contradict the arguments of narrow dogmatists?

The Cracked Bell Monster
HXZZ II 61

Besides illustrating the capacity of inanimate objects to come to life, this item is of interest as an example of Ji Xiaolan's determination to extricate a moral lesson from the most unpromising of subject matters.

* * *

Li Huating from Wenshui in Shanxi province contributed this.

There was a derelict temple not far from his home which was said to be inhabited by an ogre, and everybody gave it a wide berth after dark. A bunch of sheep traders happened to put up there to shelter from the rain. During the night they heard a hooting sort of noise, and in the darkness saw something round and bloated in shape; what its features were they could not make out. In any case it lumbered towards them, its gait extremely cumbersome. Being all young roughnecks, the sheep traders did not turn a hair; they met it with a hail of brickbats, which made a ringing sound when they struck home. The monster faltered and began to retreat. Seeing what a poor show it put up, they chased it with whoops and cheers. It came to a halt at the broken down gateway to the temple, where it remained motionless. On near view it turned out to be a cracked bell; inside it were a lot of bone fragments, which they took to be the remains of its meals.

The next day the sheep traders told their story to the local inhabitants. The bell was melted down and its metal cast to make utensils. That put paid to the menace. This thing was remarkably clumsy and inept, yet it still sallied forth to molest people, only to end up destroying itself. It seems it had observed that among weird things expert in assuming other forms there were some who got up to mischief, and had tried to copy them.

We had a maidservant from a village in Cangzhou prefecture. She said that in the past her village had been the base for a band of robbers. One ordinary villager saw what rich pickings they got, and he too turned to robbery. When the authorities made a big raid to mop up the robbers, the hardened ones put up a fierce fight and got away, while this one was captured and put to death. I would say he had a lot in common with the cracked bell.

2

GHOSTS

Despite ancient Greece being a wellspring of scientific thought, it also invented a pantheon of gods of such fascination that they continued to people European painting, sculpture and poetry for a good two thousand years. Less inspiringly, in China the courts of heaven were ruled over by beings who hardly differed from emperors below except in the lengths of their beards, while out in the field many of the gods who watched over various aspects of life on earth were historical personages elevated to divinity after they passed away. Dragons and demons had the particular province of managing natural forces like rain and drought. As a whole, the spirit world in China was conceived of as hierarchical, in imitation of the social order on earth, especially the bureaucratic order; indeed the workings of the nether world seemed to be an exact replica.

In contrast to gods, ghosts were an order of beings who dwelt in daily proximity to humans. Their existence was more accepted than explained. An explanation was available, however; it derived from classical cosmogony. The most coherent theory subscribed to by early philosophers was that the space between heaven and earth was filled by a rarefied vapour or ether, given the same name as "breath" (qi), for in common with breath it carried a charge of energy. Given this coincidental resemblance to the atoms with their electrons of modern physics, qi is often translated as "matter-energy", though when the energy aspect is emphasized "life force" might be preferred. In this early version of the theory, it was the qi of earth which produced the myriad forms of creation, and the qi of heaven which infused vitality in the forms and enhanced their particular properties. The Neo-Confucians of the Song dynasty dispensed with the dual role of heaven and earth, replacing their function by the one agency of li, *or organizing principle.* Li *worked entirely autonomously, and not only patterned the physical world but also determined norms for social and moral behaviour. By recognizing only universal norms, the concept of* li *left no room for the abnormal, which is why Ji Xiaolan and thousands like him who took the view that there were more things in heaven and earth than were dreamt of in that philosophy were displeased with it: at the lowest level it made life less interesting, and interest is what Ji lived for.*

If Ji thought the notion of li *was applied too dogmatically, he fully accepted the partner notion that* qi *filled and formed the universe, from which ghosts could not be excluded. However, since by definition ghosts enjoyed only an afterlife, they were deprived of the vitality of living beings, that is to say their matter-energy was diminished. That presumption underpins some of the stories that follow. The Neo-Confucian view ruled out that afterlife: they held that the* qi *of living beings dispersed forthwith on death and mingled with the* qi *of heaven and earth: end of story. The basis of all ghost tales, contrariwise, is that the story continues: ghosts retire to a parallel universe where some seem to live uneventful lives until disturbed, while others actively intervene in the earthly world because they have unfinished business, usually a grudge or grievance of some kind, most dramatically one that led to unnatural death.*

At this point we cross into the territory of popular beliefs and individual yarn spinning, both of which are equally represented in Ji's collection. Chinese intellectuals seem to have been more addicted to spinning yarns about the supernatural than their counterparts in other cultures, particularly in the Qing dynasty, when it became a literary genre: Ji's collection was one of many similar compilations. Apart from straightforward retelling of unearthly happenings and experiences for their story value, the literati also used the ghost setting as a framework for making or debating a point, or pointedly criticizing the morals and manners of their day: who after all was better placed to observe what went on in private than the unseen ghost? Some examples of the ghost in this reproving role are given below.

On a few occasions Ji Xiaolan speaks on his own behalf to raise general questions about the spirit world, attempting to follow a logical train of thought. One example given here is particularly interesting because it shows he has absorbed some of the geographical knowledge imparted by the Jesuit scholars employed for their expertise at the Chinese court in the seventeenth and eighteenth centuries: before their arrival very little was known about the western hemisphere or the globe as a whole. More starkly than elsewhere, we see enacted in these think-pieces the contest between his scepticism and his credulity. Ultimately, and rather disappointingly, he usually gives way to the bureaucratic instinct to keep options open.

However, the occasional exercise of free thought in respect of particular conundrums does not imply any doubt whatsoever on Ji Xiaolan's part about the reality of ghosts and spirits. The first item below shows that it would have been almost unfilial of him to doubt: belief was practically written into his family constitution.

One more thought: perhaps the density of population mentioned in the Introduction to this volume might explain the number of stories about ghosts being in competition with not only humans but also foxes for living space.

Belief by Heredity
LYXXL VI 28

This account goes back to the last stage of the Ming dynasty, and concerns my great-great-great-uncle Ai Tang. Locally he enjoyed the reputation of a scholar, and was a dedicated follower of the Zheng Xuan-Kong Yingda tradition of Confucianism. In both the heat of summer and cold of winter he stayed up till midnight poring over his books. One evening he dreamed of finding himself before a government office, over whose door there was a board reading "Bureau of Ceremonials". Inside a dozen men, all vaguely familiar to him, were sorting documents. When they saw Master

Ai Tang, they exclaimed in one voice:

"You're much too soon, you don't take up your place here for another seven years!"

Master Ai Tang woke up with a jolt, realizing that meant he had only that number of years to live. Thereafter he daily sought the company of Buddhist and Taoist monks. He once invited a Taoist adept whose views were very congenial to share some wine with him. After the Taoist went on his way he ran into a servant of Ai Tang called Hu Mengde, and said to him:

"Just now I forgot to give a book to your master. You can take it back for me."

Master Ai Tang found the book contained spells and incantations for controlling supernatural forces. He shut himself up to learn and rehearse them. When he had quite mastered the spells, he set about performing them for his own amusement, and in this way whiled away his remaining years. He fell ill and died in the tenth year of the Chongzhen reign [1637], as predicted.

Half a day after expiring, Ai Tang came to life again, to tell those about his bier:

"I have been taken to task in the underworld for profanely using the spells of the Thunder God, and the court there has ordered that this book be returned. Please burn it immediately."

When the burning was carried out he expired again. But a short time later he revived once more, to say:

"The judges have inspected the book and found that three pages are missing. I have been commanded to come back to retrieve them."

There were indeed three pages among the ashes that had been only partially burned. Once these too were committed to the flames, Ai Tang finally passed away.

My father Yao An inserted this episode in our family annals. He had heard it from his great-grandfather, who in turn had heard it from his own father, the very person who had burned the book. I find it hard to believe that on this evidence anyone could deny the existence of ghosts and spirits.

A Drunken Ghost Gives Clue to Its Constitution
LYXXL II 14

It was night time when a butcher by the name of Xu Fang set down the two crocks of wine he was carrying on his shoulder pole, and took a rest under a big tree. The moon shone bright as day. From some way off there came a kind of hooting sound, and a ghost of frightening aspect emerged from the shrubbery. Xu Fang hid behind the tree, gripping his shoulder pole in readiness to defend himself. The ghost came upon the crocks, and danced in delight. It wasted no time in opening one and draining its contents. Turning to the second crock, it had only got the stopper half out before it collapsed in a heap.

Xu Fang was beside himself with fury, and guessing the ghost was now defenceless, he attacked it with his shoulder pole: it was like striking nothingness. As he rained hefty blows on it, its recumbent body gradually dissolved into a dense pool of vapour. Fearing it might still be capable of transformation, he hammered it with another hundred blows. The vapour spread out flat on the ground and gradually began to disperse, its remnants like pale ink, like diaphanous silk, thinning all the time, until not a trace was left, doubtless marking the ghost's total extinction.

In my view, ghosts are the vestiges of a person's vital energy. This energy dissipates with the passing of time, which is why it is stated in the *Zuo Commentary on the Spring and Autumn Annals* that new ghosts are large, old ghosts are small. We know of people seeing ghosts, but I have never heard of them seeing ghosts that date back to far antiquity: that is because their vital energy has utterly dispersed. Alcohol is in itself a dispersal agent, which is why physicians use it as a supplement in medicines for quickening the blood, inducing sweating, treating depression and chills, and suchlike purposes. As for this particular ghost, its vital energy was on the wane, and was further dispersed through drinking a whole crock of wine: the dominant yang element in the wine caused turbulence and vaporized the weak yin, so total extinction was a matter of course. It was the alcohol that caused annihilation, not the beating.

When I heard this tale I had with me a teetotaller. He commented: "A ghost's form is volatile. It was due to the effect of alcohol that it fell down and suffered the beating. Men go in fear of ghosts, but being given to drinking, this one was subjugated by man. Wine bibbers should take note!"

A heavy drinker was also present. He said: "Though ghosts have no substantial form, they still have consciousness, so they are not free from the swings of emotion. In falling down dead to the world and gravitating to oblivion, this ghost was discovering its proper nature. One can look for no greater fulfilment from drinking than this. The Buddhists regard nirvana as the highest bliss: what do those who hurry and scurry know of that!"

I imagine this would be what Zhuangzi meant by "This is one way of looking at things, that is another way"!

An Epicurean Ghost
HXZZ I 28

Mr Sun Duanren, my former examiner, is a talented writer of great learning and elegance, and at the same time a heavy drinker. His compositions when drunk are no different from those when sober. The notables of the academy rate him as second only to the great poet Li Bai in turning out masterpieces while under the influence.

During his service as Commissioner for Education in Yunnan province, Mr Sun was enjoying a tipple by himself in a bamboo grove one moonlit night when he saw a shadowy figure staring intently at his wine pot and beaker, as if dying for a drink. Though he realized at once it must be a ghost, he was not alarmed; he simply put his hand over his beaker, saying, "I'm running low on wine today, I'm afraid I have none to spare." The figure shrank back and disappeared.

After Mr Sun sobered up he regretted what he had done. He reflected: "Since he came in quest of wine, it shows he was not your common or garden ghost. Besides which, he readily settled on me as provider, which shows he holds me in some regard. Why should I have been so offhand in rejecting his company?"

Thereupon he sent for three brimming bowls of the best wine and set them out on a little table in the bamboo grove for the ghost to enjoy the next night.

When he inspected the bowls the following day, he found that the wine had remained untouched. He sighed: "This gentleman is not only cultured, he also has his pride: just because I played a little joke on him he refused to take a single drop!"

One of Sun's secretaries pointed out: "Ghosts and spirits only savour bouquets, of course they can't actually drink!"

"In that case," responded Sun with some warmth, "I'll get my drinking in before I become a ghost, not leave it till I can only enjoy the smell!"

Mr Sun's nephew, Sun Yushan, told me this story when he was my assistant in Fujian. It brings our wine-loving Sages of the Bamboo Grove very much back to life.

* * *

The Seven Sages of the Bamboo Grove were a group of libertarian free-thinking intellectuals of the third century AD who were devoted to wine and music.

Do Ghosts Exist?

LYXXL VI 6

In the fourth year of the Qianlong reign [1739], I was a pupil at the Gathering Clouds Retreat [in his father's mansion] in Peking, along with Li Yunju and Huo Yangzhong, both from Dongguang county in Hebei province. One evening the conversation turned to the supernatural. Yunju took the view that ghosts and deities existed, Yangzhong held they did not. While they were debating the issue, Yunju's attendant unexpectedly intervened, holding forth in this wise:

"There are many strange happenings in the world, things that I would not have credited had I not experienced them in person. I was passing through the overgrown graveyard in front of the temple to the tutelary god when I accidentally put my foot through a coffin. That same night I dreamed that the tutelary god had me arrested, saying that someone had complained that I had damaged his abode. I realized that he was referring to my breaking the coffin. I disputed the point with the plaintiff, saying: 'The fact is your abode should not be in the middle of the pathway; it is not that I encroached on your domain.'

"The ghost disputed in turn: 'No, the fact is the pathway was made over my abode; my abode was not originally in the middle of it.'

"The tutelary god smiled at me, saying: 'Everyone walks along that path, so I cannot blame you for doing so. On the other hand, everyone steps on his abode without breaking it: how come *you* should break it? In the circumstances, I cannot let you off entirely: in compensation you should burn paper money for his use in the nether regions.'

"After some reflection the god added: 'The ghost cannot repair his coffin himself. You should lay a board over it, and spread a layer of earth on top.'

"The next day I did as the god instructed, and also burnt the money offering, whereupon a squall arose and whirled the ashes away. On a following night I once again passed through the graveyard, and heard a voice inviting me to take a seat. I was sure it was the same ghost, and fled as fast as my legs would carry me. The ghost laughed heartily, making a sound like the hooting of an owl. To this day my hair stands on end when I think of it."

Yangzhong said to Yunju: "Your attendant backs you up: my one voice cannot contend with your two voices. But when all's said and done, other people seeing things is not the same as me seeing things."

Yunju replied: "Supposing you were to hear a case in court, would you require to have seen with your own eyes all the events described before you believed them? Or would you accept the testimony of witnesses? Since the former is out of the question, isn't accepting the testimony of witnesses tantamount to equating what others have seen with what you have seen? I ask you, how would you dispose of the matter?"

Thereupon everybody laughed, and the debate concluded.

One Ghost Is Reproved, Another Ghost Reproves
LYXXL V 30

When my honoured father Yao An was posted to Yunnan province, one of his secretaries reported an uncanny apparition which occurred in the government compound on moonlit nights, namely a woman heavily made up and richly attired in red standing under an ornamental citron tree; when she sighted people, she slowly sank into the ground. The general view was that the spot she stood on should be dug up to see what was buried there. My father took a beaker of wine and poured a libation on the earth under the tree. He addressed the woman politely in these words:

"Since you hide when you see people, it shows you have no intention of creating mischief. So why do you have to frequently manifest yourself, and court the danger of having your remains exposed?"

The ghost did not appear again.

Another happening took place in a large and airy studio in the grounds of the government compound, which had long been left empty. My uncle An Wuzhang had accompanied my father to Yunnan, and on one hot summer night slept there in the buff. He dreamt of a man approaching him, bowing, and saying:

"It is true that our kind and yours belong to the different realms of the material and immaterial, but our families live here with us, and we observe the distinctions between the sexes. What prevents you, good sir, from conducting yourself as becomes a gentleman?"

My uncle awoke with a start, and dared not sleep there again.

My father remarked: "The ghost under the tree could be persuaded by reasoned argument, and equally the spectre in the studio could instruct the living by reasoned argument. This prefecture is situated off the beaten track in a circle of mountains, and the customs here are plain and simple, like back when the world was young. Hence the unearthly beings too stand for no nonsense."

Distinguished Scholar Allows a Ghost's Rebuttal
GWTZ I 18

Mr Wang Zhirui, from my home region of Hejian, was a star pupil of the great scholar-official Li Guangdi. His learning was profound and his conduct principled: in a word he was a gentleman of the old school. Mr Wang was still preceptor in the Imperial Academy of Learning at the turn of the Yongzheng-Qianlong reigns [1735–1736], when I accompanied my father to the capital, but to my lasting regret I never met him.

According to legend, one night Mr Wang happened to go to the yard at the rear of his hall of residence to pull up some radishes he had planted, to go with the wine he was drinking. He thought he saw a shadowy figure, whom he suspected of thieving. But the figure suddenly disappeared, convincing him instead that it was a ghost. Thereupon he launched into a tirade about overstepping the dividing line between the realms of light and shade. He heard a voice respond from a stand of bamboos:

"You, sir, have gone deeply into the *Book of Changes*, and will know that the opposition of yin and yang is the way of Heaven. People go about by day, ghosts go about by night: that is the dividing line between light and shade. People occupy a space without ghosts, ghosts occupy a space without people: that marks the partition between them. Now there is nowhere in the world where there are no people, and equally nowhere where there are no ghosts, but as long as they leave each other alone, there is no obstacle to their peacefully coexisting. If a ghost were to intrude into your living quarters in the daytime, you would be within your rights to reprimand it. In this case, it is late at night, and the place is an empty space, that is to say the time is when ghosts are active, and the place is that which ghosts occupy. You neither carried a lantern nor raised your voice as a warning; so, taken by surprise, I could not prevent your stumbling across me. It is you who have trespassed against a ghost, not the other way round. My discreetly avoiding you should have satisfied you. Why should you have reprimanded me so rudely?"

Mr Wang laughed and said: "You have made a fair point. We'll leave the matter be." With that he pulled up his radishes and retired to his room. Later on he recounted the incident to his student, who responded:

"Since the ghost was able to speak, and you for your part were not frightened, you could have got his name out of him, and adopting a superior tone, questioned him to ascertain whether the stories about the courts of the dead are true or not: that would have been a solid contribution to knowledge."

Mr Wang replied: "At the same time, that would have been to presume an intimacy between men and ghosts: where then would have been my insistence on light and shade being separate realms?"

Ghost Remonstrates with Reprobate
LYXXL IV 27

In the twenty-first year of the Qianlong reign [1756] a provincial graduate from Fujian province travelled to the capital to compete in the triennial doctoral examination. He arrived at year's end, and being pressed for time was unable to find suitable lodging, so he rented a room in a run-down temple north of the Altar to Agriculture. One night a couple of weeks after he moved in, he heard a voice outside his window, saying:

"Excuse me if I wake you, sir, but I have something to say. I occupied this room for a considerable time, but to start with I was willing to yield it to you, mindful that you were an educated man who had undertaken a very long and strenuous journey in order to make your mark in the world. Then I observed that you, good sir, spent all day out and about, but I did not hold that against you, as you were new to the capital and would probably want to look up various friends and relatives. More recently you have often come home drunk, and a certain doubt crept into my mind. Just now, when I heard you tell the priest that you frequented drinking houses to watch plays, I realized that you are simply a ne'er-do-well. I have had to move into a niche behind the Buddha's throne, which is cramped and difficult of access. I can no longer continue to deny myself by giving place to a person such as you. If you do not move out tomorrow, be warned that I have laid by a stock of missiles."

The priest in the room across the passageway heard these words, and advised the scholar to seek accommodation elsewhere. Thenceforth the priest did not dare let out this room again, citing this incident to anyone who enquired.

The Ghost Hermitage

LYXXL VI 10

Dai Zhen contributed this.

Towards the end of the Ming dynasty a gentleman named Song penetrated deep into the mountains of She county in Anhui province while exploring for a propitious grave site. As dusk fell storm clouds gathered, and seeing a cave at the foot of an escarpment, Song made for it to seek shelter. A voice issued from inside the cave, announcing: "A ghost lives here, you had better keep out."

"So what are *you* doing in there?" Song enquired.

"I *am* the ghost!"

Song asked if they could get acquainted. The ghost responded:

"Your yang aura and my yin aura will conflict if we come together, and you would be sure to suffer a nasty chill. I suggest you light a fire as a precaution, and sit at some distance from me while we talk."

When they were so settled, Song asked:

"How come you live here? Surely you have a grave to go to?"

"I served a term as magistrate in the Wanli period [1573–1619]. The way my fellow officials fought over spoils and intrigued for preferment disgusted me, so I resigned from my post and stayed home for the rest of my days. On my death I pleaded with the King of the Nether World to spare me from reincarnation, and was allowed to exchange the rank and salary due me in the next life for an official position down below. What would you know, the greed and rivalry there was still the same! So I resigned again, to retire to my grave. But I could not put up with the awful racket the horde of ghosts made milling about in the cemetery, and had no choice but to seek solitude here. Though the cold wind and endless rain make it bleak and comfortless, it is a paradise compared to the turmoil of officialdom and the traps and pitfalls of common life. Being all by myself in these barren hills, I even forget what year it is. I couldn't say how long ago it was I cut myself off from ghostland, and am even vaguer when I left mankind behind. I have luxuriated in being released from all worldly ties and able to immerse myself in nature. But now that humankind has made tracks to my haven, I shall have to move on again on the morrow. This peaceful sanctuary is lost to me forever!"

The ghost refused to be drawn further, and even ignored Song's enquiry after his name. Song had brush and ink with him; before he left he wrote two big characters over the mouth of the cave: Ghost Hermitage.

A Ghost Defiled
LYXXL IV 25

A tenant farmer of ours by the name of Zhang Tianxi came upon a skull lying in an open field, and just for fun urinated in its mouth. All at once the skull bounded up from the ground and gave voice, saying:

"You must know that humans and ghosts go their own ways: why should you abuse me? Besides, I am a woman, you are a man: it is even more disgraceful that you should so defile me."

The skull bounded higher and higher in the air, until it knocked him in the face. When Tianxi fled in terror, the ghost followed him home. Every night afterwards cursing and complaining came from the top of his wall and the eaves of his house. Tianxi succumbed to ague and became delirious. The whole family knelt and prayed, which mollified the ghost to some extent. Someone thought to enquire the ghost's former name and dwelling place. The ghost complied in full. The whole family then kowtowed, saying:

"Then you must be our great-grandmother! Why should you plague your descendants?"

What sounded like a choking sob came from the ghost: "Are you really my own family? When did you move here? Tell me how you are related to me."

The Zhang family explained the ins and outs of the matter. The ghost sighed deeply:

"It was not my own idea to pursue you; the whole tribe of ghosts in the neighbourhood egged me on, seeing this business as a chance to scrounge some food. There are a number of them in the sick man's room, and another lot gathered outside. If you will prepare a ladle of broth, I will do my best to persuade them to leave. You see, these ghosts are regularly starved of nourishment, but if they go on the rampage without good reason, they get into trouble from the gods. Given a chance like this to cause ructions, they will take it, hoping in that way to get offerings to pacify them. In future you should be careful to avoid bother like this, and not fall victim to their designs."

The family did as they were asked. The ghost reported: "They have all gone now, but the foul taste in my mouth is unbearable. You should go back to that place and find my bones, wash them clean, and give them a proper burial."

Her words ended in sobs. She was heard no more.

Ghosts Need Protection from Foxes
RSWW II 26

The venerable scholar Liu Tingsheng contributed this.

There was a huntsman in the Eastern City who awoke in the middle of the night to hear a sound like the pattering of rain against his window paper, followed by a rustling noise below the window. He threw on his clothes and barked out a question, demanding to know who it was. To his surprise the answer came:

"I am a ghost, and have come to ask for your help. Please do not be afraid."

Asked what the matter was, the ghost continued:

"Ghosts and foxes have never ever lived together. The grave vaults which the foxes make their dens are not lived in by ghosts. My own grave is roughly a mile north of the village. A fox took advantage of my temporary absence to move his family in, and had the gall to chase me away when I desired to enter. If I did battle with him, I would be sure to lose, having been a studious type. If I brought a plaint against him with the tutelary god, even were I to have the luck to have it allowed, again I would lose, because in the end the foxes would exact revenge. The solution, as I see it, would be for you, on your next hunting expedition, to circle round the spot a few times, not too close but close enough for the foxes to get the jitters and clear out. If you should run into them when that happens, do not rush to catch and kill them, for in that way it might become obvious that you have been primed to the task, and the foxes would again work up a grudge against me."

The huntsman did as requested, and afterwards dreamt of the ghost thanking him.

To sum up: The ghost clearly had justice on his side in wishing to reoccupy the home of which he had been dispossessed, but he lacked the strength to prevail, hence he avoided open conflict. Yet after he had rallied sufficient support to prevail, he still pondered on the long-term consequences, and did not use that superiority to the maximum. By neither chancing his arm in a stand-up fight nor looking for out-and-out victory, he did prevail in the end. When the weak and helpless come up against the strong and ruthless they might take a pointer from that ghost!

A Hanged Ghost Turns Temptress
LYXXL IV 21

The wife of an exiled criminal in Urumqi had hanged herself from a window frame in the Tiger Peak Academy. The director of the academy, a certain Chen Zhili, who had previously been magistrate of Ba in the district of Chongqing, was reading by candlelight one night when he heard a rustling sound coming from the ceiling over the window recess. He looked up to see two slender female feet slowly coming down through a gap in the paper. Gradually the knees appeared; still gradually, the thighs followed.

Chen had heard about the suicide. He said in a stern voice:

"Furious and resentful at your adultery being exposed, you died by your own hand. Would you torment me? I am not your enemy. Would you seduce me? I have never consorted with ladies of easy virtue, so I am proof against that temptation. If you are foolhardy enough to descend, I will strike you with my staff!"

Thereupon the legs slowly withdrew, and a faint sigh was heard. But soon after, the woman peeped through the crack, showing her face, which was indeed extremely pretty. Chen looked up and spurned her, saying scornfully: "Have you no shame, even in death?" The apparition straightway withdrew. Chen blew out the candles and retired to bed, hiding a dagger in his sleeve lest she visit him, but in the end she did not come down again. The next day Chen Tiqiao from Xianyou in Fujian visited him, and the conversation turned to this matter. As they spoke, a wail like the ripping of silk came from the roof space. The ghost left him alone after that.

But there was more to come. Chen Zhili's manservant slept in an outer room. He took to talking in his sleep, and in time succumbed to a wasting illness. Chen wept sorrowfully when he was on his deathbed, because this servant had followed his master a thousand miles to his posting. The servant waved his hand airily, saying:

"A fine looking woman has been visiting me in secret. Now she is going to take me home as her husband, so I depart this life joyfully. Do not grieve for me."

Chen stamped his foot in frustration, saying: "I chose not to move my quarters because I trusted to my mettle. I never imagined you would become the target for her devilry. If I'd only known that my leniency would have such an awful consequence!"

Subsequently Mr Yang Fengyuan of Liu'an in Anhui province, who graduated together with Chen, took over the directorship of the academy. He chose alternative quarters for himself, quoting Mencius' motto, "Do not stand under a high wall that is in danger of toppling."

A Governor Regrets Interviewing a Ghost
LYXXL III 12

Governor-General Tang Zhiyu was reviewing a case of homicide on which the verdict had been handed down. He sat alone one evening, reading the papers by lamplight, when he heard the faint sound of weeping. It seemed to be nearing his windows. He called on a maidservant to go out and see who it was. She gave a shriek and fell down in a faint. The governor parted the door curtain and saw a ghost splattered with blood kneeling at the foot of the steps. When the governor shouted a rebuke, the ghost kowtowed and said:

"My murderer was so-and-so. The magistrate condemned the wrong man for the crime. I cannot rest until the real culprit is brought to justice."

The governor replied, "I have taken note of what you say," and the ghost departed.

The next day the governor reopened court proceedings. The attendants produced the clothes and shoes the dead man wore: they matched those he had seen the night before. Now confirmed in his belief, he changed the verdict, indicting the man whom the ghost had named as the guilty party. The original examining magistrate put forward a host of arguments to the contrary, but in vain: the governor insisted that mountains would move sooner than he would alter his verdict.

The governor's private secretary suspected that there was more in this than met the eye, and he discreetly sounded his superior out. Only then did the governor reveal all that had happened. There was nothing the secretary could do at that point. Some nights later he requested a further interview. He asked the governor:

"Which direction did the ghost come from?"

"It just appeared at the foot of my steps."

"Which way did the ghost leave?"

"It took off like a shot over the wall."

"Ghosts have shape but no substance: it should have simply melted away on the spot, instead of scaling the wall."

A search was then undertaken, starting from where the ghost scaled the wall. No broken tiles were discovered, but due to it having recently rained, faint smears of mud were found on a trail over the roof ridges that ended at the boundary wall of the compound. The secretary showed these footprints to the governor, saying: "These were surely made by a cat burglar in the pay of the culprit." The governor needed little reflection to realize he had been taken in, and he restored the original verdict. To keep the matter quiet, he did not pursue further enquiries.

Ghosts Need Passes
LYXXL I 41

When I was serving in Urumqi, one of my military aides shuffled a batch of papers together and proffered brush and ink for me to sign them. He explained:

"When personnel die on station here, their coffins are shipped back to their place of origin. We customarily supply this documentation, otherwise their souls will not be allowed through the passes."

Because these certificates had to be transmitted to the Court of the Dead, they could not be endorsed in red ink, and the seal too had to be black. Their content was totally absurd, viz:

"To whom it may concern: This is to certify that so-and-so of such-and-such a place, of so many years of age, died of sickness on such-and-such a date in this jurisdiction. Presently his family are transporting his coffin back to his native place, this voucher being issued for said purpose. On the strength of this voucher we expect that the ghost-minions guarding the passes along the route will, after duly checking that the details are correct, allow transit for this soul, and not hold it up in order to extort payment, thus causing unwarranted difficulties."

I said: "This is no more than an invention of petty clerks to extract a fee for issuing these things." So I advised the commanding general to abolish this practice.

A week or so later someone reported that ghosts in the untended graveyard west of the city were wailing because they could not get home without such a certificate. I denounced that as a pack of nonsense. Another week passed, and there came a further report to the effect that the wailing had reached the city limits. I scorned this report as before. Another week or so later I heard ghost-jabbering coming from over the wall of my own quarters, but still I thought this was a put-up job on the part of the petty clerks. After another similar interval the sound came right up to my window. The moon was shining as bright as day; I rose and looked out: truly there was no one there. My colleague, the Manchu censor Guan Cheng advised:

"The stand you took was entirely proper: not even the commanding general could gainsay it. However, the wailing of the ghosts was heard by one and all: they truly blame you for their not getting their passports. Why don't you try approving a sample batch for now, to shut the mouths of your detractors. If the ghost wailing goes on as before, your hand will be strengthened."

Reluctantly I followed his advice. That night all was quiet.

In a similar occurrence, my military aide Song Jilu suddenly fell down in a faint when he was in the dispatch office. After he eventually regained consciousness, he said he had seen his mother arrive. Soon afterwards a messenger delivered an official missive. It was from the Hami administration, to say that Jilu's mother had died on her journey to see her son.

There is more in this world than can be explained: our theorists' discourse is confined to its normal workings. Among the 160 poems in my collection *Occasional Verses from Urumqi* there is one which reads:

> The feathered grass rustles in the wind and merges with the cold clouds
> Who determines the boundaries of mountains and passes?
> Shadowy ghosts come and go as their permits allow
> Han Yu knew not of that when he wrote his "On Ghosts".

This poem arose from those two incidents.

Sheep Have Souls Too
LYXXL V 43

That domestic animals should be killed for food is accepted as normal, but to slaughter them more than need be will lay up bad karma. Likewise those who kill them without due warrant can face redress. A garrison sergeant in Urumqi called Ru Daye contributed this:

An orderly whom Major Jimusa sent into the mountains to gather snow lotus became disoriented and could not find his way back. One night the major dreamed of his orderly bathed in blood. "On a certain mountain," he said, "some Mongol bandits struck me down and sliced me up and ate me. My remains still lie under such-and-such a pine tree south of the bridge. I beg you to send a search party to retrieve them."

The major sent a lieutenant to investigate, and indeed he found a bloody mess under the designated tree, but on inspection the bones proved to be those of a sheep. It came out that a group of soldiers on herding duty had stolen a sheep belonging to the local authorities and killed it on this spot. The orderly was assumed to have died elsewhere, but some days later he came back, having met a hunter who gave him directions. Only then was it realized that the sheep had possessed the orderly's soul as he slept in order to expose the herders' crime.

The Paradox of Ghostly Capacities
GWTZ I 30

We do not know whether the fox spirits regard as real the transformations they make by their own magic, or what they think of each other's transformations. What we do know for sure is that fox spirits have always been expert at changing into vamps to bewitch people.

As for ghosts, they are composed of the vestiges of the human life force. Their ability to draw on spiritual power is therefore no greater than that of living men. Living men cannot create something out of nothing, change small into big or ugly into charming. Yet according to what is written in many and varied accounts of encounters with ghosts, coffins are transformed into palatial chambers, into which men can be invited, and their tombs transformed into courtyards where men can reside. Ghosts who have died a violent death, and whose appearance on death is gruesome and repulsive, can transform themselves into beauties. How come they acquire such powers as soon as they become ghosts? Or, is it that instead of just acquiring these powers, they are somehow *taught* to exercise them? I find that even more inexplicable than the transformations of fox spirits.

I remember when I was on my way to Liangzhou in Gansu province, my driver pointed to a mountain col and said: "Some time ago I camped out hereabouts with a wagon train, and in the moonlight we could see people's houses far away on the mountainside, all surrounded by tamped earth walls, each house clearly outlined. When we passed close by the next day, they were just grave mounds."

So it seems that even in quite uninhabited places, ghosts can produce such phenomena by and for themselves. Were the ancient sages aware of such possibilities when they advocated the making of funerary models to furnish the needs of the dead in the afterlife?

The Problem of Foreign Ghosts
RSWW I 7

When people die, their ghosts are enrolled in the registers of the underworld. However, the planet earth has a circumference of thirty thousand miles and a diameter of ten thousand miles. The number of different countries is incalculable, their population must exceed that of China a hundredfold, and the spirits of their dead likewise exceed China's by the same multiple. How is it then that visitors to the underworld see only Chinese ghosts, no foreign ghosts? Could it be that they all have their own Kings of Hell in their homeland? Senior Secretary Gu Demao's portfolio includes matters related to the netherworld; I asked him this question, but he was unable to answer.

Those people who live forever have their names recorded in the register of immortals, Chisongzi and Guangchengzi being two such, both famed in high antiquity. How is it that immortals we now hear about are all of recent origin, while those recorded since the time of Liu Xiang of Western Han have dropped out of view? Could they have faded away to nothing, like Wei Boyang the alchemist of Eastern Han whom Zhu Xi discussed? The venerable Lou Jintan is a Taoist elder; I asked him this question, and he could not answer either.

Ghost Portraits
LYXXL II 24

The subject of this entry, the artist Luo Pin, was famed as one of the "Eight Eccentrics of Yangzhou". Prints of his portraits of spectres sold extremely well among the literati. In their monstrous appearance these spectres differed little from the nightmare creations of mythology; what was special was Luo's claim to have seen them with his own eyes in broad daylight, though his observations are so childish they are comical.

* * *

Luo Pin of Yangzhou is able to see ghosts. He says:

"Everywhere there are people, there are ghosts. Grim ghosts who have died a violent death, and have been suspended in limbo for many years, are mostly found in isolated and unoccupied buildings. They should be given a wide berth, because they will attack you. The common sort of ghost who drifts about aimlessly seeks the shade of walls in the forenoon, when the yang element is in the ascendant, but in the afternoon when the yin element dominates, wanders off in all directions. They can pass through walls at will, avoiding the use of doors, and if they encounter human beings they will give way to them, being afraid of their yang aura. These ghosts are found all over the place, and are not harmful."

Luo goes on to add: "Ghosts of the latter type congregate in densely populated places: I have rarely seen them in the wilds. They prefer to gather round kitchen stoves, presumably to enjoy the scent of food. They also favour latrines, I don't know why— perhaps because humans don't go near them more than necessary?"

Mr Luo has published an album of *Portraits from the Spectral Zone*, which one suspects to have been painted from imagination. One portrait shows a spectre whose head is enormously bigger than his body, which seems particularly fanciful. Yet I remember my late father telling of a Mr Chen from Yaojing who had his window shutters hooked back when he retired to bed one summer night. The window was all of ten feet wide. Suddenly a gigantic face looked in through it, filling its whole space; where and how its body was positioned could not be seen. Chen snatched up his sword and stabbed at the apparition's left eye. The apparition receded before this thrust, and disappeared. An old servant witnessed this incident from his room opposite: according to him, the apparition rose up from the ground under the window. They therefore dug a hole ten feet deep on that spot, but found nothing.

Figure 9. Luo Pin's big-headed ghost. Reproduced by permission of the Hong Kong Museum of Art from the collection of the Hong Kong Museum of Art.

So the existence of such a spectre was after all authenticated, but I confess I am out of my depth in this nebulous sphere: would that I knew where to turn for counsel!

ADDENDUM: Ji Xiaolan's letter to his distant nephew Yisun (*Family Letters*, FLP 2012 edition, p. 78, story not discovered in *Perceptions*)

When you were in Tongguan [Shaanxi province], you saw two female ghosts, and now back in Hejian you have met with a drowned ghost. You might wonder why ghosts like to play pranks on you: the reason is your uncle loves talking about foxes and ghosts! In your letter you ask about ways of catching ghosts. Unfortunately I am only the faithful chronicler of the ghost world: I record everything I hear. Not being Zhong Kui [the legendary ghost catcher], I don't know any formula for catching the ghosts I write about.

I am reminded of the old caution handed down to us, to the effect that a nervous disposition can create imaginary ghosts. For example, while a man afraid of ghosts was out walking one night, he heard the rustle of his own clothes, and suspected it might be a ghost making the noise. When he turned his head he could see nothing behind him, which only increased his fear. He stepped up his pace, which only made the rustling get louder. By the time he got home he was a nervous wreck. True, after he stopped walking the sound also stopped, but he still just put that down to the ghost withdrawing on seeing his family. That is quite a funny story.

Since you were bold enough to fire off a musket at ghosts in Tongguan, it proves you don't belong to that lot who are timid and fanciful. If people do often come across ghosts, it means they lack a robust constitution. Their only recourse is to nourish their vital powers and do good deeds—ghosts will not trouble them then.

In Urumqi there is a stretch of wilderness called "ghost

country". Once upon a time a merchant was passing through this area at night, when he suddenly caught sight of a shadowy figure in the trees. Suspecting it was a ghost, he called out, "What is your business here?" The reply came, "I got here at dusk, and being afraid of ghosts I waited for company before I went on." The merchant then joined up with him.

As they walked together, they became quite sociable, and the other man asked the merchant what urgent business he might have to venture out on such a cold night. The merchant replied:

"Long ago I borrowed twenty strings of cash from a friend. Today I got a letter from him saying that he and his wife were both ill, and their situation was critical. He pressed me to return a certain amount, so he could pay for doctors and medicine. I raised the cash in a hurry and am now travelling overnight to get it to him. I was afraid the least delay would cost them their lives. Though my shortest way led through this ghost country, it was a risk I had to take."

These words disconcerted his companion. He took a step back and said:

"I am a hanged ghost. Originally I meant to hex you and make you my surrogate, but hearing what you just said, I realize you are a gentleman of benevolence and honour. I dare not molest you; instead I offer to lead the way for you."

Shocked and horrified, the merchant refused the offer, but the other persisted: "You must know this is a ghost hollow. Up ahead lurk many violent ghosts who would do you harm. That is why I volunteered to guide you. I have no other motive."

Reluctantly the merchant consented. At all dangerous places on their route the ghost gave him prior warning. Only when dawn broke did he take his leave.

From this it can be seen that a single charitable thought can ward off harassment from ghosts. Please do not dismiss it as a fairy tale. If you stick to doing what is right and good, ghosts will always give you a wide berth.

Figure 10. Zhong Kui the Ghost Catcher by H. Y. Ting. Reproduced by permission of the Art Museum of The Chinese University of Hong Kong from the collection of the Art Museum of The Chinese University of Hong Kong.

3

HAUNTINGS

Ji Senior Braves Ghosts
RSWW III 16

It is, or was, characteristic of Chinese thinking to fit particular phenomena into a cosmic or at least historical framework or pattern. There is no greater order of things than the correlation but also opposition between the two fundamental forces at work in the universe, namely yin and yang. Yang is the polarity for light, fire, strength, masculinity, etc.; yin stands for the opposites of dark, water, weakness, femininity, etc. Since ghosts are denizens of the nether world, they belong to the yin force.

In the following entry, Ji Xiaolan's father places the question of ghost haunting in that context. He elaborates on the principle that yang is superior to yin, and will therefore keep ghosts at bay, by enumerating the moral qualities that carry a positive yang charge. By implicitly attributing these qualities to himself, he embarks on self-promotion, an indulgence that his son seems blind to. We might note in passing that despite Ji senior's refusal to be frightened of ghosts, his firm belief in their existence would have been a powerful influence on his son, given the profound filial respect that Xiaolan continually expresses.

* * *

The compound of the Commissioner for Education in Fuzhou had been the eunuch-run tax office in the previous Ming dynasty. Behind closed doors the despotic eunuchs took innocent lives, so to this day the place is beset by uncanny hauntings. When I served there as Commissioner for Fujian province, my servants were all disturbed at night by them. In the twenty-ninth year of the Qianlong reign [1764] my late father Yao An came to stay with me. Hearing that a certain room was haunted, he immediately chose it as his bedroom, and enjoyed untroubled sleep the whole night through. I found an opportunity to mildly reprove him, urging him not to risk his precious health in a trial of strength with evil spirits. My father put me right, saying:

"The Confucian dogmatists' dismissal of ghosts is out of touch with reality, and casuistic to boot. Though ghosts do exist, they need must fear men, because yin cannot triumph over yang. If ghosts are sometimes able to harm men, it is because men's yang is too weak to rise to the challenge. Now the supremacy of yang is by no means solely owed to physical robustness and an intrepid disposition. In the character of man, yang is manifest in charity, yin in viciousness; the open and honest is yang, the deep and devious is yin; the just and upright is yang, the selfish and mean is yin. Therefore the hexagrams in the *Book of Changes* symbolize the superior man as yang, the petty man as yin. If the mind of a man is set on being fair and honourable, he emanates pure masculine yang, and though there be malignant spirits, it is like installing a brazier in a cold dark room and fanning the flames: the bone-chilling cold will evaporate of itself.

"You are quite widely read. Have you ever in the histories and biographies come across decent men and great scholars being plagued by ghosts?"

I bowed in gratitude for this instruction. Even today, whenever I recall my father's lectures, it is as if I stand obediently before him.

Haunted Houses
RSWW III 19

In drawing on his personal experience for this narrative, Ji exhibits his own willingness to accept the reality of houses of ill omen (a more precise translation than "haunted houses"). He has no qualms, sees no need for scepticism, for explaining away, such was the atmosphere of the time. Indeed, now as then it seems that there is hardly a person in China who does not know of a haunted house near where he or she lives. The fact that it is Ji's children who witness the apparition strengthens rather than weakens the case, for children were believed to be more clairvoyant than adults.

* * *

In the summer of the thirty-sixth year of the Qianlong reign [1771], I returned from army service in Urumqi to the capital, where I rented a house on the east side of Zhuchao Street, next to that of Judicial Commissioner Long Chengzu. In the second row of five rooms, the door curtain of the most southerly one was always being lifted a foot off the ground, as if curled up by a wind, though the door curtains of the other rooms remained still. No one could suggest an explanation for that. My children cried when they came into this room, saying they saw a fat monk sitting on the bed, smiling playfully at them. Why a sinister apparition dressed as a monk should take over a family's living space was even more inexplicable. For another thing, after nightfall we often heard a woman wailing from Long's house over the other side of our wall; those next door also heard the sound, though they thought it came from our side. These things remained a conundrum, but one thing I was sure of was that this was not a good place to be in, so I moved to Mr Zhe Nan's Two Tree Studio.

All those who subsequently took up residence in those two neighbouring houses suffered misfortune. For instance, Bai Huanjiu, President of the Board of Punishments, just dropped dead without warning one day—that was in Long's house.

I believe that the notion of "haunted house" is not without foundation. My late tutor Chen Baiya commented:

"Those who live in lucky houses will not necessarily be lucky, but those who live in haunted houses will not escape tragedy of some kind. In the same way, a warm breeze and balmy air won't necessarily cure you of illness, but perishing cold and foul air will straightway make you take to your bed. The tonic effect of good medicine won't necessarily make you strong and healthy overnight, but the stimulus of an over-potent drug will bring you down with diarrhoea."

His words make a lot of sense. It would be wrong to deny the wisdom of not tempting fate by setting it against the doctrine of what will be will be. As Mencius said: "The man who truly understands what destiny is will not stand under a wall that is in danger of toppling."

How to Invite Haunting
RSWW I 50

This is essentially no more than a piece of amusing gossip, but the rituals of exorcism have changed little in the intervening centuries: much the same ceremonies are still conducted in Chinese communities.

* * *

In the twenty-second year of the Yongzheng reign [1734] I visited the capital for the first time, accompanying my father. A story about a censor of highly nervous disposition was going the rounds. Apparently he started by renting a house near the Yongguang Temple; the house being surrounded by open ground, he was fearful of being a prey to burglars, so at night he had servants supplied with hand bells and rattles patrolling the perimeter in shifts. On top of that, he himself went round with a lantern in both the freezing cold of winter and the muggy heat of summer to ensure that his servants did not slack on the job.

When this got too strenuous for him, he moved to a house on Xiheyan, a commercial street next to the palace where the buildings are packed closely together. There he was afraid of a fire breaking out, so he installed vats of water in each room, and as before both placed his watchmen and patrolled himself.

When this once more became too much of a strain, he rented another house on the east side of Hufang Bridge, not far from where we lived. Seeing that the long rooms had dark corners, he suspected they might be haunted. He first engaged Buddhist monks to chant the holy scriptures and perform a service to placate hungry ghosts. The din of clashing cymbals and beating drums went on for days, which was said to release these ghosts from their torment. Next he hired Taoist priests to set up an altar to summon a heavenly general, post magic signs and chant spells. Once again cymbals clashed and drums beat for days on end, this time in aid of driving away fox spirits.

In fact there had previously been no disturbances in this house, but all this rumpus provoked the ire of malicious spirits. They threw brickbats and roof tiles, and made off with utensils: the censor got not a night's peace. His crafty servants took their chance to lift valuable items on their own account, so his losses were hard to calculate. In the general opinion, this was a case of human behaviour instigating a haunting.

The censor moved to a house in Rope Makers Lane before the year was out. After that we had no news of him, so do not know what provisions he made there. My father was fond of quoting the dictum: "When all's well in the world, silly people insist on meeting trouble halfway." That would seem to apply to this gentleman!

4

FOXES

The fox has been promoted worldwide as the animal with the greatest cunning and savvy. The first legends it spawned are lost in the mist of antiquity, but no doubt all originated in observation of its furtiveness and the silent way it hunts alone. Folk tales about Reynard the crafty fox appeared in Europe with the beginnings of literacy among the laity, but nothing matches the way foxes fired the imagination as was the case in China, where they were credited not only with having human intelligence but also with accruing supernatural faculties in step with their increase in age. In his look back at historical precedents, Ji notes that fox worship had spread to every corner of the empire by Tang times. He passes over the fact that by then the fox spirits were already said to adopt a bewitching woman as one of their guises, an idea which the literati took up to create in their fiction an ideal of femininity, a woman beautiful in body and virtuous in conduct, most famously realized in the much anthologized story by Shen Jiji (740–805) entitled Ren shi, *the name of the heroine. Before cohabiting with a handsome young scholar, this fox fairy had moved in the world of entertainers and courtesans, a connection supported in later ages by prostitutes choosing fox idols to occupy their shrines. The fox fairy as ideal female persisted in biji literature alongside her other role of predatory demon, bent on sapping a man's vitality in order to enhance her own powers: this neatly reversed the notion and practice of certain Taoist cults of performing multiple sex acts with young women, preferably virgins, to prolong their life span. Ji Xiaolan's sketches being exemplary in nature, romance does not enter into them, except* satirically in one translated below, but he does extensively exploit the idea of the caring fox fairy in order for her to advise, educate and remonstrate.

Male fox spirits are also enlisted for their wisdom, culture and decorum, the purpose being to contrast with lapsed humanity. Some of them, though, are malicious, like the one in a sketch assigned here to the "Homosexuality" section, where a fox spirit sodomizes a shepherd boy.

The popularity that fox fairy stories enjoyed in the Qing dynasty, most notably in Pu Songling's Strange Stories from a Chinese Studio, is continued in the present day in the form of endless television adaptations.

THE LOW-DOWN ON FOXES
RSWW IV 36

Men and animals are two different orders of beings; the fox spirit comes somewhere between them. The unseen and the visible worlds are two different spheres; the fox spirit exists somewhere between them. Immortals and demons take different paths; fox spirits live somewhere in the divide. Hence encounters with fox spirits can be regarded as abnormal, and also as normal.

No documentation is available for high antiquity, but the chapter in the [Han dynasty] *Records of the Historian* called "The Hereditary House of Chen She" relates that Wu Guang lit a torch and proclaimed in the voice of a fox, "The great Chu kingdom shall rise again and Chen She shall ascend the throne," which shows that the fox spirit was known at the time, otherwise he could not have impersonated it. And Wu Jun of the Liang dynasty [sixth century] wrote in his *Tales of the Western Capital* of the Han prince Liu Yue digging up the grave of the late Zhou dynasty general Luan Shu and in the process injuring the foxes who had their den there; afterwards he dreamed of a spirit in the guise of an old man coming to exact revenge. This proves that the belief that foxes could assume human form was common in the

Han. Zhang Zhuo's *Happenings in Court and Country* of the Tang dynasty claims that the common people served fox gods from the beginning of Tang, there being an adage at the time, "Without a fox spirit, there is no village." This indicates that legends about fox spirits were most widespread in Tang. The Song dynasty collectanea *Taiping Miscellany* has twelve sections devoted to foxes, of which ninety per cent relate to the Tang: that confirms the point.

All these records differ in their contents. We owe it to the Hanlin Academy scholar Liu Shitui for the most complete account of the origins and history of the fox legends. Now it seems that in the south of Cangzhou county there was a schoolmaster who made friends with a fox, and Shitui met with the fox on the introduction of this schoolmaster. The fox was of small stature, seemingly fifty to sixty years old, his apparel somewhat in the style of a Taoist priest, neither ancient nor modern. In their exchange of initial courtesies he was modest and composed. After they had made some small talk, the fox asked to what he owed the favour of Liu's visit. Shitui said:

"The stories told of contacts between mundane humanity and your honourable kind are all at odds, and suffer from vagueness. I understand that you, sir, speak plainly and hold nothing back. So I hope you will dispel our perplexity."

The fox smiled and said:

"When Heaven created the myriad forms of life, they were all given names: foxes were called foxes, just as men were named men. It is as simple as that: what is there to hold back? As for my own kind, you will find good and bad among them, again as among mankind there are the virtuous and the immoral. Men are not shy of talking of evil among men, so why should foxes avoid mention of evil among foxes? We can speak quite freely."

"Are there different kinds of foxes?"

"All foxes may cultivate the Way, but the most adept are called 'silver fox'. It is similar in your society to uneducated peasants outnumbering learned scholars."

"Are your silver foxes adept from birth?"

"It is a question of heredity. Those born of foxes who have not attained the Way are ordinary foxes. Those born of foxes who have attained the Way are innately capable of transformation."

"Once they have attained the Way they must be able to retain their youthfulness. Yet we read in our tales about both male and female *old* foxes. Why is that?"

"The expression 'attained the Way' means the human way. In eating, drinking and sex, in the sequence of birth, ageing, sickness, death, in all these aspects they are the same as humans. Making the ascent to immortality is another matter: among human kind it is like one or two people out of a multitude aspiring to office. The fox's transmutation by means of disciplined exercises is parallel to rising to eminence through persevering study. Those foxes who by beguilement draw upon the vital energy of others to make up their deficiencies are like men who take shortcuts to achieve success. The foxes who sojourn in the Blessed Isles and ascend to the Court of Heaven are in the first camp, while those who cause trouble in the world in violation of Heaven's law are in the second camp."

"Who oversees rewards and punishments, and imposes interdictions?"

"Minor rewards and punishments are in the hands of seniors; major rewards and punishments are overseen by the gods of the underworld. If there were no interdictions, then given that foxes may make themselves invisible and leave no trace of their presence, there is nothing they might not get up to!"

"Since the drawing on others' vital energy by beguilement is improper, why is it not included in the interdictions, instead of waiting till people get harmed before intervening?"

"This can be compared to getting people to part with their valuables by trickery: if the other party is compliant, the law of the land does not run. On the other hand, if murder is committed in the act of robbery, the offender pays with his life. For instance, the trickery carried out by the wineshop's landlady as recorded in the [Han dynasty] *Lives of the Immortals* in no way transgresses the criminal code of the underworld."

"I have heard of fox spirits bearing the children of men, but never of women bearing the children of fox spirits. How come?"

The fox smiled sarcastically: "That is not worth discussing. It is simply a matter of rather getting than giving."

"When lady foxes bestow their favours on men, does this not arouse jealousy in their own spouse?"

The fox guffawed: "You speak too rashly, sir. You do not understand the subtleties. Young females are free to choose their own mates, while those in a stable married relationship do not dare stray from the straight and narrow. As for occasional amorous dalliances that go beyond the bounds of propriety, the life of the feelings among us does not greatly differ from that in the human world, so that can be understood by analogy."

"Some fox spirits take up their dwelling in human homes, others live in the wilds. What is the explanation?"

"Those who have not attained the Way still retain animal characteristics, hence it suits them to keep apart from mankind: they are only comfortable in mountains and forests. Those who have attained the Way are in every respect the same as humans, so it suits them to be close to humans: they are only comfortable in towns and cities. Those who have reached a higher state of perfection can live either in towns or in the hills. It is like men who have obtained great wealth and eminence: anything and everything is within their grasp; they can choose to live in some hamlet in the back of beyond or in a metropolis."

Liu Shitui and the fox spirit then embarked upon free discussion, the fox's main theme being to urge men to study the Way. He said:

"To transmute into human form, we fox spirits have to toil and moil for one or two centuries, whereas your kind start out as human beings, so are already halfway advanced along the path we have to tread. Yet you fritter away your time, and wilt and wither like the grass in the fields. It is extremely regrettable."

Liu Shitui was well versed in the Buddhist scriptures, and he turned the topic to that religion. The fox refused to be drawn. He said:

"The Buddhist goal is highly elevated, but your cultivation might fall short of that goal, in which case you enter the wheel of transmigration, and all features of your previous existence are erased. You can have more confidence if you opt for aiming not to die. I have indeed had many meetings with very wise priests, but have resisted the temptation of trying something new."

As Shitui took his leave he said: "It was my great fortune to meet you today. Would you care to give a parting word of advice?"

His companion hesitated a long time. Finally he said:

"After the golden age of the three ancient dynasties, inferior people thought it a mark of vulgarity not to make a reputation for themselves, whereas the sages and wise men of old were even-tempered and mild-mannered, and avoided any suggestion of striking attitudes. The Song dynasty Neo-Confucians put on intimidating looks and gave rise to endless imbroglios with their challenges. It would be worth bearing that in mind."

Shitui was disconcerted, probably because he was similarly overbearing, and frequently expressed himself too dogmatically.

The Fox's False Colours
LYXL VI 16

Tian Baiyan contributed this.

Zhu Ziqing from Jinan made friends with a fox spirit, but he only heard his voice and never saw his physical form. The fox often participated with Zhu in literary salons. Words flew there in lively debate, but none could best the fox in argument. On one occasion the fox was asked to reveal his form. The fox said:

"You want to see my true form? I can't show that to you. Do you want to see my phantom form? Since it is phantom, seeing is the same as not seeing, so why insist?"

They all stubbornly pressed their demand. The fox asked, "What do you imagine my form is like?"

One said, "Bushy eyebrows and hoary head." The image of a

venerable elder straightway appeared.

One said, "Having the aura of a transcendent." A Taoist adept appeared.

One said, "Having the star-shaped headdress and feathered cloak of an immortal." A chamberlain at the court of Taoist heaven appeared.

One said, "Having rosy-cheeked innocence." A little child appeared.

Another jokingly said, "Zhuangzi speaks of the goddess of Guyi Mountain having the soft shapeliness of a virgin. I think that might suit you." Immediately a graceful maiden appeared.

Finally one said, "These instant apparitions are all very well, but they are merely false creations. We still want to see your true self."

The fox replied, "Where in the length and breadth of the empire would you find anyone willing to show their true self? Do you wish me to be the sole exception?" He then took his exit, roaring with laughter.

Ziqing remarked, "This fox claims to be seven hundred years old. He has seen a lot in his lifetime, of that we can be sure."

What a Fox Fears
GWTZ I 33

This was contributed by Li Cangzhou.

A fox spirit had resided in a certain gentleman's library for several decades. He kept the owner's books and scrolls in very good order, and protected them from the ravages of bookworms and rodents better than any devoted bibliophile. He could converse with people, but never manifested his physical form. Sometimes an empty place was reserved for him at banquets, and he would actually keep company with the guests. He spoke in quiet and dignified tones, but made such fine distinctions and telling points that his dining companions were quite bowled over.

On one occasion the master of ceremonies proposed a game

of forfeits. The idea was, everyone had to say what they feared, penalty in the form of draining a beaker of wine being paid for answers that were nonsensical or not particular to the individual. The guests variously came up with dogmatists, self-styled luminaries, filthy rich people, the high and mighty, sycophants, self-depreciators, sticklers for propriety, and close-lipped and prudent people who never gave more than a hint of what they thought. The fox's turn to answer came last. When he said "I fear foxes", great hilarity broke out around the table.

The guests objected, "It is all right for humans to fear foxes, but foxes are your own kind, so what is there to fear? You will have to down a bumper as a fine." The fox spirit laughed sardonically and responded in this wise:

"It is precisely those of one's own kind who are to be feared. The farmers of the south and the huntsmen of the north do not fight over territory; boatmen on rivers and lakes do not contend for passage with carriages and horses. The reason is that they have nothing in common. By contrast, all those who contend for property will be sons of the same father; those who contend for favour will be wives of the same husband; those who contend for power will serve the same throne; those who contend for profit will sell in the same market. That is to say, those in the same groove will get in each other's way, which will lead to some being crushed.

"Now, trappers of pheasants don't use chickens or ducks to lure wild pheasants, they use tame pheasants; likewise deer hunters lure deer with deer, not with sheep or pigs. So in order to sow dissension or plant agents in a rival camp, you also have to employ persons of the same stripe as those you seek to undermine. If they do not come out of the same mould, they will not be able to get into your rival's good books and win their trust, and discover your rival's weaknesses for you to exploit them. With those considerations in mind, how can foxes avoid fearing foxes?"

Those at the table who had known frustrations and adversities in their own careers praised the fox's insight. Just one guest set a full cup of wine in the fox's place, saying:

"I can't find fault with what you say, but your fear is a universal one, not peculiar to yourself. You still have to down a bumper."

The company broke up in good humour.

In my opinion, the fox's penalty should be reduced to half a cup. Granted, the business of edging rivals out and putting them down is common knowledge, yet possibly few are aware of agents who masquerade as close confidants while actually being snakes in the grass, all the time pretending to be in perfect accord with you while actually plotting to worm out your secrets.

A Female Fox Takes a Dim View of Romancing
LYXXL I 13

A young scholar from Ningbo named Wu was in the habit of trawling the bawdy houses. In the course of time he entered into a liaison with a fox fairy, and had regular assignations with her, but still consorted with harlots. One day the fox proposed to him:

"Since I am able to transfigure myself, I can impersonate any woman you hanker after, just by getting one look at her. Whenever you bring any such female to mind, she will appear before you in response to your thought. Wouldn't that be better than buying her favours with your gold?"

He tried the experiment, and in a trice the fox fairy indeed transformed herself into the exact double of the real woman in question. Thereafter Wu did not seek his pleasure abroad. There came a time, however, when he said to the fox fairy:

"To taste the delights of the pleasure quarters in this way is very satisfying, to be sure. All the same, it is brought about by conjuration, and I can't help feeling it is at one remove from the real thing."

She replied: "Not so. Sensual pleasures are as transient as flashes of lightning and sparks from a flint stone. Not only is my imitation of another woman a conjuration, in fact even that woman in your thoughts is a conjuration. And even as you see me now, I too am a conjuration. To go further, even the famed enchantresses and courtesans of olden days were all phantoms of the mind. White poplars and green swards, yellow plains and blue mountains—where in the world has not at some time been the scene of singing and dancing? The joys of tender lovemaking, the sadness of mourning over the grave of a beloved, the pain of devoted couples on parting, are all over in the time it takes to bend and stretch an arm. The union of beaus and belles, whether measured in hours, in days, in months or years, must eventually end in separation. Their separation, whether it comes after decades together or just a brief encounter, is like releasing their grip on a cliff edge: of a sudden, there is nothingness. Are not the charms of rosy cheeks and warm bosoms just as deceptive as baseless daydreams? Even with couples tightly bound together by predestination, though they may enjoy a long lifetime together, still the bloom of youth fades, white hairs encroach, the body's clock cannot be turned back. That being so, the enchantresses of their salad days can surely be counted phantom creations too, can they not? Why do you single out my impersonations of certain females as such?"

Wu's eyes were opened in a flash. Though some years later the fox fairy took leave of him, he never returned to whoring.

Fox Fairy as Tutor
LYXL III 6

The academician Cheng Yumen contributed this.

A certain scholar became intimate with a fox fairy. Right from the outset of their relationship she was totally frank with him. She said:

"I am not after increasing my own vitality by draining you of your potency, nor will I pretend that we were destined for each other. I simply rejoice in your good looks and refinement, and cannot restrain myself, that is all. On the other hand, since I fell for you on first sight so deeply that I cannot let you go, it might be predestiny after all."

She did not come to him constantly, saying: "I am afraid you might ruin your health if you become addicted to sex." And sometimes when she did come, she left again if she found him studying or writing, saying: "I don't want to interrupt you in your proper endeavour."

She continued to display such consideration for nearly a decade. They were as close as a married couple. No children having resulted from his mundane marriage, the scholar asked the fox fairy in jest, "I wonder if you might produce a child for me?" She answered:

"There is no way of telling. An embryo is formed when the male and female vital essences meet and fuse together. If in copulation the male essence issues and the female essence does not, or vice versa, no pregnancy results. If both essences issue, but not together, the first to issue disperses before fusing can take place, and again no pregnancy results. When both essences issue together, and the male essence forges ahead, the female essence envelops it; the male being dominant, a boy child is conceived. If the reverse happens, a girl child is conceived. That is the natural wonder of reproduction, and is beyond human engineering. Hence there are instances of conception from one act of coitus, and also of no conception from a thousand acts of coitus. That is why I say there is no way of telling."

"What about twin births? How do they happen?"

"In that case both essences are very vigorous. If they happen to collide head-on, then they split into two branches. If they collide side-on, in one situation the male essence is greater in quantity than the female, and it absorbs the female essence; in another situation the balance is on the other side. Hence it is more common for twins to be both male or both female, though sometimes one is male and the other female."

"Sexual arousal has to precede the issuance of vital essence. Intercourse might take a young bride by surprise on her wedding night, yet she conceives on this first occasion. So how does her vital essence get to flow?"

"On the wedding night both parties are joyful. Initially the intercourse may be difficult, but it soon becomes easy; or there may be outward distress but inward willingness. Given harmony in their desires, their essences are both secreted, so it follows that occasionally a first encounter results in conception."

"Why is it that a woman can conceive only after the menstrual blood has cleared up?"

"The essences are like seeds of corn, blood is like the soil. Old blood saps the vitality, new blood nourishes it. I should say I overheard a fairy consort discussing the fundamentals of reproduction while I waited on her: that is how I got a rough idea of how things work. You could apply the old adage to me: 'common folk often have a better idea of how to go about something than the sages do.'"

After the scholar reached the age of thirty, his whiskers sprouted vigorously. The fox fairy complained: "This face of yours is so hirsute it prickles like the spikes on ears of wheat—it's quite unbearable! It makes me cringe just to look upon it. Could it be a sign that our common destiny has run its course?" The scholar assumed she was joking, but she did indeed cease to visit him.

Now Cheng Yumen had a full beard himself, and when he took a concubine my colleague Ren Zitian referred to this story about the risk attendant on whiskers to make fun of him. Yumen was of course familiar with it, and he joined in the laughter. He went on to say, "Actually the fox spirit had a lot to say for herself: you've only told the half of it." He proceeded to narrate her discourse in detail, as set out above. Since it made very good sense, I thought it worthwhile to leave a record of it, relying on my memory.

A Fastidious Unseen Boarder
RSWW II 5

The academician Zhou Lanbo once stayed in a villa attached to the General's Parade Ground in the West City. He would sometimes hear poetry being recited upstairs at night, but assuming it was a fox spirit, was not unduly concerned. When Lanbo moved out, the fox also decamped. Later on, Tian Baiyan rented the villa, and after some months the fox returned. Baiyan made offerings of wine and dried meat, and spread out on a table a flowery address of welcome he had composed:

"I have heard that an immortal's carriage was once drawn up outside this humble dwelling. I have also heard that he then flitted like a cloud to distant parts, like Buddhist monks unwilling to stay in one place in order to avoid worldly attachments. As for myself, I have got nowhere in my official career, and have drifted along like duckweed for ten years, resorting to loans to eke out an existence; that is how I settled on this poor domicile. For a number of evenings now I have heard faint coughing and chuckling, and surmise your supernal conveyance is once more at the door. It could hardly be that you are bent on intruding on me because of my frivolous conduct: perhaps instead you have come to join me because we kept congenial company in my previous existence? Since you have deigned to graciously notice me, how would I dare to rebuff such an illustrious guest?

"I merely hope that we can keep separate our domestic arrangements, so that the mundane and spiritual do not conflict, but each might find tranquillity, much as mosses and lichens live peaceably together on the same rock face. I here lay bare my true feelings for your enlightened appraisal."

The next day a note fluttered down from the upper storey. It read:

"Although I, your servant, am not of your kind, I take great pleasure in the belles lettres of the human race, and being so acculturated do not wish to associate with vulgarians. For several decades past, this house has been the lodging of literary men, which exactly suited my taste. So I brought my family to settle here. After Mr Lanbo forsook me, those who succeeded him as tenants were of a different character: my eyes could not bear their look of horse-traders, my ears could not bear the racket of their music, my nose could not bear the stink of meat and wine on their breath. Therefore I had no option but to take refuge in the hills and forests. But hearing recently that you were the youngest son of Tian Shanjiang, and so must draw on a deep well of culture, I have been attracted back by your presence, and have absolutely no intention of disturbing you.

"In future I might misplace your bookmarks when searching for references, borrow your brush to scrawl some poor thing of my own, and use your ink slab to grind my ink, but that would be all. If I cause the slightest offence, you will have every right to complain to the gods. In thus unburdening myself, I hope to avoid the kind of suspicions that might lead to estrangement."

The note was signed: "Kang Mo presents his compliments". Thereafter not a whisper was heard.

Afterwards Tian Baiyan showed this note around. The handwriting was sloping and the ink pale, indicating that it was hastily written. One comment was: "Baiyan keeps a low profile as a minor official. He is fond of joking and making fun of the world. He concocted this story as a vehicle for his satire. It is meant as a homily, wouldn't you think?"

It is too much of a coincidence that there was another story of the same time and of the same Shandong authorship which similarly had the theme of contrasting a cultured fox spirit with uncouth humans, so maybe one copied the other, or one expanded on the other's theme, one cannot tell. In any case, the story is worth preserving for its social criticism.

* * *

In a letter to his uncle Yinan (Family Letters, FLP *2012 edition, p. 68), Ji reveals his personal involvement in this story. He says the incident took place in Urumqi, after he himself moved in to live with Tian, and Tian wrote the letter to the fox spirit on his suggestion. It was he, not an unnamed person, who thought the fox's reply might be a spoof on Tian's part, but Tian swore it was genuine, and neighbours confirmed that foxes had previously lived in the house, so Ji was reassured.*

A Spoof (or Pastiche)
HXZZ III 27

Dong Qiuyuan contributed this.

A certain scholar was taking a night-time stroll in the countryside near his home in Dongchang prefecture when he came upon a stately mansion. Working out that this was actually the site of so-and-so's family burial ground, he wondered what the mansion was doing there—could it be a transformation brought about by fox spirits? He was an avid reader of the tales in Pu Songling's *Strange Stories from a Chinese Studio* about fox fairies looking for romance with humankind, and hung about hoping such an adventure would come his way. After a while a procession of carriages approached from the west, all sumptuously decked out. A middle-aged lady in one of the carriages drew back her window curtain and pointed to the scholar, saying:

"This gentleman would suit very well. Please invite him in."

A young woman was seated in the back of the carriage; her angelic beauty made the scholar joyful beyond measure. Passing through the gate, he was immediately received by a pair of maids. Since by then he was persuaded that he had entered the world of fox spirits, he followed the maids inside without making the usual enquiry after the host's name and antecedents. Somewhat disappointingly, the master of the house did not put in an appearance; he was simply waited on in a luxuriously appointed room, and served with fine food and drink. As he waited for his nuptials to begin, the scholar's heart fluttered like a feathered pennant flying from a mast.

When evening at last came round, a band of musicians struck up. An old man then parted the door curtain, made a bow, and announced:

"The bridegroom has arrived at the gate to be welcomed into his new family. Being a cultured gentleman, sir, you are surely familiar with the marriage rituals. If you would deign to perform the office of best man, all parties to the marriage would be greatly honoured."

The scholar was devastated, but seeing that there had been no mention of marriage, he could not object on the ground of breach of promise; equally, because he had been feasted well, he could not brusquely rebuff the invitation. So he grudgingly did the minimum required of him, and left without farewell.

Because by then the scholar had been missing for a day and night, his family was on the point of sending out search parties when he got back home and resentfully recounted his adventure. His hearers all clapped their hands and laughed: "The foxes did not have you on, you had yourself on!"

[…]

5

FORTUNE-TELLING

From the earliest times human beings have wanted to know what the future holds for them. The Chinese have been pre-eminent in that regard. Animal shoulder bones and tortoise shells whose cracks when heated were read as auguries have been dated back to the second millennium BC. The fall-out of milfoil stalks was used at the same time; they later evolved to form a series of hexagrams (the working parts of the Yi jing, *or Book of Changes) and more popularly were the likely origin of the inscribed sticks shaken from a pot still used to tell fortunes. In addition to nearly universal practices such as astrology and palmistry, other modes have proliferated in China. Physiognomy, geomancy (feng shui) and spirit writing (planchette) come within our compass here. Also popular have been the analysis of dreams, of birth dates and times, and—surely peculiar to China—the deconstruction of the characters used for a person's name or written down at random, not to mention lucky hours and days for doing all sorts of things.*

Feng Shui
LYXXL I 44

Feng shui (literally "wind-water") is the sole Chinese art of divination to be known universally by a phonetic transcription of its native name, which attests to its attraction having spread beyond the confines of China. Essentially it is used to determine whether a site is propitious or not by examining the forces of nature that dominate it, and if necessary to devise means to counteract adverse influences. Tasked principally to choose a good grave site according to the local topography, in urban use it takes into account a building's axis and surroundings. The feng shui expert draws on a spectrum of arcane sciences, among which are the theories of the Five Elements (metal, wood, water, fire and earth) and, of course, yin and yang. For an English equivalent to feng shui, "geomancy" has to serve, though its practices are different, and compared to feng shui ridiculously simple.

* * *

Vice-Minister Qian Weicheng contributed this argument:

"Is Heaven's bestowing of good fortune and visitation of ill fortune not like the sovereign's rewarding and punishing his subjects? Is the scrutiny of the gods and spirits not like the review boards of senior administrators? Now suppose there were a memorial of impeachment submitted to the throne which read: 'So-and-so has conducted himself immaculately in society and has some achievements in office, but his residence faces in an ill-favoured direction and was built on an inauspicious day. So he should be demoted and penalized.' Would the authorities approve? Would they reject?

"Alternatively, supposing a recommendation were forwarded which read: 'So-and-so has many flaws in his character and has brought shame on his office, but his residence faces in a well-favoured direction and was built on an auspicious day. So he should be promoted and rewarded.' Would the authorities approve? Would they reject?

"Is it conceivable that gods and spirits would approve of propositions which the bureaucracy would be sure to throw out? For this reason I will never accept the notion of propitious locations."

By this analogy Qian makes a very telling point: feng shui masters would have no answer if confronted with it. Yet in my experience there really is a jinx on some houses. There is a house on the south end of the street opposite the Buddhist Jigu Temple in the capital city that I went to five times to condole the bereaved; and another house on the west side of the north end of

Liuli Street that I have visited seven times for the same purpose. Cao Xuemin of the Imperial Clan Court once occupied the house near the Jigu Temple: soon after he moved in, two of his servants died a sudden death on the same night, which frightened him into moving out again. Director of Schools Shao Dasheng rented the house on Liuli Street: he frequently saw uncanny things in broad daylight, but stubbornly refused to be daunted; in the end he died there. What rational explanation can be found for those things?

The Grand Secretary Liu Tongxun offered this comment:

"In the *Book of History* it says Duke Zhou took auguries to choose the site of the new capital, and in the *Book of Rites* there is reference to auspicious days for journeying. If there were no such thing as auspicious or ill-omened, why did the sages practise divination? I'm afraid it is simply that present-day diviners cannot master the art."

That is a well balanced view.

Shaman

LYXXL IV 37

The counterpart to the spirit medium in the Western world was known as a shaman, or sorcerer, able to invoke spirits who spoke through his/her voice. The credibility of persons of this calling remained higher in late imperial China than in the West by virtue of their standing in high antiquity, when they performed at kingly courts the functions of divination, ritual, and interpretation of abnormal phenomena. Their respectability was upheld by the prestige of the canon in which their deeds were recorded, and not least by the Book of Changes, *essentially a manual for divination, being incorporated in the Confucian classics. In the higher echelons of later society, and most notoriously at the court of some emperors, certain of their functions were assumed by charismatic Taoist priests, but common sorcerers and witches still enjoyed considerable standing among the general population.*

* * *

The female shaman Hao was the most guileful of old country wives. Back when I was a boy I saw her at the house of my aunt Lü in Cangzhou. She claimed that she was possessed by a fox spirit who could foretell weal and woe, and knew every detail of people's private lives. Hence she had a very big following. The truth was she had a network of cronies who cultivated acquaintance with serving maids and nosey old women for the purpose of spying out secrets for her: that was the way she was able to carry out her trickery.

A pregnant woman once asked her whether her child would be a boy or girl. Hao promised her it would be a boy, but it turned out to be a girl. When the woman took her to task for making the wrong prediction, Hao glared back at her, saying:

"You were supposed to have a boy child, but on such-and-such a date your mother gave you a present of twenty cakes. You gave six of them to your parents-in-law but kept fourteen for yourself. The recorder in the underworld gave you a black mark for unfiliality and exchanged the boy for a girl. Why don't you face the facts?"

Not knowing that she had been spied on, the woman was flummoxed, and admitted she was in the wrong. That example typified Hao's adroitness in covering up for herself.

One day Hao had just lit joss sticks to invoke her guiding spirit when she suddenly snapped upright, and spoke in a penetrating voice:

"I am a true fox spirit. Though we do have commerce with mankind, in fact we are independent beings who have perfected ourselves by rigorous exercises that draw upon subtle cosmic forces. Do you think we would deign to ally ourselves with rustic old crones, and interest ourselves in piddling domestic matters? This old dame is as cunning as they come: she swindles you out of your money by a lot of hocus-pocus. She has gone so far as to take the name of my kind in vain, so today I really possess her body, and make known the tale of her deceit."

The fox spirit went on to spell out all Hao's knavery and name every one of her hangers-on. After the voice ceased speaking,

Hao awoke with a start, as if from a dream. She slunk away in confusion, and it is not known what became of her.

PLANCHETTE

With shamans, the spirit control speaks through the medium's voice; with the planchette the spirit control communicates through the written word. The one thing common to all the mechanics of the operation is that the message is scratched on a tray of sand. The more elaborate mode of operation is that the characters are formed by a stylus suspended from a T-frame, on whose ends two persons, the medium being one of them, rest their fingers; a variation of that is the use of a forked branch in place of the T-frame. Alternatively, the medium alone might manage the contraption, or even inscribe the characters by hand. Disappointingly, our author never specifies the mode of operation involved in the examples he deals with (for his readers he would not have needed to). Naturally the movement of the stylus is believed to be actuated by the spirit control. The use of the planchette was already popular among the scholarly class in the Song dynasty, the great poet and man of letters Su Dongpo being one of its biggest fans, and was extremely widespread in the Qing dynasty: entries related to the planchette make up roughly one tenth of the contents of Perceptions. *In the novel* Dream of the Red Chamber *one is even set up in a courtroom to persuade the on-looking public of the justice of the verdict the magistrate intends to deliver. It is also said that candidates for the degree examinations sought to know from the planchette what topic would be set for their essay.*

The control may identify itself as a fountain of wisdom, a deceased relative, or a poet/poetaster with whom the enquirer can swap verses, as is mentioned in Ji's concluding comment to the first item. He himself engages in such verbal duels in several other entries, which my readers will be grateful for my not attempting to translate; needless to say, Ji invariably comes off best, though he is sometimes very impressed by the genie's versifying and knowledge of literature.

The separate strokes of intricate Chinese characters cannot be inscribed on a tray of sand, because the stylus cannot be continually lifted; instead the stylus leaves a continuous trail of loops and squiggles. The task of interpreting the scratchings was normally performed by the inspired medium, though in some performances Ji records onlookers familiar with "grass" or cursive script seem to be able to make out the words by themselves. Needless to say, some mediums were plain charlatans, as is illustrated below, but in general all classes of society gave them some credit. The practice still has a tenuous hold on life today.

Planchette 1

LYXXL IV 2

In the days before my father took his higher degree, he met up with a planchette diviner, and asked if distinction lay ahead of him. The judgement made by the planchette was: "A career extending ten thousand miles." When my father followed up to ask in what year he would pass his examination, the answer was: "For that you will have to wait for ten thousand years." My father guessed that might mean his success would not come in the normal course of events. When he did graduate with honours, it was indeed at a special examination held by the Kangxi emperor to mark his sixtieth birthday [1713], the emperor's longevity being "ten thousand years". So that judgement was explained. Later on my father served as prefect in Yao An, Yunnan province, before retiring to care for his ailing mother; and Yunnan being so remote, the first prediction of "ten thousand miles" distance was also vindicated.

Most magic is performed by legerdemain; only the art of the planchette is genuinely well founded, though how well it works depends on the literacy of the presiding genie. The claim of the genie to be some god or immortal is all an act, and even the pretension of being the spirit of a historical personage cannot be easily sustained, for when faced with queries about that person's poems or essays, they usually have no answer, and fall back on the excuse of having forgotten such dim and distant details.

If the person who assists the medium writes a good hand, the calligraphy of the response will be skilled; if that person is an able poet, the versification of the reply will be accomplished; if that person excels in neither respect, then though the response will be coherent, it will still be stiff and wooden. I myself have some skill in versifying, but my calligraphy is poor, while my cousin Tanju's competence is the reverse. When I assisted with the planchette, the verses that came back were deft and fluent, but the calligraphy sloppy, whereas in Tanju's case the calligraphy was immaculate but the poetry plodding. Actually neither of us was particularly intent on what we were doing; it would seem that the genie of the planchette needed to draw on the mental resources of the enquirer for inspiration. As is said, the spirits are not effective by themselves, their efficacy depends on human collaboration. The milfoil stalks and tortoise carapaces used by the ancients in divination were in essence no more than dry plants and rotting shells: they awaited the contribution of humans before they could function as predictors of weal and woe.

Planchette 2

HXZZ I 33

Wang Xuchu contributed this experience of his.

At a planchette session he attended, the spirit control claimed to be Zhang Ziyang, founder of the Southern School of Taoism, but when Wang questioned him on Zhang's main work, *The Ultimate Truths*, he could not answer, merely pronouncing "The occult path to immortality cannot lightly be divulged."

Coincidentally, the wife of Wang's servant had run away from home, taking their nest egg with her, and his servant asked, "Is it too late to catch up with her?"

The spirit of the planchette replied, "In your last life you offered a man a tempting sum to buy his wife; then you entrapped him into drinking and gambling, and in that way went on to strip him of his possessions. Now that same man has come into your present life, and has enticed your wife to run away with him, which is your retribution for buying his wife. The stealing of your nest egg is retribution for your stripping him of his possessions. This fate is written in the ledgers of the underworld. If you pursue your wife you won't catch her—better let the matter drop."

Wang Xuchu himself followed with another question: "It goes without saying that Your Holiness does not speak inadvisably, but if this argument is accepted, would not all thieves and adulterers be able to evade prosecution by pleading justification in a previous existence, so encouraging malfeasance?"

No answer came from the planchette.

Another person present was suspicious. After the session he confided: "This medium is known to keep company with crooked, scheming knaves. How do we know that one of them has not holed up with this woman and told the medium to spin this yarn?"

He secretly employed an agent to keep watch on the medium. When dusk fell, the medium indeed repaired to a back alley. The agent climbed onto the roof of the house to spy: he saw a crowd of men gambling inside, and the servant's wife, dressed up to the nines, was going round filling their wine cups. The agent slipped away to summon the watch to surround the house. Those inside were arrested without a struggle.

Now the law places prohibitions on magicians and shamans because frauds and tricksters infiltrate their ranks. In the Ming dynasty the Jiajing emperor's favourite, the Taoist Lan Daoxing, brought about the downfall of the corrupt prime minister Yan Song by manipulating the planchette, and was not greatly blamed for doing so, because Yan Song was so hated. Thus it came about that a wizard pulled off with ease what upright officials like Yang Jisheng and Shen Lian could not accomplish even at the sacrifice of their lives. That he was able to write Yan Song's death warrant shows how great Lan's power was. Fortunately his target was Yan

Song; if he had used that power against unsullied officials, would even ministers as great as Han Qi, Fan Zhongyan, Fu Bi and Ouyang Xiu have been able to stand against him?

I conclude that communing with the spirit of the planchette is a game the educated class can play at, by swapping verses for instance, much as they might watch a stage performance. If it is used to predict fortunes, upright men should go in fear of the consequences!

Planchette 3
LYXL VI 11

The desirability of the job of gatekeeper to a provincial magistrate, on which this narrative centres, calls for some explanation. In the present instance, the gatekeeper's employer is a compiler in the Hanlin Academy, that is to say, his duties are scholarly, not administrative. Hence those who come to his door would be mostly colleagues paying social calls: they would be admitted without question. The gatekeeper's opportunities for tips elsewhere, as from traders, would also be meagre. Since, by contrast, a provincial magistrate's remit encompassed all the duties and powers of the state, in his bailiwick those wishing audience would mostly have come as petitioners—whose access the gatekeeper could either expedite or obstruct. But a gatekeeper to a yamen did much more than keep the gate. He was also the direct channel for orders, directives and reports from and to the magistrate, and as a member of his personal staff was superior to local clerks and runners. Little wonder then that our academician's gatekeeper thought his dream had come true when he heard of his master's transfer. Looking down from his Olympian height, our author declares himself baffled that the job should be the object of such contention. If he had been a magistrate himself he would have known better.

* * *

One's lot in life being predetermined, the gods and spirits are able to predict its grand lines. Still, some minor happening whose first signs have yet to emerge, something which has not yet been conceived of by the persons concerned, which does not alter the measure of one's good or bad fortune, which is not bound up with one's karma, in fact is so frivolous and trivial that it is hardly worth mentioning, and definitely not what the clerks in the underworld could go ahead and enter into your dossier—can often be predicted, too.

In the thirty-fifth year of the Qianlong reign [1770], a compiler in the Hanlin Academy chanced to attend a planchette session, and took the opportunity to ask how his career would progress. The presiding spirit dictated the following verse:

> Jubilation leads to leaning on a stick
> Where peach and plum blossom the eyes are bedazzled
> A pair of butterflies in search of nectar
> Cross paths when over the garden wall.

The academician could not make head or tail of that.

Shortly afterwards the emperor examined the fresh cohort of academicians, and reassigned this compiler to a country magistrature. His colleagues then concluded that the second line of the spirit's verse had been proved right, it being a classical allusion to Pan Yue planting peach and plum trees on his appointment as magistrate in Heyang county, but the other lines still defied deciphering.

When this person's fellow graduates called to sympathize with him for his outside posting, they were surprised to see his gatekeeper hobble out, leaning on a stick. What had happened is explained by the fact that to servants of court officials their counterparts in the provinces were in a state of grace, so the instant the gatekeeper heard of his master's posting he jumped for joy, exclaiming: "Today I join the ranks of the immortals!" He was so carried away that he slipped and fell down some steps, injuring his ankle, which was why he walked with a stick. Thus the first line was explained.

Some days later it was rumoured that two of the academician's menservants had been dismissed at the same time, though for what offence was not clear. But an insider soon divulged the reason:

"These two servants were both manoeuvring to get the lucrative job of gatekeeper, but the crippled incumbent stood in their way. They separately hit on the idea of dolling up their wives and having them introduce themselves into the master's study after he had retired for the night, there to lead him on and captivate him. So after nightfall one wife prepared a tray of sweetmeats, while the other brewed a pot of fine tea. They each groped their way in the dark to the study corridor, where they collided head-on, spilling the things they were carrying. To cover up their embarrassment they both flew off the handle and started cursing each other. Their master refused to listen to excuses: he simply sent them all packing."

Thus the third and fourth lines of the verse were borne out. The planchette's verse turned out to be uncannily accurate, but how such outcomes could be predicted remains a mystery.

A seamstress employed by my lady wife had formerly worked for this academician's family. According to her, it was true that the two menservants had plotted to usurp the gatekeeper's position, but the idea of offering up their wives as a bait had not been their own. They had consulted on the quiet with a wily fellow servant, who mapped out that plan for them. He had advised them both that their master was at leisure on a certain evening, and then would be a good time for the wives to make their move. But he did not let either manservant know of the other's intentions, and so brought about their common downfall.

After these two menservants had been got out of the way, the wily servant palled up with the crippled gatekeeper, and proposed they go whoring together. The gatekeeper realized he had something up his sleeve: he told the wily servant to go on ahead and wait for him, while he secretly informed their master of which brothel he could be caught in. So the wily servant also got his comeuppance.

Alas, to think of the lengths to which these four people went to do each other down, all the plotting and counterplotting it involved, just over the job of gatekeeper to a country magistrate!

We are forcibly reminded of the parable of the mantis intent on snapping up a cicada ignoring the oriole coming up behind it. This postscript is added to highlight the perfidy common in our society.

Planchette 4

HXZZ I 20

In the eighteenth to nineteenth year of the Qianlong reign [1753–1754] Cheng Nianlun came to Peking to see the sights. He ranked in the top league of chess players, but Mao Xiangzhu of Rugao said of him: "Actually he is only second class, like me, but as there is no grand master at present, he thinks himself top dog."

One day my student Wu Huishu and friends set up a planchette session. They asked the planchette genie if he could play chess. "Yes," came the answer.

"Would you condescend to play against a mere mortal?"

"Agreed."

As Nianlun was staying with me at the time, he was prevailed upon to play against the genie.

[Here our author explains parenthetically how in the absence of a shared board it is possible to play by calling out the moves of counters to positions on a numbered grid: for example, the intersection of the ninth vertical line with the third lateral line would be called as 9-3.]

Finding the genie's first moves quite baffling, Nianlun suspected an impenetrable gambit devised by supernatural intelligence, and feared for his reputation. He pondered and brooded, and was reduced to sweating and trembling before he resolved to place his own counters, though still with his heart in his mouth. However, as the game went on he seemed to decide there was nothing out of the ordinary in the genie's play, and he launched an attack that comprehensively routed the genie's troops. At that the room exploded in uproar.

To our surprise the following confession appeared on the

sand, in a big sprawling hand:

"The fact is, I am a common or garden ghost, I just pretended to be the Taoist master Zhang Sanfen for a lark. As I had a rough idea how to play chess, I rashly accepted the challenge. I never thought this gentleman would wipe the floor with me like he did. I am signing off now."

Wu Huishu commented with some feeling: "So in our capital even the ghosts are liable to pull a fast one!"

I joked: "To come straight out with the truth on being exposed shows, rather, he is that rare thing in the capital, an artless ghost."

Phrenology

LYXL I 1

"Phrenology", the pretended science of telling character types from bumps and hollows on the subject's skull, is probably the Western method of prognostication closest to that described below, but in the Chinese case the examination extends to the bone structure of the whole body. More fanciful ways of telling fortunes by resemblance to bird and animal types in terms of skull shape, facial features and gait also exist, but they would have been beneath our author's notice.

* * *

In the fifth month of the third year of the Jiaqing reign [1798], as I was preparing to accompany the emperor to his summer hill resort, the venerable member of the Censorate Zhao You told me of a blind man called Hao, a house guest of Grand Secretary Peng Yunmei, who circulated among the elite, plying his trade of telling fortunes by his subject's bone structure. His deductions had proved surprisingly accurate. The only exception was in respect of the Honourable Hu Changling: Hao placed him correctly as having the rank of fourth grade, but did not know he had graduated as Number One Scholar. Among roving soothsayers his skills could be said to be a cut above average.

Hao claimed he came from my home prefecture of Hejian,

so I inquired about him locally, but no one had heard of him, possibly because he had been away too long. Hao also claimed that his teacher, a monk whose powers of divination were phenomenal, could tell a man's office and stipend on the strength of a few words of conversation. Apparently this monk swore never to emerge from his refuge deep in the mountains. I found that a bit too mythical, and was not inclined to credit it.

Now, on the topic of telling fortunes by a person's physiognomy, that practice is already mentioned in the [third century BC] *Zuo Commentary*, and manuals on the subject are listed in an appendix to the [first century AD] *Han History*; but I know of no reference in antiquity to schools of divination based on reading a man's pulse or feeling a man's bone structure. The Pulse Reading school first appeared in the Northern Song dynasty, but accounts of its origin and transmission are incoherent and far-fetched, and false attributions are obvious. I discussed it in detail in my *General Catalogue for the Compendium of the Four Sets of Books*, and need not elaborate here. The Bone Structure school is also of indeterminate origin. The 136th chapter of the *Taiping Miscellany* [printed AD 981] quotes an early source as saying that the future emperor Gao Huan of Northern Qi [sixth century] met a blind old woman while out hunting with Liu Gui, Jia Zhi and others; she went round feeling their bones, and predicted they would all be exalted. When she got to Gao Huan she said they would owe their high position to this man. So it seems that this technique of divination was already established in the Southern and Northern Dynasties [fourth to sixth centuries].

Also in the Tang dynasty miscellany *The Tide of Fortune* it is said that in the fourteenth year of the Tianbao reign [756], a blind man from Dongyang prefecture called Ma palpated Zhao Ziqing's skull and divined his office and stipend. And Liu Mengde's *Entertaining Tales* says that at the end of the Zhenyuan reign [785–805] there was a blind hermit who could tell with certainty whether clients would be noble or base by feeling their bones. The Tang collection of anecdotes *Amazing Stories* says that in the Kaicheng reign [816–840] there was an eyeless man called

Long Fuben who was able to tell fortunes from voice and bone structure. All that goes to prove that this practice was widespread in the Tang dynasty.

Since this Bone Structure school goes back such a long way, it could have been handed down to the present day. That being so, even fortune tellers with a smattering of knowledge could get things right, because they have more to go on than the Pulse Reading school: no more than that.

What There Is to Be Predicted
LYXXL II 45

Early Confucianism conceived of Heaven (tian) both as the force which impersonally governed the dynamics of the universe and as an overseer of man's moral conduct which (or who?) expressed pleasure or displeasure in determining individual fate. Hence the common expression on the part of the recipient: ting tian you ming (*submit to Heaven and resign to Fate*).

* * *

Leiyang, my grandfather's cousin, had this story.

A man once met a recorder from the underworld. The man asked:

"Is it true that everyone's fortune is predestined?"

"It is, but only the grand lines of prosperity and life span. As for being able to predict what people will eat, as is claimed in Tang dynasty fiction, that is simply the contrivance of conjurors. If such trivialities were to be written in everyone's fate, the whole wide world would not have enough space for shelving all the necessary files."

"Is a person's fate subject to alteration?"

"It can be altered by great goodness or great wickedness."

"Who decides fate, who alters it?"

"The individual concerned determines it, and also alters it. The gods and spirits have no such authority."

"Reward and retribution sometimes works out, sometimes does not. Why is that so?"

"In the mundane world, good and evil are reckoned in terms of one lifetime, as are fortune and misfortune. In the courts of the underworld, good and evil relate also to the previous life, while fortune and misfortune relate to the next life. Hence there sometimes seem to be incongruities."

"Why are the consequences of conduct different in different persons?"

"They depend on the slated destiny of the person concerned. Let us take the example of official careers. Two persons may merit promotion: the minister is promoted one grade and is elevated to prime minister; the sheriff is promoted one grade and merely becomes registrar. Or two persons may merit demotion: in the one case an upgrade due to that person cancels out that demotion; in the other case no upgrade is due, so there is an actual demotion. The action taken is the same, but the apparent outcome may be different."

"Wouldn't it be better for people to know their destiny?"

"Impossible. If destinies were known, the flow of human affairs would be stilled. If the reclusive Zhuge Liang had known in advance the key role he would play in founding the kingdom of Shu, instead of being admired he would have been thought meddlesome; likewise the turncoat Six Ministers who negotiated the abdication of the last Tang emperor instead of being despised would have been recognized as bowing to the will of Heaven."

"Why then are the workings of destiny occasionally revealed?"

"If they were not, the lack of belief in otherworldly powers would free the human heart of all restraints, and in dark and secret places all sorts of misdeeds would be done."

My late father Yao An commented when he passed on this story: "This may well have been Leiyang putting his own view in the mouth of the underworld official, but in terms of rhyme and reason I would say he summed things up pretty fairly."

Taboos in Top Places
LYXL II 22

The central portal of the main hall of the Hanlin Academy was never opened: if it were to be, it was said an ill fate would befall the Directors. In the thirty-eighth year of the Qianlong reign [1773] when the *Compendium* project was launched, the portal was opened on the order of the master of ceremonies to admit a prince of the blood for his inspection. Not long afterwards the Director Liu Tongxun died, followed by his Manchu Co-Director.

Soil solidifies into balls within the gravel embankment in front of the academy, and there is a belief that if these balls are broken open, harm will come to academicians. In the twenty-eighth year of the Qianlong reign [1763] one such ball was exposed by heavy rain eroding the embankment, and it split open from children throwing it about. One of our senior members, Wu Yunyan, soon passed away.

There was a taboo against members with living parents setting up their desks in the south-west corner of the Yuanxin Pavilion: if they did, their parents' lives would be shortened. The Deputy Censor Lu Xixiong, who was then a member, adamantly refused to believe that, and as a result lost his father.

The gate in the left-hand corner of the academy grounds was always kept locked. If it was opened, the steward would suffer demotion. No one dared put that belief to the test, so I do not know if it was valid.

Other institutions of state have their own taboos....

Such taboos are invariably well grounded. There must be some kind of causal link involved in these things, but what exactly it is defies explanation.

* * *

The superstition about mud balls may have been connected with the "Mud Ball Palace" in Taoist alchemy, which was where the God of the Brain lived in the human body.

If You Believe That ...
HXZZ IV 56

Li Xuan, a colonel from Gansu province, was expert in a predictive system developed in the Song dynasty that followed the explanations in the *Book of Changes*. His forecasts mostly proved valid.

During the campaigns to pacify the Western Regions, when he was attached to the headquarters of General Wen Fu, a soldier accidentally started a fire which spread to consume a strip of dry grass over ten feet wide in front of the palisade gate. General Wen had Li divine what sort of portent that was. Li responded:

"It is no great matter: it is only that you will soon dispatch a secret memorial to the throne. Fire picks up speed over dry grass, signifying a missive sent post-haste. The smoke rises into the air, pointing to the destination of the throne. It must be a secret memorial because the rule requires that the draft copy be burnt."

Our general remarked: "I have nothing to submit any secret memorial about."

"The fire was sparked unintentionally, so likewise without preparedness."

The prediction turned out to be true.

The method used by Li Xuan to foretell a person's life course was to have the subject pick up an object at random. It did not follow, though, that two persons who picked up the same object would get the same forecast. When we were both back in the capital, a Hanlin academician picked up a tobacco pipe. Li observed:

"The pipe stores fire, and its smoke travels through the stem drawn by breath. That shows you will not be left out in the cold. However, your position will not be very prominent, because you will depend on others puffing you up."

"How long will I have in office?"

"Pardon me if I speak frankly. To begin with, the fire in a pipe has little combustible material: once it goes out, it is dead ashes. It cannot stay hot for long."

"How long do I have to live?"

"Brass vessels can indeed last for ages, but I have never heard of a hundred-year-old pipe." Li shook his head.

The academician snorted with anger, got up and left. A year or so later, his end came as predicted.

A vice-president of a board who attended the same session picked up the same pipe to see what Li's construction would be.

"The pipe has gone out, which means you are employed in no meaningful work; the fact that the pipe has been placed on the bed shows that your career was at one point brought to a standstill. Yet since the pipe has been picked up and handled again, someone has given you a boost, and revived your career. Heat will come back again, but what follows will be the course previously described."

Subsequent events bore Li out once again.

BEYOND BELIEF

Conjuring
LYXXL I 24

Conjuring tricks are no more than the hand being quicker than the eye, but the magic of transposition, moving objects from place to place, is genuine. I remember seeing a magician perform in my maternal grandfather's house when I was a young boy. He placed a filled wine cup on a table, patted it with the palm of his hand, and the wine cup sank into the table, its rim becoming level with the table top. But when we felt the underside of the table, there was no bottom of the cup protruding. On the magician removing the cup, the surface of the table was unmarked. That trick could have been put down to misdirection or masking, but what followed was of a different order.

The magician took up a big bowl of fish stew and threw it high in the air, whereupon it disappeared. He said he couldn't get it back when we asked him to, because it was in the study, stowed away in a drawer of a layered chest for keeping paintings. He invited the gentlemen present to fetch it themselves. At that time there were a lot of guests and their attendants milling about, and since the study had numbers of valuable antiques in it, it was securely locked. Besides that, the layered drawers were only two inches in depth, while the bowl was three to four inches high, so it was quite impossible for it to fit in one of those drawers. Everyone thought he was talking through his hat.

In any case, the keys were brought and the study opened. The bowl was found sitting on a side table, only now it contained five Buddha's hand fruits, while the dish that had contained the fruits was now filled with fish stew, and was secreted in one of the layered drawers. Now if that wasn't transposition, what was it?

What reason says cannot happen, nevertheless sometimes does happen, as this example demonstrates. Reason should then be flexible enough to accommodate the fact. That fox sprites and hill goblins should steal people's possessions is not thought abnormal, neither is it abnormal for a sorcerer to be able to subjugate such spirits; and since he can subjugate them, he can have them do his bidding. Given that the sprites and goblins can steal things for themselves, it follows that they can steal things for others. What is there abnormal about that?

Egg-Laying Cocks
GWTZ II 3

In Yuan Mei's collection of supernatural tales called *What the Sage Did Not Speak of* there is a reference to cocks laying eggs. I know now there really is such a thing. The egg is as long as a finger, and in shape like a Fujian peanut, never perfectly round. There are flecks in the shell, and when held up to the sun, you can see its yolk is deep red, like amber. It is very effective for treating cataracts. Decheng, President of the Board of Works, and Wang Chengpei, Senior Vice-President of the Censorate, are among those who have used it as an ingredient in their medications. However, these eggs are in short supply: you can pay ten ounces of silver for one. Adisi, Minister of Agriculture, stated:

"Though these eggs are hard to find, actually they can be produced by human intervention. You shut a big strong cock up in a coop, and let loose a lot of hens around it, so that the hens are close by, but out of reach. In time the cock's sperm compacts, and comes out by itself as an egg."

That sounds reasonable enough. Still, poultry as a species are subject to the influence of the warm south-east wind, which is why one can come out in sores from eating them. A cock's egg is formed by a build-up of thrusting vitality that cannot find relief, so must be imbued with heat. In which case, how can it improve eyesight, when vision is thought, rather, to be impaired by heat? Besides, the *Materia Medica* does not mention the cock's egg, nor does it feature in the classic medical handbooks, so how is it known to cure eye defects? The answer escapes us.

Vice-President Wang added:

"Some people pass off snake's eggs as cock's eggs, but their yolk is not red when held up to the sun, so their falsity can be proved that way."

That is an indispensable piece of knowledge.

* * *

In Ji Xiaolan's letter to his younger cousin Xiulan (Family Letters, 1937 edition, pp. 60–61) he reveals he had a personal involvement with the cock's egg story. Apparently his student Li Xiusheng brought him an egg of the above description. When Ji doubted its provenance, Li brought the fowl concerned, actually a golden pheasant, to his house the next morning; by the afternoon it had indeed laid such an egg. Ji then consulted an authority as related above. His conclusion in the letter is a guarded acceptance, to the effect that strange things do happen. We do not know if he could tell the difference between a male and a female golden pheasant.

Invading Dreams

GWTZ I 54

Dreams take shape when the higher conscious soul mingles with the lower animal soul, but their workings are mysterious. My late brother Qinghu wrote a poem on the legend of the King of Chu enjoying the goddess of Mount Wu in a dream. It ran:

> When another dreams of me
> I have no means of knowing it.
> When I dream of another
> How can that other know of it?
> That weakling king's dream was wishful thinking
> Would a goddess have been up for trysting?
> Whatever happened on Mount Wu
> I doubt that making love was part of it.

That goes far to restore the good name of the goddess. Nevertheless, it really does happen that the dreams of others can be entered into. Once upon a time my servant Li Xing was taking a stroll outside his village on a moonlit night when he caught glimpses of a neighbour's young wife moving through a stand of jujube trees. He thought she must be on her way to guard their vegetable plot from thieves, and her parents-in-law or husband might be with her, so he did not presume to call out to her and engage her in conversation. He caught sight of her again crossing fields in a westerly direction; after a few hundred yards she entered a high clump of sorghum. Li Xing suspected she might be meeting someone in secret there, so was even more reluctant to approach. He contented himself with watching from a distance. She soon emerged on the other side of the sorghum, found her way blocked by a stream, and turned back. For quite some time she stood still, irresolute, then followed the stream north for a hundred paces, until she ran into a swampy patch and had to backtrack again. This time she headed north-east into a bean field. There she zigzagged about, falling over several times. Li Xing realized she had lost her way, so called out to her:

"Where are you going in the dead of night, Mrs So-and-so? The way north doesn't lead anywhere, and you could sink into the bog."

The young woman looked back and said:

"I can't find my way out. Would you kindly lead me home?"

Li Xing hurried over to her, but she was nowhere to be seen. Concluding she was an apparition, he was frightened to death, and ran back home in panic. As he passed the young woman's house, he saw her sitting outdoors with her mother. She said she had fallen asleep over her spinning loom, dreamed she went out into the woods and fields, lost her way, and went round in circles. When she heard Li calling from behind her, she woke up. Everything she said corresponded with what Li Xing had observed.

The explanation seems to be that when physical exhaustion reaches its peak, the conscious mind loses dominion, and the primal energies are set free, resulting in the separation of higher soul from body. When it is the lower soul that leaves the body, we have the phenomenon of spectres, which is different from the present case of volatile phantoms generated by fluctuations in consciousness, phantoms that may be visible to others. Our story here is just like that of Dugu Xiashu, described in *Tales from East of the Yellow River*, who saw his wife carousing with young dandies on his return journey, but found her still at home, awakening from a dream of that happening.

Faery Lands
LYXL II 12

The fabled Three Isles and Ten Atolls in the Eastern Seas, the Five Cities and Twelve Towers in the Kunlun Mountains where immortals dwell, have long been the stuff of poetry. Now, Chinese books can be read in Korea, the Ryukyu Islands and Japan, and I have seen the Japanese *Guide to the Five Capitals* and *Map of the Lands and Seas*: these maps cover an area of thousands of miles, but there is no mention of the fairy mounts or blessed isles that the Japanese would have read about in Chinese texts. I have also had many conversations with envoys from Korea and the Ryukyu Islands, and questioned them on this subject. They all say that besides Japan there are dozens of nations and countless big and small islands in the Eastern Ocean, beyond the range of Chinese shipping; their own trading vessels voyage far and wide to visit them, but they have had no reports of the places mentioned. However, there is a trough in the ocean bed off the Ryukyu Islands, seemingly the Perilous Sea of legend where ships are sucked under; yet that too can be traversed in safety when the seas are calm, and there has been no talk of "silver palaces that can be glimpsed but not attained to". In that case, the Three Isles and Ten Atolls are surely products of the imagination.

According to the *Er ya*, our earliest lexicon, and the *Records of the Historian*, the Yellow River has its source in the Kunlun Mountains. I have ascertained there are two possible sources for the Yellow River: either the Hetian or Congling range. Some maintain that Congling is its true source, and the water from Hetian flows into it; some think it is the other way round. In any case, since the two streams merge, there is no telling major from minor. Both ranges are now within the territory of the Qing empire, and colonization of the land under the military has gone on for forty years or more. Even the remotest and least accessible mountain areas are under the plough or used for herding. No matter which of the two ranges is the true source of the Yellow River, it is certain that Kunlun must be in their area. Yet there has been absolutely no sighting or report of the so-called Jasper Lake, Hanging Garden, Pearl Tree or Ambrosia Fields. Consequently the tale of Five Cities and Twelve Towers in the Kunlun would also be an absurdity, would it not?

That is not the only thing. The Holy Vulture Mount, in present day Badakhshan, has on top of it some stone stupas containing the relics of various Buddhas and Bodhisattvas, and their inscriptions in Sanskrit correspond exactly with the authentic Buddhist scriptures. There are also over 600 cells comprising the Thunderclap Monastery, where the Western Buddha is said to have dwelt; they are occupied by Moslem nomads. Our troops reached there in their campaigns against two rebel tribal chiefs, and they found nothing out of the ordinary: the descriptions of magnificence were all due to writers' grandiloquence.

Again, legend has it that the Moslems built a city of bronze in their homeland. The Moslems on the west say the bronze city is far away to the east, while the Moslems on the east say it is far away to the west. So they address their prayers in each other's direction, and to this day none have actually gone to the bronze city. I deduce that the Jesuit Verbiest's *Map of the World* [1674], with its five continents, Seven Wonders and weird denizens, probably belongs to the same category.

On the other hand, the Hanlin compiler Zhou Shuchang says:

"It takes a person with affinities to Buddhism to see the Buddha's world; it takes a person with the potential for transcendence to perceive a wonderland. You cannot determine their existence or non-existence on what the vulgar herd hear and see. I once met a Taoist priest who had toured the Kunlun range, and what he said he saw there was no different from what the ancient texts said."

In that respect I have to confess my ignorance.

* * *

Matteo Ricci was the first Jesuit missionary to gain acceptance in China proper, largely on the strength of the map of the world he presented to Chinese scholars in 1584. At the time the Chinese were almost wholly ignorant of the western and southern hemispheres. A succession of more detailed maps by other Jesuits followed, copied from originals by master Dutch cartographers. This industry served a double purpose: first to impress their hosts with their practical knowledge, and second to make the Chinese more receptive to Christianity by drawing them out of their cultural isolation and into the ecumenical community. The map produced by Ferdinand Verbiest in 1674 was in two volumes, the first illustrating the physical geography of the world, and the second being an explanation of the human geography, describing the education, economy, customs and institutions of various countries and continents, as well as grand buildings and constructs. Flora and fauna were also introduced; presumably Ji Xiaolan was referring to examples of the latter as "weird denizens" (though Verbiest may have included some creatures of the Christian bestiary).

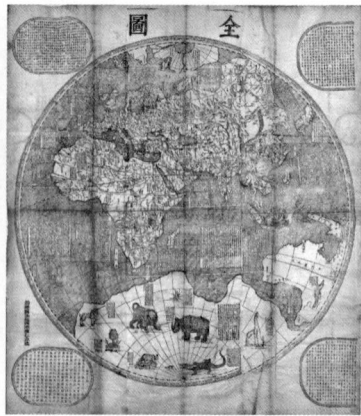

Figure 11. Ferdinand Verbiest (1623–1688), Belgian Jesuit who served as a second rank official at the Chinese court, and his *Map of the World*.

The Evil Eunuch

LYXXL III 25

The turpitude of the Ming dynasty eunuch Wei Zhongxian was of a magnitude unequalled in our history. Because he knew his evil deeds would be exposed some time, one story has it that he secretly stabled a mule capable of covering a hundred leagues in a day for when he would have to flee from arrest, and also kept in the wings a double of himself who could die in his stead. In the event he did make good his escape by these means at Youjiadian in Fucheng county. I think that is a load of nonsense. In terms of the way of Heaven, unless we are deceived about the thoroughness of divine justice, there is absolutely no reason why he should have been spared. From the point of view of the realities of life on earth, Wei Zhongxian bestrode the court for seven years, so who did not know him? Supposing he sneaked away to hide in the house of one of his former confederates, it is the rule that loyalty among low characters dissolves when their power is broken: he would simply have been trussed up and handed over to the authorities. Alternatively, if he holed up in the backwoods, the sudden appearance among country folk of a eunuch who looked different and spoke differently would be bound to cause a sensation, and he would have been apprehended in a matter of days. Then again, if he were to have sought refuge beyond our frontiers, he would not have had the advantage of Yan Shifan who colluded with Japanese pirates, or of the Gansu General Chou Luan who had secret connections with the Anda nomad raiders: barred by high mountains and deep seas, with passes and ports sealed, how would he have got out?

Let us look for comparison at the case of the Jianwen emperor, overthrown by his uncle in the Ming dynasty: it was said even of him that he escaped with his life when his palace burnt down. However, Jianwen was not reputed to have had moral failings, nor to have lost his people's affections. Those who had served under his reign still thought well of their former sovereign. His uncle, the Prince of Yan (later the Yongle emperor), on the other hand, had usurped the throne by force of arms, and set about the slaughter of good men and true with a will: no one would have wanted to take his side. So it is not beyond the bounds of possibility that Jianwen had a relay of protectors who took him in and hid him. In contrast, Wei Zhongxian's barbarity stank to high heaven, and his poison infected the whole land: his demise would have been met with universal rejoicing. The Ming dynasty had fifteen years to run after his downfall: if he had lived, how could he have remained undetected in all that time? For all these reasons I firmly reject the notion that he went to ground.

Mr Wang Yuefang of Wen An county observed:

"At the beginning of the Qianlong reign the county college was beset by a violent storm: thunderclaps reverberated round the Confucian temple in its grounds, shafts of lightning fired the sky like flickering bands of red silk, and a ball of lightning passed through the portals and circled round continually inside. The Director of Studies, Wang Zhuqi, said: "This is surely something freakish!" He braved the rain to enter the temple, and saw there a big centipede crawling over the Sage's spirit tablet. He took it up with tongs and threw it down the steps. There came a deafening clap of thunder, and the centipede lay dead; the sky immediately cleared. When the centipede was examined, the three characters *wei zhong xian* were found inscribed in red on its back."

Now *this* story I am willing to believe.

Red Lamas and Yellow Lamas
LYXXL VI 17

The "Red Hat" Tibetan lamas dated as a sect from the eighth century, and represented indigenous religious beliefs and practices, which had some communality with Hinduism. The "Yellow Hat" sect of the fourteenth to fifteenth centuries was led by reformists bent on purifying Tibetan Buddhism. They enjoyed the patronage of the Qing court: the title of Dalai Lama was conferred in 1653 by the Shunzhi emperor, and that of the Panchen Lama in 1645.

* * *

There are two kinds of lama priests, distinguished by the colour of their robes, the Yellow and the Red. The Yellow ones preach moral conduct and expound the doctrine of karma; though forming a different sect, they come from the same stock as the *Chan* Buddhists. The Red ones, in contrast, are devoted to the practice of magical arts. Liu Baozhu, Secretary of the Board of Western Tribal Affairs, tells how he offended a Red lama when he was stationed in Tibet, and subsequently was warned that the lama would take his revenge during Liu's ascent of a mountain. Liu took the precaution of ordering his sedan chair bearers and mounted escort to go ahead of him, while he covertly followed on horseback. Sure enough, one of the horses reared up and brought its hooves down on the empty sedan chair, reducing it to matchwood. I heard that from Liu's own mouth.

On my own account, I personally witnessed a demonstration of Red lama witchcraft during my garrison service in Urumqi.

A Red lama was called in to find a horse that had strayed. He chanted a spell over a little wooden stool, which eventually started to move, jerking about like the arm of a well sweep when a bucket is lowered into a well. Telling the horse's owner to follow him, the lama led the way in the direction pointed by the stool, and behold, they found the missing horse in a gully.

Given records of sword-swallowing and fire-eating sorcerers in the Western Regions dating back to the Former Han dynasty [206 BC–AD 25], I presume their wizardry had been passed down to the present day; it is not part of Buddhism proper. That would explain why the Yellow lamas call the Red lamas diabolists. My adviser told me: "In fact those Red lamas are Brahmins, condemned in the Buddhists scriptures as heretics." That seems to be not far from the truth.

The Black Art of the Red Lamas
GWTZ I 49

There is an interesting parallel with the black art described in this item in the Neoplatonism mentioned in Chapter One. According to Keith Thomas: "Neoplatonic theory also emphasized the influence of the imagination on the body, of the mind upon matter, and of words, incantations and written charms upon physical objects. By the exercise of his imagination, and the use of magic, symbols and incantations, the operator could transform himself or his victim. Since the world was a pulsating mass of vital influences and invisible spirits, it was only necessary that the magician should devise the appropriate technique to capture them. He could then do wonders." (Religion and the Decline of Magic, p. 224)

* * *

My fellow graduate Jiang Xinyu contributed this.

In the course of his travels a merchant was invited to go boating on a lake. When he arrived at the spot, he found a pleasure boat, musicians playing flutes and drums, and a hostess dressed in red plying the guests with drink. On looking closely at her, he recognized her as his wife. He could not understand how she could have ended up there, a thousand miles from home. He did not dare address her, out of fear of bringing shame on himself. For her part, the woman acted as if she did not know him, betraying no disquiet or embarrassment. She seemed entirely at ease when she tuned her instrument and sang her songs, or flipped back her sleeve to lift her cup. Only her voice was different, though too the merchant's wife covered her mouth when she laughed, while this entertainer did not. Nevertheless, she had exactly the same reddish mole as small as a grain of millet on her right wrist as his wife had. Completely nonplussed, the merchant managed somehow to sit through the party, and returned to his lodging to get his things together for his journey home.

Before his preparations were complete, he received a letter from home saying that his wife had died half a year ago. He guessed then that the woman he had seen on the boat was a ghost, and was not inclined to pursue the matter. All the same, his close companions noticed that his mind was unsettled, and eventually wormed the reason out of him. Their consensus was that the resemblance could only have been coincidental.

Some time later, news came of a stranger touring the Jiangsu-Zhejiang region who did not seek audience with dignitaries, and neither mixed in society nor engaged in trade. He simply shut himself up with a bevy of concubines. From time to time he might release one or two of these women to a matchmaker for her to sell for him. People thought he must be a trafficker in women, but since he did not interfere with others, they left him to his own devices.

One day this stranger got very flustered and bought a boat in a tearing hurry to take him to the Eye of Heaven Mountain in north-west Zhejiang, there to ask the venerable abbot to perform a service of deliverance. On account of his written supplication being cast in cryptic and evasive terms, the abbot could not tell what the matter was. For another thing, it contained the passage:

"It is on the Buddha's prompting that I now pray for his protection. May his cloud of compassion shield me from the punishment of the Thunder God."

This made the abbot suspect that an undisclosed motive lay behind the stranger's prayer. The abbot returned his donation, declined to hold the service, and sent him on his way. The man was indeed struck dead by a thunderbolt on his return journey.

Afterwards, the stranger's attendant disclosed:

"This man learned a black art from a red-cassocked foreign monk. By reciting a spell he could possess the corpse of a woman just laid to rest, and bring this corpse alive again by implanting in it a wanton ghost or fox spirit he also captured. She then served his pleasure. When he was able to procure a new female, he sold off an old one, making a mint of money. It was because he dreamed of a warning from the gods that the measure of his iniquities was full and he faced imminent destruction by High Heaven that he rushed to the monastery to seek clemency, but it was already too late."

It was thought that the merchant's wife was one of his victims. The President of the Board of Tibetan and Mongolian Affairs said that the Red Sect lamas of Tibet did indeed have the magical power of taking possession of women, which is why the orthodox Yellow Sect condemned them as devilish.

REINCARNATION

Given the key Buddhist concept of the impermanence, insubstantiality and illusoriness of all phenomena, material and psychic alike, it follows that human cravings will be frustrated, and result in suffering. The ultimate release from suffering is through attaining obliviousness, or "nirvana", which literally means "blowing out", as a flame is blown out. The passage to nirvana is not completed in one lifetime but in a series of lifetimes (an established tenet of Hinduism) following a gradient towards total awareness, the ascent being made by mental discipline and blameless conduct. Obviously there had to be some link which carried over progress or regression from one lifetime into the next; since that could not be a conscious permanent soul, it was conceived of as a chain of causation, or "karma", which acted mechanically like a flame from one candle used to light another candle.

However, with the spread of the Buddhist religion (it came to China in the first century AD), its doctrine accommodated to the common preference for future bliss over extinction, paradise over nothingness, and a pantheon of Buddhist gods emerged, devotion to whom could succour and save: for example, constant pious evocation of the Amita Buddha's name could attract his blessing. In China Buddhism became mixed up in the popular mind with religious Taoism, the majority of the people turning from one to the other as occasion required. The following items reflect the conjunction of reincarnation with the accounting of merits and demerits by an underworld bureaucracy, as is postulated in Taoism, and the ancestral belief in the controlling power of Heaven.

An Overview
LYXXL V 14

If there is no reincarnation, then counting from far antiquity the number of ghosts would have gone on growing day by day until the whole wide world would not be able to fit them all in. If to the contrary there *is* reincarnation, when one person dies here another is born there, one bodily form promptly exchanging for another. In that case there should be no ghosts active in the world: presumably everyone, including street hawkers and peasant women, would be continually reborn. But then again, ghosts are commonly seen in desolate graveyards, so it seems there must be exceptions to the rule of reincarnation.

When he was lying ill in bed, my cousin An Tianshi's unfettered soul gravitated to the nether world, and he raised this question with a keeper of the rolls. The keeper said:

"There is reincarnation for some and no reincarnation for others. The three pathways for reincarnation are: felicity awarded for benevolence; retribution exacted for sins; and the ongoing consequences of charity or injustice. For non-reincarnation there are also three pathways: for sages and saints destined for immortality; for those condemned to the bottomless Avici hell; and for those neither blessed nor damned. The last are left to wander in cemeteries. If some vital energy remains, they linger; when their vital energy drains away, they disappear. Like dew on the grass, like bubbles in water, they exist only fleetingly; like wild flowers, they bloom and fade unnoticed. This sort of ghost has no possibility of being reborn.

"Exceptionally, there may be stray souls who attach themselves to women who become pregnant: this is called 'stealing life'. Exalted Buddhist monks and Taoist priests may borrow someone else's body to begin a new life: this is called 'appropriating a habitation'. These are incidental transformations, and are unrelated to the normal operation of reincarnation. As for the heavenly hosts descending to support a rightful dynasty, or hordes of demons wreaking death and destruction, those events belong to the tides of destiny, and do not count as reincarnation."

Tianshi had resolutely rejected the notion of reincarnation, but after he recovered from his illness he recounted this experience, concluding: "What the keeper of the rolls said makes sound sense."

A Personal Affirmation
RSWW III 5

The story of Gu Feixiong's rebirth in response to the depths of his father's grief is told in the Tang dynasty *Yuyang Miscellany* and the Song dynasty *Trifles of Northern Dreams*; it is also recorded in a poem of his father, Gu Kuang. It is unlikely to have been fabricated. In recent times Shen Yunjiao, Vice-President of the Board of Civil Service, composed an epitaph for his mother, surnamed Lu. It states that his mother had not been married more than a year before his father died, and the child she was then carrying, a boy named Heng, also died at the age of three. His mother wept bitterly at Heng's death, saying:

"The reason I have clung onto life was because of you, but now you are gone. I still cannot bear the thought that our Shen family line should be thus cut off!"

When the boy was placed in his coffin, his mother made a mark with red pigment on his arm, and offered this prayer:

"If Heaven does not determine to cut off our posterity, you will bear this mark as a token when you are reborn."

This took place in the twelfth month of the seventh year of the Yongzheng reign [1729]. Later in the same month a neighbouring family of the same clan gave birth to a son: on his arm was a bright red mark. Madam Shen then adopted him as her son to carry on the family line. This child was the said Shen Yunjiao. He was my colleague when I was President of the Board of Rites, and in conversation he explained this happening in every detail.

Now there are indeed absurdities in the holy scriptures of Buddhism to begin with; its adherents go on to exaggerate blessings and reparations in order to induce people to give alms, in the process compounding the falsities and deceptions. Still, the doctrine of the transmigration of souls is supported by unshakeable evidence. From time to time the powers that control people's fates give particular signs to demonstrate the morality of the Divine Way. Through the above example of rebirth they show proof of the influence of a distressed widow's constancy and devotion. Those Confucian dogmatists who loudly deny the existence of spirits have no way to account for such events.

8

CURIOSITIES

The Rat's Lesson
RSWW IV 34

Physicians and alchemists applied themselves to producing drugs that enhanced sexual prowess from very early in Chinese history. Names of aphrodisiacs are recorded for the Han dynasty, Emperor Cheng (first century BC) being said to have died from an overdose of one kind, and similar preparations continued to be marketed down the ages. Their ingredients could be very peculiar: one preparation popular in the Ming dynasty called "red lead" was made from the menstrual fluid of young virgins, whose first period was deemed to have the greatest efficacy. Ming emperors were notoriously addicted to drugs as elixirs and sexual stimulants, which might have boosted the latter kind's popularity. In the item that follows, since Li Qingzi easily recognizes aphrodisiac pills when he sees them, and expresses no surprise at their presence, we can deduce that their use was also widespread in the eighteenth century.

* * *

Li Qingzi told me the following story.

"I once spent a night in a friend's study. As dawn approached, two rats started bounding after each other, whirling round the room like a flying chariot, cavorting and catapulting, knocking over urns, jugs and washbasins. The noise of their crashing and shattering was most unnerving. After some time, one rat leapt several feet in the air, fell to the floor, leapt up again, fell flat and ceased to move. Blood issued from its eyes, ears, nose and mouth, something that puzzled me. I hurriedly called a servant to clear up the mess, and then I noticed that the aphrodisiac pills which had been emptied into a dish had been nibbled at. I realized that the rat had swallowed this drug in mistake for food, and had been driven to a sexual frenzy. The female rat could not stand up to this harassment and made her escape, leaving the male rat no release for its lust, and it had died from spontaneous combustion.

"My friend expressed amazement and amusement when he appeared on the scene. But on reflection he looked worried. 'I never thought it would come to this,' he said. 'I must watch out for myself.' He tipped the remaining stock of the drug down the sink."

Heat-inducing chemicals are both potent and poisonous. I have seen too many people come to grief through taking such stuff. Even our great men have not been free of this habit, as the case of Han Yu taking sulphur preparations in his old age shows. Obviously the reaper was not yet ready for this friend of Li Qingzi, so the rat's warning came in time for him to mend his ways!

Bestiality
HXZZ II 6

Prostitution was rife in Urumqi. From low hovels in shady lanes came the constant racket of tinny music, and those places were ablaze with light right from the drum for the first watch of the night to the temple's dawn bell. Libertines could satisfy any desire in those precincts: the authorities did not suppress the business, nor could they have.

There was a certain dealer in textiles from Ningxia called He, a young and handsome man. He was rolling in money, and not stingy with it either, but he was averse to taking pleasure in the bordellos. He took instead to keeping a dozen sows, which he fed very well and washed very clean. Every day he shut the pigsty door and copulated with them in turn. The sows, for their part, nuzzled up to him, as if he were their favourite boar.

Young He's servants regularly spied on him without him knowing it. When one day a friend who had had too much to drink jokingly questioned him on this matter, he drowned himself in a well out of shame.

Mu Jintai, deputy magistrate of Dihua county, commented: "If I had not personally officiated in this case, I wouldn't have credited it, even if our most reliable historian Sima Guang had told me."

[...]

It is amazing that human appetites can run to such extremes. Reason cannot account for all the anomalies that happen in this world, nor can we rely on fellow feeling to understand all possible eccentricities.

APE LIPS

GWTZ I 14

Of the traditional Eight Delicacies, only bear's paws and deer's tails are generally available. Camel humps from beyond the frontiers are already rare (this refers to the single-hump camel, not the ordinary double-hump camel). The lips of the orang-utan used to be known to me only by name.

In the fortieth year of the Qianlong reign [1775], General Min Shaoyi presented me with a set of the same, packed in a brocade box as a mark of the object's prestige. It turned out that, rather than just the two lips, the whole face from forehead to chin had been stripped off and cured; it was complete with mouth, nose, brows and eye holes, the whole resembling the actor's face mask. My chef did not know how to prepare the "delicacy" for the table, so I passed it on to a friend. This friend's cook was also in the dark, so it was passed on again. I have no idea where it ended up, and still can give no advice on how it should be cooked.

FASHIONS

GWTZ I 13

In the Tartar Jin dynasty they valued Shenyang sturgeon, and we still do; they also valued swan meat, but now we do not. In the Khitan Liao dynasty they thought highly of yellow weasel, and still did in the Ming dynasty, but now we do not. In the Ming dynasty they liked to eat "Xiao bears" and penned deer; penned deer means they were farm raised, but what Xiao bears were I haven't a clue—my enquiries in the most epicurean households have met with blank looks. To sum up, it seems there is no fixed scale for what is valued or despised: it all depends on the fashions of the time.

When I was young, I remember that ginseng, coral and lapis lazuli were all inexpensive, but now they have shot up in price, whereas turquoise and tourmaline were both extremely expensive, but now get cheaper by the day. At that time Yunnan jadeite was not regarded as jade, no more than jasper is, while now it is a treasured possession, priced far above true jade.

Formerly it was the white squirrel that was prized for its fur, now it is the black kind; similarly long-haired sable used to be in demand, but now it is the short-haired kind. The snow weasel was once only slightly dearer than squirrel, far and away cheaper than the corsac grey fox, while now it is as dear as sable. Once it was the fiery red coral that was sought after, now it is the cherry red, and the most valuable coral of all is the colour of mother-of-pearl. What we are talking about here is a difference of fifty or sixty years: think what a gap of hundreds of years makes!

Scholars have privately suspected some error in the term "ant-egg sauce" which occurs in the *Rites of Zhou*: they haven't caught up with the fact that customs and taste change radically over the years.

A Lion

RSWW IV 48

In the fourteenth year of the Kangxi reign [1675], a western nation [Portugal] presented a lion as a tribute to the throne, and the most venerable mandarins of the time composed poems to mark the event. Legend has it that the lion very soon escaped, and ran as fast as the wind: having broken free from its chain in mid morning, it exited through the Jiayu Pass at the western end of the Great Wall at noon. That is no more than a fairy tale.

The Kangxi emperor returned to the capital from his southern tour by way of the Wei River, and likewise had the lion transported by boat. My late maternal grandmother Madam Cao got a glimpse of it through a chink in the window of her family's pagoda on the river bank. Its body was like that of a chow dog, its tail like a tiger's but somewhat longer, its face round like a human face, not as long and lean as that of other wild animals. They had chained it to the main mast of the boat, and tied a pig up for it to eat. The pig had squealed when it was still being driven along the bank, but fell silent as it neared the boat. When dragged up in front of the lion, the lion lowered its head and sniffed it: by that time the pig had already died of fright.

When the oars were unshipped and the boat prepared to sail, the lion suddenly let out a thunderous roar, making a sound like countless martial gongs resonating in unison. The dozen horses in my grandfather's stable heard the roar through the stable walls, trembled and lay head down in their stalls, not daring to stir till hours after the boat left. Not for nothing is the lion called the king of the beasts.

As soon as the lion arrived in the capital, the then Vice-President of the Civil Service Board, Alibei, who ranked alongside the great artists of old, painted it from life, giving it a vivid personality. The painting was previously hung in my senior Bo Xizhai's house, Alibei having presented it to his grandfather. Afterwards the picture was sold to me, and I asked a connoisseur to write in a title. Alibei had not signed the picture, because of the precedent of a lion being presented in the Yuan dynasty. The connoisseur inscribed "A Yuan dynasty true image of the lion". Bo Xizhai commented: "The painting skill of the Vice-President is not inferior to that of the Yuan work, so one cannot find fault with this appreciation."

Cangzhou Wine

LYXL V 4

To avoid giving the wrong impression of our author, he drank very little himself: he is here simply retailing local lore.

* * *

The statesman and poet Wang Shizhen called Cangzhou wine "Magu wine", likening it to the wine brewed by the immortal Magu for the birthday of the Queen Mother of the West, but local people do not use that name. Cangzhou wine has been famed for generations, though opinions of it differ considerably, because visitors passing through Cangzhou by boat buy their wine in shops on the quay, and the thin village brew available there is not up to proper wining and dining. Another reason that applies to officials is that the natives are wary of the insatiable appetite for requisitioning on the part of government, and ban the supply of genuine wine to the yamen: they will not produce it on pain of flogging, nor sell it at ten times the going price. Even the yamen of the Governor-General of Zhili province could not get a drop of it, let alone others.

Market traders are not able to brew the true Cangzhou wine, it is the monopoly of the old established families whose expertise is passed from generation to generation: only they have the secret of the right times and temperatures. The water is drawn from the Wei River, but not from its muddied currents. They have to lower their tin containers to the river bed under the South Stream Tower to catch the flow from the pure underground spring, the same as the monks of Jinshan Temple draw water from the springs feeding the Yangtze River for their tea making. This is needed to give the wine its delicate body.

As to cellarage, Cangzhou wine is sensitive to excessive cold and heat, damp and dryness: its taste is spoiled if subject to any of those. New wine does not drink well, it needs to be shelved for more than ten years to reach its peak. One pitcher can fetch a price of four or five silver taels, though in practice this wine is mostly given as gifts, it being considered infra dig to market it. Besides, it is nowadays harder to get hold of, because the prominent clans like Dai, Lü, Liu and Wang, and families like Zhang and Wei have all fallen on hard times, and less wine is brewed by them.

If the kegs of Cangzhou wine are transported, whether carried by shoulder yoke or shifted by cart or boat, the jolting ruins the taste, and it has to rest undisturbed for two weeks to recover. When drawn into a wine jug for drinking, it should be scooped out smoothly with a ladle: if stirred up, the taste is again spoiled, and the wine must be allowed to settle for several days.

My late father Yao An once remarked:

"There are so many cautions to be observed with Cangzhou wine, so much fuss and bother to go to before you can take a sip in the appropriate poetic setting that it is hardly worth all the trouble. I'd rather send an errand boy to a wine shop for a pitcher of whatever wine is on offer: that way you can enjoy your drink in peace and contentment."

No doubt he had in mind all the conditions I have referred to.

The test of wine that is brewed from the spring under the South Stream Tower is that you can drink yourself silly without feeling queasy or getting a hangover. It simply makes you feel relaxed, and you sleep like a top afterwards. That is not the case with wine brewed with plain river water. As to assessing the vintage, the wine of two years vintage can be warmed twice, that of ten years vintage can be warmed ten times without detriment, though the taste will deteriorate on the eleventh warming. Wine aged only one year will not stand up to a second warming, and likewise two year old wine will not tolerate a third warming. There is absolutely no deviation from that rule, though don't ask me why.

Dong Siren, the uncle of my senior Dong Qujiang, was a great drinker. When he served as prefect of Cangzhou, he was aware that the good wine was not supplied to officials, and exhausted all his arts of trickery and exhortation without managing to get the ban lifted. But after he was dismissed from office and returned to Cangzhou to stay with Dr Li Ruidian, he partook liberally of Li's home brewed fine wine. Dong Siren said to Li, "I profoundly regret that I wasn't dismissed sooner!" Though this was said in jest, it goes to show that to enjoy the fine wine of Cangzhou is a rare privilege.

THE WILD WEST

Throughout recorded history, regions little explored by "civilized" peoples have been suspected of harbouring if not frightening monsters then weird and wonderful creatures. The Christian bestiaries of the Middle Ages catalogued such beings, and the Mappa Mundi located many of them. In China the standard source for strange creatures was the Shan hai jing (The Classic of Mountains and Seas). There are some remarkable coincidences between the creatures illustrated there and those shown in the Mappa Mundi, including the headless man with his face on his chest known in English as Blemya and in Chinese as Xing Tian. Interestingly, the latter has fascinated celebrated literary men as far apart as the early poet Tao Yuanming and the modern rebel Lu Xun, not to mention Shakespeare, who had Othello tell Desdemona of "The anthropophagi, the men whose heads do grow beneath their shoulders". Xing Tian features here too.

Ji Xiaolan was exiled for three years to Urumqi, a remote western outpost of the Qing empire in the midst of vast uninhabited deserts and mountain ranges, which was rich territory for strange encounters and the growth of tall stories. There follows a small sample of these which Ji culled for his collection, as well as some things on the ground that interested and surprised him.

Tibetan Wild Men
GWTZ I 4

Something to add to the literature on the yeti, it seems, with the bonus of a graphic description.

* * *

Gang Chaorong, a felon exiled to Urumqi, contributed this.

Two men who set off to Tibet on their mules to sell their merchandise got lost in the mountains, and could not tell in which direction they were heading. Suddenly a dozen men jumped down from a crag into their path, apparently bandits intent on waylaying them. As they neared, they were seen to be of giant stature, their bodies covered with furry hair, some of yellow, some of green hue; their faces were only half human, their speech was unintelligible, rather like the twittering of birds: they were certainly ogres of some kind. Thinking their end was nigh, the merchants prostrated themselves in fear and trembling.

The band looked at each other and laughed; they made no move to pounce on the merchants and sink their teeth into them. They simply clasped these men under the armpit and frogmarched them off, driving the mules before them. When they got to a mountain col, they set the merchants down. One of the mules was pushed into a pit, the other they slaughtered and butchered with their knives. They kindled a fire and roasted the meat, then sat in a circle and started wolfing it down. The merchants were not forgotten: they were brought over and meat was placed in front of them. Being tired and hungry, and discerning the band meant them no harm, the merchants thought they might as well eat too. After they had had their fill, the band lay back and wheezed, making a noise like the whinnying of horses.

Two pairs from the band then propped one merchant each between them, skimmed over the crests of sheer mountains, as agile as monkeys and fleet as birds, and deposited the merchants by the side of a post road, gave each of them a stone, and were gone in the twinkling of an eye. The stones, as big as melons, were solid turquoise. When the merchants got back home and sold the stones, they fetched a price double that of the goods they lost.

This took place around the thirtieth year of the Qianlong reign [1765]. Gang Chaorong had met one of the merchants concerned, who recounted their adventure in great detail. These might have been mountain fauns or forest dryads: judging by their actions, at least they were not ogres. Quite possibly these wild men dated back to far antiquity: dwelling in remote mountains and deep valleys, they had never been in contact with civilization.

Figure 12. A hairy savage, as depicted in *The Classic of Mountains and Seas.*

The Headless Man
LYXL I 3

Though this tale of the headless man did not originate in Urumqi, its location is still in the wild west. According to legend, Xing Tian rebelled against the Lord of Heaven, had his head cut off, but refused to accept subjugation.

* * *

My grandfather chanced to ask me about Xing Tian brandishing shield and axe, and in reply I related his description in *The Classic of Mountains and Seas*. Grandfather said:

"Don't think that what you read in ancient books is stuff and nonsense: Xing Tian really existed. In times gone by a noble of the Kochin tribe called Daermadadu was hunting deep in the hills to the north of the Gobi desert when he came across a stag in full flight, an arrow sticking in its side. He drew his bow and killed it. He was about to retrieve its corpse when a horseman charged up. The man in the saddle was headless: his eyes were on his nipples, his mouth was in his navel. His speech came out of his navel in squawks and twitters. Though his words were unintelligible, his gestures conveyed that he had shot the stag, and he laid claim to it. The Kochin noble's escort were frightened out of their wits, but he himself had a well earned reputation for bravery, and in turn he used gestures to say that the other's arrow had not brought the stag down, and it was his own arrow that had put paid to it, so they should cut the stag up and share it equally. The headless man got his meaning, and gave an approximation of a nod. The upshot was, he departed with half the stag.

"What tribe the man belonged to, where he came from, no one knew. Judging by his aspect, he could have been none other than a descendant of Xing Tian, isn't that so? The world being so big, there is no end to its marvels. Confucian pedants are too rigid in believing only the evidence of their senses."

[...]

* * *

In his comment, Ji Xiaolan notes that the great Han historian Sima Qian expressed doubts about the existence of monsters described in such texts as *The Classic of Mountains and Seas*, but goes on to argue that Sima's scepticism was due to the texts at his disposal having been corrupted by later expansions and fanciful additions. His implication is that he agrees with his grandfather. I do not translate his comment because the annotation would be heavy, and serve no great purpose.

Figure 13. Xing Tian, as depicted in *The Classic of Mountains and Seas*.

Little People
LYXXL III 26

Horse herders deep in the mountains around Urumqi often see little people about a foot high, of both sexes, old and young. At the time of year when the red willows come into blossom, the little people break off a branch, bend it into a ring and wear it on their head; then they form ranks and kick their heels in lively dance, at the same time making a "yo-yo" sound as if singing to a set tune. Sometimes they sneak into an army encampment to steal food, and if they are caught at it they kneel down and blubber. If they are restrained, they starve themselves to death. If they are released, they do not immediately take to their heels, they just go a few steps, stop and look back. If they are then chased away with angry shouts, they once more kneel down and blubber. Not until they get far enough away from their captors to think they will not be overtaken do they take off like the wind, putting streams and mountain ridges behind them. But their dens or lairs or dwelling places have always been a mystery. These creatures are not elves, neither are they feral animals. It would seem they are akin to the *jiaoyao* pygmies mentioned in the *Book of Liezi*. Their names are not known, but because they look like children, and they are fond of headdresses of red willow, they are called "red willow kiddies".

In the course of a tour of inspection of livestock farms, assistant magistrate Qiu Tianjin obtained the body of one of these little people, had it cured and transported back to the city. Close inspection revealed that his whiskers, eyebrows and hair were exactly the same as those of normal humans. That goes to show that the *jing* homunculus mentioned in *The Classic of Mountains and Seas* really did exist. And if there are extremely small people, it necessarily follows that there are extremely big people: the Longbo country of giants described in the *Liezi* must also have truly existed.

Animals of the Wild
HXZZ II 37

There are lots of wild cattle in the Urumqi region. They are bigger than normal cattle, form herds of hundreds, and have horns as sharp as spear tips. When on the move they are led by the strong bull, with the smaller and weaker following behind. If they are attacked from the front, they break into a headlong charge which even musketry and cannon fire cannot withstand. No matter how seasoned and stalwart the soldiers are, they cannot keep ranks and contain them. On the other hand, if the herd is taken from the rear, they will never turn back on you. The biggest beast is elected as the herd's leader, like bees having their queen, and they follow his every move. It can happen that the lead bull loses his footing, and falls into a deep gully; the whole herd then throw themselves in after him, piling on top of each other and killing themselves.

There are also wild mules and horses which like the cattle form herds, though they are not so bellicose, and take flight whenever they see people. They look like familiar mules and horses, but when they are saddled and bridled, they lie prone and cannot be got to their feet. However, some have occasionally been found with saddle marks on their back and shoes on their hooves. No one really having any idea of what the explanation was, some thought they must have been mounts for immortals. It took a long time to realize they were domesticated mules and horses that had strayed into the mountains, gradually turned feral and joined a herd. The flesh of mules is firm and succulent, quite edible, but I have not come across people eating horseflesh.

There are also wild goats, to which the "Western Regions" section of the *Han History* gave the name "ibex". Their meat tastes the same as that of ordinary goats.

There are also wild boar; their ferocity comes a close second to that of wild cattle. They have extremely hard hides, proof against spears and arrows, and their teeth are keener than sharp knives— when they get a horse's leg in their jaws they can bite it off. There was an old boar in the Jimusaer Mountains that was almost as big as a bull, and no one who got near to it came away unscathed. It used to lead its herd of some hundreds out at night to devastate crops. Colonel E'erhatu once took seven hounds into the hills to hunt this boar down. They came upon it unexpectedly, and in a trice the seven hounds were lying dead. Then the boar turned its sharp tusks on the men; they only escaped with their lives by whipping up their horses and fleeing helter-skelter. I proposed erecting a wooden stockade and concealing a cannon behind it to blast the boar when it approached, but it was objected: "If the boar is not hit, it will root up the posts like rotten wood with its tusks, and then the men behind will be in peril." So I dropped that idea.

There are also wild camels with only one hump. When diced, the meat of this hump is quite delicious. No doubt that was what Du Fu was thinking of when he wrote in his "Ballad of Fine Ladies", "The purple camel's hump emerges from a green-glazed chafing dish." People nowadays say that the meat of the twin-humped camel is one of the eight top delicacies, but they have got the wrong camel.

The Mystery of the Straying Horses
GWTZ I 44

One night a livestock farm in Urumqi was hit by a violent storm, and driven by panic, dozens of horses broke out of the corral and got clean away. Seven or eight days later they turned up at Hami, the far end of the mountain range. The brands they bore proved they were definitely those from Urumqi. Now their starting point was twenty days journey from Hami, so how did they cover the distance in less than ten days? There had to be a shortcut through canyons and defiles, a path so far unknown to men. The then commanding general, Wen Fu, sent out patrols of garrison troops to explore, but they returned when their rations ran out, saying that they had found no passage at all.

Some opined: "The patrols were afraid of making a long trek, so they hung about in the nearby hills for a week or so, and only pretended they had kept going."

Another view was: "The garrison troops were afraid of the labour of cutting a road through the mountains, and also of the extra expense of moving to new outposts along the route, so they deliberately denied the existence of a passage."

A third view was: "Along the present road from Hami to Urumqi there is a string of habitations: the villages, towns, post stations and hostels are similar to those in the homeland, besides which the desert is as flat as the palm of the hand, whereas a mountain route would be hazardous, and the territory a bare wilderness. In other words, it would be a bad deal all round. That's why they did not put themselves out."

A fourth view was: "Since such a shortcut would reduce the distance by road by more than half, the quota of garrison troops, the number of horses at the posting stations, and all transportation allowances would also be cut by more than a half. That would severely damage the interests of all those in government employ, so they put a spoke in the wheel."

However that may be, it still leaves unsolved the puzzle of how the horses ended up in Hami after only seven or eight days. One explanation offered was: "Since the loss of the horses carried a heavy penalty, the people in charge of the livestock farm offered fulsome sacrifices to the god of the mountains. The god goaded the horses on to make such speed that they emerged very quickly. It is not that they found a new route." But if the god could urge them forwards to Hami, why couldn't he urge them back to Urumqi?

Part II
The Official's Milieu

10

OFFICIALDOM

It is a truism that the intellectual class in imperial China conventionally aspired to officialdom, the honourable motive being to provide a cadre for good and principled governance, the self-serving motive being to prosper through the authority officials wielded. They had a long ladder to climb, however, to gain that status. The steps on the ladder were an ascending series of examinations: the first step was the "bachelor" degree, examined twice every three years in the candidates' local prefecture; the second step of the "master's" degree was examined once every three years in the provincial capital; and the third step was the "doctoral" degree, which took place in Peking. Only a small minority of candidates passed at each stage, and the winnowing process resulted in a mere handful receiving the top degree. Nevertheless, each degree conferred some privileges and legal protections, and qualified the holder for some kind of respectable employment. Generally speaking, appointment to the post of district magistrate or its equivalent in the central government was fairly sure for the holder of the doctoral degree, still possible for the holder of a master's degree, but out of the question for those who held only the bachelor's degree, unless they received other special recognition. That leaves aside the acquiring of titles by purchase, which was allowed in order to replenish imperial coffers.

The literature of the Qing dynasty is generously populated with scholars who doggedly resat examinations well into old age, and even so talented an individual as Ji Xiaolan himself failed the doctoral examination at his first attempt. The examination mountain having been climbed, appointment did not follow immediately or automatically:

there were simply not enough jobs to go round. Hence the creation of the class of "expectant" or "intendant" officials, waiting in the capital for a vacancy to occur. They were a prey to the moneylenders on whom they relied for support in what could be a very long wait, and who, though needed, were thoroughly detested, as is evident in one of the pieces that follow.

The problem then arose of how these high interest loans were to be repaid. Nominal official salaries were derisory, a mere pittance. Supplementary salaries were more generous, but still covered only a small fraction of actual expenses, for the magistrate had to employ a personal staff out of his own pocket, provide hospitality for visiting dignitaries, give presents to superiors, and pay for a host of other things. The magistrate's real income came from "customary fees", irregular but condoned out of necessity. Simply put, they consisted of a percentage taken from practically all fees levied by his yamen on the population under his jurisdiction ("yamen" being the name given to the complex of offices and residences which were the official's headquarters). That was just the way things worked, and had to work. Hence the saying, "Three years as an upright magistrate, ten thousand taels of snow-white silver."

The abilities tested by the state examinations were knowledge of the Confucian classics and skill in literary composition. No fields of practical knowledge were included in the curriculum. Therefore a new magistrate had to engage personal aides able to handle matters of law, taxation, water conservancy, and so on, and also secretaries to draft reports, run his office, etc. These experts were often holders of the first degree who had schooled themselves in such fields. The local employees, the runners and lictors, like the magistrate himself, received a pitiful wage or no wage at all: they therefore held their hands out when their duties were to be performed. So the magistrate was formally responsible for the honest and efficient conduct of all business in his county domain, but in practice was at the mercy of his subordinates, who were given to subverting due process if there was something in it for them.

Because of the plethora of regulations, prescriptions and prohibitions governing the conduct of government business with which it was impossible to fully comply, officials at every level were vulnerable to impeachment for dereliction of duties or out-and-out corruption. If only out of self-preservation, they had to devise their own modus vivendi, a tacit compact to join together in common cause, a fact which led to another saying: "Officials always stand by each other." The following story set in ghostland illustrates the tactics of procrastination, compromise and evasion used to evade blame, and "The Four Protections" gives a glimpse of the mantras followed by higher review boards.

Mutual protection did not of course rule out jockeying for position and power within the ranks of the bureaucracy. Where promotion depended on attracting the notice and securing the patronage of ministers and ultimately of the emperor himself, there was bound to be conflict, rivalry so intense as to make individuals engineer the execution of opponents. That trend was, to be sure, inherent in the power structure of most, if not all, countries, but seems to have been most developed in the hothouse of the imperial Chinese bureaucracy.

Looking back in his old age on the faults, failings and gross injustices of the system which he knew from the inside, our author can only cling to the pious hope that wrongs will be righted in the infernal regions.

Passivity

LYXXL I 10

Zheng Suxian from North Village dreamed one night of going to the courts of the dead just as King Yama was judging the cases of souls awaiting sentence. An old woman from Zheng's neighbouring village was brought before the court. King Yama's stern visage at once relaxed. He cupped his hands in respectful salute, ordered a cup of tea for her, and commanded his assistant to arrange for her to be reborn in a good family without delay. Zheng took this assistant aside and privately asked him what merit this old peasant woman had earned. He replied:

"All through her life this old woman has never thought of

profiting herself at the expense of others. You might say the motive of self-profit is practically inescapable even in men of virtue and eminence, but profiting oneself needs must entail harming others. Thus various sleights and subterfuges come into play, and all sorts of wrongs and injustices are created. This impulse has been the root cause of names going down in infamy, of corruption spreading throughout the land. This old woman, though a simple peasant, put pontificating Confucianists to shame by being able to contain her selfish tendencies. Is it any wonder that King Yama should treat her with courtesy?"

Always quick to get the point, Zheng Suxian was unsettled on hearing these words, taking them as a caution.

Zheng went on to tell us that before the old woman was heard, a gentleman proudly wearing his robes of office took the stand. He declared that wherever his duties had taken him he accepted only a cup of water, and now faced his underworld judges with a clear conscience. King Yama mocked him, saying:

"Officials were set up to tend to the people's needs, and all of them, right down to the superintendants of posting stations and water gates, have the duty of promoting the beneficial and eliminating the harmful. If merely not taking money makes you a good official, would not placing in your front office a wooden idol which did not even crave a cup of water serve the purpose better than your good self?"

The official defended himself: "Though I cannot claim achievement, at least I have done no wrong!"

King Yama replied: "Your constant concern has been self-protection. There has been many a criminal trial you have assisted in where you have kept quiet in order to avoid suspicion: is that not betraying the people's trust? You have neglected many a task as too troublesome: is that not betraying the nation's trust? How would a review board assess your performance? No achievement is in fact a black mark!"

The official was crestfallen, his self-importance instantly punctured. King Yama softened his tone, and said with a smile: "I only take you to task for your arrogant manner. To be fair, you still rank as a good official of the third or fourth grade. In your next life you will retain some kind of office." Thereupon he ordered the man to be passed on to the underworld king in charge of rebirth.

On the basis of these two cases I deduce that the spirits can discern every dark shadow in the human heart, and no passing selfish thought, even in worthy persons, will escape reprimand. As it says in the *Book of Songs*, "The watchful spirits are ever by your side." Do not doubt it!

Rivalry
LYXXL V 15

The astrologer Yu Chuntan was phenomenally accurate in telling fortunes. When taking a boat trip in the Xiangyang-Hankou region he fell in with a cultivated gentleman. They had a lot in common, and got on very well together. In the course of their acquaintance Yu noticed to his wonderment that this gentleman neither slept nor ate, and suspected he was either an immortal or some sort of ghost. Late one night when they were alone, Yu Chuntan put that question to him. He answered:

"I am not an immortal or a ghost. In fact I am comptroller to the Star-God Wenchang, the arbiter of officials' careers. I had business in the Sacred Mountain of the south, and because I found there was affinity between us, was able to tarry a while to enjoy your company, that is all."

Yu pursued his questioning: "I prided myself on my skill at foretelling people's destinies, but I once calculated that a certain person would achieve great eminence. My prediction was not realized. Since you are in charge of the ledgers, you would know why this man's career did not prosper."

The gentleman replied: "He was indeed destined for eminence, but his career prospects suffered a discount of seven parts out of ten because of his zeal for advancement."

Yu said: "Surely zeal for advancement is the rule among officials: why does it count so heavily against him in the other world?"

"Zeal for advancement shows itself differently in two types of officials. The strong and overbearing type will make the most of his authority, and in doing so will be ruthless and inflexible. The weak and irresolute type will above all safeguard his position, and in doing so will be devious and cryptic. Now these two types will inevitably engage in factional strife to contend for honours, and in the process will shut out the nonaligned, regardless of their probity and competence, the only question being whose side they are on. No consideration is given to whether an undertaking is worthwhile or not; all that matters is one's own side coming out on the top. The malpractices that stem from zeal are too many to enumerate. So its evil is greater than common venality and harshness: let alone his rewards, even the life of the man you speak of will be shortened!"

Yu made a mental note of the gentleman's words. Two years later, the man did indeed die.

Debts

RSWW I 59

Tenth Brother Wang, a soldier who did sentry guard duty in the southwest quarter of the capital, is a former servant of my late father's. He told how in the sixth year of the Qianlong reign [1741] he was resting in the August Temple one summer night to take the cool air, when he saw two dim figures sitting on the steps. Suspecting they might be up to no good, he kept a close eye on their movements. At the time there was a religious festival put on by the Shanxi moneylenders in progress at the nearby Shaoxing Lodge, and the noise of gongs and drums filled the air. One of the men said:

"They may be making merry now, but their loansharking and

sharp practices are going to bring terrible retribution, I'm afraid."

The other man answered: "Yet some are worse than others. I have heard our judges discussing this matter. Expectant officials up from the provinces find themselves in financial straits: either they have to wait years for a posting, in which case their funds run out, or their posting is far away, in which case their travel expenses are too much for them. So like it or not, they have to raise loans. It is hard for us to imagine the stress they are under. If a moneylender exploits their exigency, puts the screws on them, leaves them no choice but to knuckle under to signing notes of promise, his villainy is on a par with barefaced robbery. In the mundane world the punishment would only be a flogging, in the nether world he would go straight to the lowest hell.

"There is another kind of debtor, of dissolute character and extravagant habits. He counts on being able to repay his debts by bleeding his subjects dry on taking up office, and on the strength of this prospect takes out loans to maintain his life of luxury. As he continues to spend money like water in spite of having mountains of debt, there comes a day when his credit runs out and his creditors come dunning at his door.

"Once his appointment has been confirmed at a palace audience, this expectant official has no chance of absconding. He can do no other than humbly submit to being meat on the chopping board for the moneylender to slice. Since he has piled up such huge debts, and his ability to repay is in doubt, from the outset he is charged high interest to balance the risk of defaulting. The moneylender has compelling reasons to act as he does, whereas the borrower's difficulty is of his own making. In the mundane world there is a clear legal code by which the moneylenders are judged in this instance, but in the spirit world they are not blamed too severely."

Listening to this conversation, Tenth Brother Wang suspected that the two men were not of human kind. After a while, the singing and music stopped and the two men got up. Instead of asking for the barrier gate to be unlocked, they walked straight through it. Shortly afterwards Wang learned from a clamour in the street that after the celebrating ended and the crowds dispersed, a man had been found to have suddenly died from heat stroke. Then Wang was sure that the men were messengers of death who had come to claim their victim.

* * *

Our author had personal reason to think ill of Shanxi moneylenders. His eldest son Ji Ruji (b. 1744) was taken to court by one in 1774 over an unpaid debt; as his father, Ji subsequently suffered demotion for not properly supervising his son's conduct.

THE FOUR PROTECTIONS
GWTZ IV 23

To clarify a legal point in what follows, if A falsely accuses B of a crime, and the trial judge decides the accusation is indeed false, A is liable to suffer the penalty appropriate to the crime he charged B with.

* * *

Mr Song Qingyuan contributed this.

Long ago when he was serving as private secretary to the statesman Wang Lansheng, a friend told him he had gone in a dream to the courts of the underworld, and seen a score of men in official regalia trooping in. The king castigated them at great length, and they all trooped out again, looking shamefaced. The friend thought he recognized a clerk of the court, though he could not remember his name. He made a tentative bow, to which the officer responded. This friend was emboldened to ask: "Who were all those people, and why did they look like that?"

The officer replied: "You too work in government service: how come you are not acquainted with any of them?"

"I have only served two terms as aide to the Superintendant of Education, I have not served in a judicial yamen."

"In that case you really wouldn't know. They are the so-called

Gentlemen of the Four Protections."

"What does that mean, 'Four Protections'?"

"There is a rule of thumb familiar to all legal aides, namely: protect the living, not the dead; protect officials, not commoners; protect the big, not the small; and protect the old, not the new. To take them in turn, the dead are already dead, beyond protection. To make the living pay with their life for a life is to add another to the roll of the dead, hence it is preferable to find mitigation to commute a death penalty. Whether or not the dead person is denied justice is not the concern.

"With regard to protecting officials, not commoners: if an appeal against a judgement is successful, the consequences for the judge who presided over the original case would be incalculable. On the other hand, if the appeal is rejected as unfounded, the punishment for the appellant would at the most be army servitude on the frontiers. Whether the original judgement was right or wrong is not the concern.

"Protecting the big, not the small, means that if a malpractice is laid at the door of a high official, the penalty paid will be the severer the higher the rank and the greater the power of the said official, besides which many others will be implicated. Whereas if the fault is ascribed to a minor official, the punishment will be lighter, in proportion to his lesser authority, besides which the matter can be tidied up more easily. Whether the minor official is really guilty of malfeasance is not the concern.

"As to protecting the old, not the new, let us say an old official leaves his post with some cases unresolved. If he is constrained to stay on, there will be doubt that he is capable of seeing them through. The new incumbent has just assumed office, and is disinclined to take on this burden of unfinished business, but if pressure is put on him, he can still manage somehow. Whether or not the new incumbent is really up to the job is not the concern.

"Now those officials all believe they act from honourable motives, and carry out the duties of elder statesmen in good faith. They do not bend the law for their own benefit, they do not have private debts or scores to pay off. But the ways of the world are in constant flux, and cannot be measured by one rule. If they hold fast to those rules, they are liable to overcompensate, see one side of the coin only. More often than not, they think to do good but in fact do harm, intend to pacify but instead sow discord. Those summoned today were indeed responsible for causing grief and woe."

"And what were their deserts?"

"As you sow, so shall you reap. The harm you do in one lifetime follows you inescapably into the next: your nemesis will catch up with you. In a future life they will themselves come up before Gentlemen of the Four Protections, and be assigned to the 'Four Non-Protections' category, that is all."

Without warning their conversation was broken off, and Song Qingyuan's friend woke up. He could not understand why he had had this dream, unless the gods might have imparted it to him so that he could sound a warning to the world.

Much of a Muchness in the Spirit World
LYXL VI 15

Liang Huotang contributed this.

A gentleman's wife died while they were travelling in the east of Guangdong province, and he lodged her coffin in a temple in the hills. He dreamed of his wife saying:

"There is a demon at large in this temple that the guardian god cannot control. The demon has power over the occupants of all the coffins placed in the monks' cells: he enslaves all the males and violates all the females. You should register a complaint with the spiritual powers that be."

When the man woke up he remembered the dream in every particular. He lighted joss sticks and addressed the spirit of his deceased wife thus:

"I ask myself if this dream was brought on by the troubled sleep of springtime, or created by my thoughts dwelling on you—

or was it rather your genuine appeal from the other side? I could be sure that it truly came from your waking soul if the dream were repeated on three successive nights."

Indeed the same dream came to him on the next two nights. Consequently he drew up a bill of complaint which he placed on the altar of the city tutelary god. For several days nothing happened; then his wife appeared in a dream again, saying:

"If your complaint is upheld, the guardian god will be judged remiss in not investigating and reporting the transgression, and the hill god and earth god remiss in not restraining the demon. According to infernal law they will have to be demoted. Hence the city god is in a dilemma, and is procrastinating. I suggest you draw up another writ, and threaten you will go to the Dragon and Tiger Mountain in Jiangxi to present it to the Taoist Grand Luminary of the True Way. The city god will have to take action then."

He did as she said, and duly served his writ.

Some days later his wife came to him again. This time she said:

"The city god summoned me yesterday and lectured me as follows: 'This demon was already installed in the cell where your coffin was deposited, so you trespassed against him, not the other way round. With male and female sharing a room, and his attendants coming and going all the time, inevitably there will be a certain potential for indecent behaviour. All the same, you have some grounds for complaint. I have had his attendants soundly beaten today, which should suffice to appease you. Why do you have to insist you have been ravished, sullying your good name into the bargain? It is always best when problems arise to make them disappear, and reduce big issues to small issues. Hurry up and tell your husband to move your coffin, so this business can be wrapped up.' Thinking things over, I have to admit that it would be advisable to let things lie. There's no need to take on the higher powers: that could well prove our own undoing. Best to do as he said and move my coffin as soon as you can."

Her husband said, "Given that the city god is unwilling to rule on this matter, what good would it have done to appeal to the Grand Luminary to intervene on our behalf?"

"Though the Grand Luminary has no jurisdiction over the underworld, if he receives a complaint he has the right to submit a memorial directly to the Supreme God, which none of the lesser gods and spirits can block or sidetrack. Understandably, the city god is afraid of unforeseeable consequences, so he has resorted to shifts and compromises that will allow both parties to back off and let the matter drop."

With that his wife made solemn farewell. Her husband moved her coffin elsewhere, and his dreams ceased.

This female ghost had no concerns beyond saving her situation, which was sensible enough for her. But the city god is a governing deity; his conduct of affairs within his jurisdiction might be clever, but is it not still unjust? Besides, if you let criminality go unpunished, one day you will have a case of scandalous proportions on your hands. So is not even his so-called cleverness half seeing and half blind?

11

LEGAL DILEMMAS AND DISPUTES

A magistrate was solely responsible for the administration and execution of justice within his jurisdiction. He was judge, public prosecutor, chief constable and coroner, all rolled up in one. In that sense he was an autocrat, but his conduct was bound by multifarious rules and regulations, and except for minor civil cases, all his decisions had to be reviewed first by his immediate superior, the prefect, and then by stages right up to the Board of Punishments in the capital. For major crimes like homicide and robbery, the magistrate had to submit his rulings within certain time limits: the first deadline was six months, the second was one year, and so on, each failure to meet the given deadline incurring a more severe penalty. Rapid conclusion of cases, on the other hand, earned a merit point for him. Anxiety over investigations that led to no prompt conviction was the necessary consequence.

Since the magistrate had many other duties to attend to apart from the judicial one (his popular title was "father-and-mother official"), he normally did not have the time to study all the reports and depositions pertaining to a case, so was dependent on summaries prepared by his private legal secretary; in any case, he himself would have had no training in the law, a highly complex subject. The persons found guilty had to sign a confession of their crime. Those who refused were quite legally subjected to torture by flogging, the application of presses to their joints, kneeling on chains, and the like, until they complied.

One task the magistrate was obliged to perform in person was to hold an inquest at the site of a violent death. The magistrate was inclined to remain in his tent, far from the grisly corpse, and let the medical examiner get on with determining the cause of death. The latter was a lowly employee, very poorly paid, and consequently vulnerable to being bribed. Perhaps that is why very incompetent murderers thought they had a good chance of getting away with their crime.

The novel of detection became a popular genre in the Qing dynasty. It is a common feature of these novels that when the magistrate is at his wits' end he is given a clue in a dream or augury, but only enigmatically: he has to work out who it points to. In a case related below he signally fails to do so. Furthermore, for the magistrate to sit in his yamen was not exciting material for the novelist; being the hero of the piece, he has to venture abroad incognito to get the "lowdown", an expression particularly apt in this context. In the fiction, his forays are invariably productive; in the parallel story told below, the whole district knows who and where he is, so the exercise is pointless.

One trick in the judge's book was the blood test, which is at the centre of one of Ji Xiaolan's entries. We learn from him its use went back two thousand years; perhaps the best known previous reference to it was in the work of the poet Yuan Haowen (1190–1257), where it was employed to test the consanguinity not of father and son but of cow and calf, again successfully. If research into this test of agglutination had continued, the Chinese would have been out and away the first to discover blood groups, but it seems the inventiveness went into methods of falsifying the results.

Civil cases could be dealt with summarily. Primed by his secretary's briefing, or for other considerations, the magistrate might abandon the role of impartial judge for that of prosecutor, as is caricatured below in the dispute set in ghostland over land rights. Besides entertaining us with such stories, however, Ji also invites us to consider juridical conundrums and dilemmas that conscientious magistrates were faced with. They would, it seems, have been of a mind to agree with Portia that "the quality of mercy is not strained."

An Old Monk Discusses Incognito Investigations

HXZZ IV 17

Ming Shuzhai proved a dutiful official when serving as magistrate in my home county of Xian. In the course of his assignment to the Taiping prefecture in Anhui province he was confronted with a difficult court case; he set out for the locale to investigate in person, dressed in plain clothes. On his way he stopped for a rest at a small Buddhist monastery. When the aged abbot there saw Ming Shuzhai, he brought his palms together in a formal salute, and called out for his disciple to prepare tea. The disciple responded from within: "The prefect is expected any time now. You can show your visitor to another room for the time being."

The abbot replied: "The prefect has already arrived—hurry up with the tea!"

Ming was taken aback. "How did you know who I was?" he asked.

"Your honour is head of the whole district. Every step you take is known throughout your domain. I am hardly the only one to know you!"

Ming persisted: "How did you recognize me?"

"Your honour cannot know everyone in your district, but who in your district does not know you?"

"Do you know what business I am on now?"

"There is a court case in progress, and the opposing parties have dispatched their minions to stake out the roads leading here. They have just pretended not to recognize you, that's all."

Ming was disconcerted. After a pause to recover himself, he asked: "Then why did you yourself not join in the pretence?"

The abbot prostrated himself, saying: "I confess I took an unpardonable liberty, your honour. I wanted to provoke exactly that question from you. You have proved yourself a model administrator; you lack universal approval in only one respect, namely your liking for incognito investigations. It is not only the criminal masterminds who spin their webs of deceit in anticipation of your arrival, even the country bumpkins form their alliances, have their favours to repay, their scores to settle. If you question someone of A's faction, they will tell you A is straight and B is crooked; if you question someone of B's faction they will tell you B is straight and A is crooked. If you ask an enemy of one of the litigants, he is sure to say that litigant is in the wrong; if you ask someone who owes a litigant a favour, he will surely say that litigant is in the right.

"Women and children, if you turn to them, are not reliable witnesses; frail and feeble old folk get their words all muddled. How can their testimony deliver a sound verdict? And if that is already your own situation, can you expect better success by deputing others to act as your eyes and ears?

"Actually, it is not only in court cases that on-the-spot investigations do more harm than good, the same holds where the material interests of country people are concerned. I am thinking particularly of dams and irrigation channels. The peasants all have an eye to the main chance: if the river flow is benign they dam the water to irrigate their own fields; if the river threatens to flood they channel it through neighbouring farmland. That way they think they will always come out on top. Who among them is prepared to think big about the lie of the land and come up with ideas for permanently taming the river's flow?

"I am an old monk. I have put the world behind me, and shouldn't meddle in the affairs of men, much less in the business of officialdom. But Buddhism is compassionate, it teaches us to give up our lives to succour the many in need. If it is of benefit to others, I am bound to speak out, though it be on pain of death. I humbly submit myself to your honour's wise judgement."

The prefect pondered deeply on his words, and in the end broke off his investigation to return to his headquarters. The next day he sent a runner to the monastery with a gift of money and rice. The runner reported when he came back: "After your honour left the abbot told his followers: 'I have taken a load off my mind,' and he peacefully gave up his soul."

It was Yang Wenchang who passed this story on to us. My late father commented: "In all legal proceedings, the truth will emerge if the facts are examined without prejudice: it is wrong to place your trust in others, or in yourself. The problem with others was stated correctly by the priest; as for the problem of trusting yourself, there is much more to be explained. If only another priest would come along to likewise enlighten us!"

A Boundary Dispute
GWTZ IV 27

Zeng Yinghua contributed this.

A group of candidates was journeying together to the provincial capital to take the triennial examination. It was the dog days of summer, so they travelled by night. On their way they rested on the steps of a ruined temple; some slept, some stayed awake. When one of them heard voices coming from behind the temple, he thought it might just be farmers watching over their melons or dates, but then again it might be robbers. He held his breath and strained his ears. One of the voices said:

"What can I do for you, sir?"

"Just now," the reply came, "I am in a boundary dispute with my neighbouring grave owner, and we've taken it to our local tutelary god. You served in a yamen as legal aide for years on end, so perhaps you could advise me on my chances of winning the dispute."

The first person laughed and said, "You really are an innocent abroad! How could there be any predictability over winners and losers? Let me give some examples of how cases like yours might go. To tip the odds in favour of the respondent over the plaintiff, the plaintiff is rebuked: 'You brought a plaint and he did not, which shows you are taking the offensive to encroach on his territory!' To tip the odds the other way, the respondent is accused, 'He brought a plaint while you did not, which shows you had first encroached on him, and you knew you were in the wrong.'

"To favour the party who arrived later in the cemetery, the party who arrived first is accused: 'You took advantage of his later arrival to move in on his plot.' To favour the first arrival, the later arrival is accused: 'The plots had long been marked out; you came in to overturn the established order, which shows you are just a troublemaker.'

"To favour the wealthier party, the poorer party is accused: 'You are an unscrupulous pauper, you hope he will buy you off to avoid going to law.' To favour the poorer party the wealthier is accused: 'You belong to the heartless rich, your acquisitiveness is insatiable. You expect to use your wealth and power to do down the deprived and friendless.'

"To favour the strong party, the weak party is accused: 'It is human nature to sympathize with the weak against the strong. By playing the injured party you hope to create a public outcry.' To favour the weak party, the strong party is accused: 'It is always the strong who bully the weak, never the contrary. Unless he had genuine grievance, your opponent would not risk your retaliation.'

"To let both parties win: 'Neither of you has land deeds or witnesses. If this wrangling is allowed to go on, when will it end? The deadlock can be broken by dividing the land equally: case resolved.'

"To make both parties lose: 'Human beings have their field boundaries, but can ghosts have their domains? All space apart from that taken up by your coffins is owned by humans, not by your kind. Let the plot lie fallow.'

"Given all these ways one might win or lose, how can there be a general rule?"

The second speaker said: "So how should I proceed with this case?"

The first speaker replied: "Of the ten versions I have given, all can be supported by pleading, and equally all can be rebutted by pleading; the arguments can go back and forth till kingdom come. We have no means of knowing how the tutelary god will decide. As for the underlings in the court of the dead, the longer the case goes on, the richer their pickings from both parties."

Silence ensued at the end of this conversation. The speaker did indeed show he was well versed in the workings of the yamen.

Whose Ancestors?
GWTZ III 31

Some affairs are so intricate that even the legendary judge Gaotao would be unable to sort them out. A student of mine named Zhe Yulan is an able administrator. When he was magistrate of Anding county in Gansu province, two families were in dispute over a hillside burial ground. Their litigation had been going on for forty or fifty years, and had spanned two generations. The plot in question was less than one third of an acre in area; it contained two graves which each family claimed to be those of their ancestors.

When the court asked for witness statements from neighbours, it was told that the plot was so deep in the hills that you had to take provisions with you to make the trek there, and no one lived for miles around. Asked for land deeds, the answer was that those had been lost in the ravages of warfare during the Ming dynasty. Both parties could produce receipts for land taxes. Their depositions stated: "Though the plot is assessed for land-and-labour tax, there is no possibility of cultivating it, and it yields not an ounce of profit. The only reason for this endless lawsuit is that we are unwilling to see our ancestral graves being taken over by others." They also insisted, "If the remains of our ancestors were not truly buried there, who would be willing to engage in decades of litigation?"

In answer to the suspicion that they coveted an auspicious geomantic position, they both replied: "In Shaanxi and Gansu we have never bothered about such a thing as feng shui. Neither party suspects the other has that in mind. Furthermore, this plot has rocks on every side, there is no room to bury another coffin there. And if the winner of this case wants to dig up the old graves to make room for new ones, that would give a handle to the loser, for who would dare to do that if the graves were genuinely those of their own ancestors?"

There was no way the court could make them budge from their entrenched position, neither was there justification for dividing the plot equally, nor yet for the government to take the land into its possession. Thus the case could not be resolved. It looked like they would get into a fight at every time of sacrifice, and after the fight apply to the court again for damages. The court would have to judge each affray simply in terms of an affray, and not enquire into its cause.

Subsequently Cai Xizhai took over as Governor of Gansu province. He advised: "This is a dispute over worship, not land ownership. They should be brought to see reason by force of argument. It should be put to them: Since you believe these are your ancestors' graves, you should be free to sacrifice over them. As to those who offer rival sacrifice, given that they are willing to regard your ancestors as their own, and the ancestors in question suffer no privation thereby, nor do you, it would surely be a fine thing to let the ancestors enjoy the offerings. Why reject it?"

This expedient was proposed for lack of alternative. So far I do not know if the proposal has been followed.

Some Tricky Cases to Consider
RSWW I 21

Liu Qixin, a minor functionary in my home prefecture of Hejian, had a rudimentary education. One day he asked someone: "What kind of creatures are owlets and tiger cats?" The answer came back: "The owlet eats its mother, the tiger cat eats its father: they stand for unfiliality." Liu Qixin clapped his hands in pleasure, saying:

"That explains it! I went down with a fever, and in my delirious state my soul took itself off to the courts of the dead, where I saw two judges sitting on the bench. A clerk of the court, documents in hand, asked for their guidance: 'In such-and-such a place a fox has been bitten to death by his grandson. Animals being without self-knowledge, it is hard to condemn them according to human principles. We are of a mind to apply the penalty for the simple physical crime, and not class it as the turpitude of unfiliality.'

"The judge on the left said: 'The fox differs from the generality of animals. Those foxes who have primed themselves to take on human form should be judged by the laws of humanity, while those who have not so primed themselves should be judged according to the laws of the animal kingdom.'

"The judge on the right said: 'I beg to differ. In other matters birds and beasts are distinct from humans, but family bonds are heaven endowed, and in that regard the same principle applies as with humans. The kings of antiquity executed the owlet and the tiger cat; they did not pardon them because they were animals. So this fox should be consigned to hell, his offence still being classed as unfiliality.'

"The judge on the left nodded: 'Your lordship is correct.'

"The clerk then withdrew with his dossier. On his way out he gave me a cuff for being where I shouldn't be, and the shock of it woke me up. I made a note of every word uttered, only I didn't understand the reference to owlets and tiger cats. I guessed they must be unfilial birds and beasts, now it turns out I was right!"

This case was a novel one, so they had to scratch their heads over it even in the courts of the dead. It reminds us that judicial cases are infinitely variable, and it is impossible to hold to one rule for all. I shall give some examples from my own experience of cases that challenge conventional guidelines.

A man travelled to distant parts, where he was falsely reported to have died. His parents sold his wife to another man to serve as his concubine. The husband returned, but could not appeal over the head of his parents for his wife to be restored. So he lay in wait outside the home of the new husband for an opportunity to see the woman alone, and contrived to elope with her. A year later the couple were tracked down and arrested. Now to disallow the charge of adultery would have been to ignore the fact that the woman had remarried; to allow the charge of adultery would have been to ignore the fact that the man was her original husband. There was no precedent for the judge to follow.

To give another example. There is a special class of robbers called "booty robbers". They do not commit the actual thefts, they rob the robbers. That is to say, they raid the thieves' den when it is unguarded, or waylay the thieves and seize their booty. On one occasion, both lots of robbers were arrested while they were caught up in a brawl, and brought before the magistrate. Now, if they were not to be judged as robbers, the fact remained that they were in forcible possession of goods; if they were to be judged as robbers, what they were taking was booty others had stolen. Again there was no legal precedent.

A third example. A woman became pregnant as a result of an adulterous affair. After finding her guilty of adultery, the judge ruled that according to law the child should be given to the woman's paramour to bring up. When the child was born, the husband killed it out of rancour. The paramour charged the husband with the premeditated murder of his son. Though there was statute to refer to, still in the end one feels that the charge the paramour brought was right in principle but lacking in understanding, while the action of the husband was understandable but wrong in principle. There was no way to strike a fair balance.

I wonder how the judges in the courts of the dead would have resolved these issues?

A Judge's Lot Is Not a Happy One
RSWW IV 41

Cases that are incapable of being determined at law are not necessarily beyond rhyme or reason, and the more they engage our sympathies, the harder it is to reach a just verdict. My student Wu Guanxian was Magistrate of Anding county in Gansu when I was recalled from service with the army in the Western Regions, and I stayed overnight in his yamen. He told me this story.

A boy and a girl, both about sixteen years old, stopped his carriage to plead for justice. The boy said: "This is my child bride. After our parents died she wants to reject me and marry another." The girl said: "I am actually his sister. Now our parents are dead he wants to make me his wife."

They could both remember their name, but they had no memory of where they originated because their parents had been itinerant beggars, moving on every day from place to place. Wu Guanxian then questioned a beggar who was with them. He said: "They had been here only a few days when their parents died, and I don't know their history. I have just heard them call each other brother and sister." But that gave no clue, for in humble families a child bride usually addressed her future husband as "brother", and vice-versa.

An experienced officer on the magistrate's staff offered his opinion:

"This business is like chasing shadows. There can be no firm evidence, neither can the truth be extracted under duress. Whether the decision is for or against marriage, it could equally be mistaken. But to judge in error that they be separated would only be to wrongly break a marriage bond; to judge in error that they be united would be to wrongly condone incest: the fault would be greater. You should not hesitate to rule in favour of separation."

The magistrate brooded and pondered, but could not think of a better way, so eventually followed his subordinate's advice.

This reminded me of something that happened while my late father was serving in the Board of Punishments. When Hai Baofang, Director of Imperial Textiles, had his property confiscated, three soldiers were detailed to guard his mansion, the premises comprising some hundreds of rooms. One wintry night, the three of them locked the outer gate and took refuge from the cold in a bedroom deep in the recesses of the mansion. They lit a lamp and started drinking together. When they were all thoroughly soused, one accidentally knocked over the lamp; in the darkness they bumped into each other, and fell to brawling. The free-for-all went on till midnight, when they collapsed from exhaustion. Come the dawn, one of them was found to be dead. Of the two others, one was called Dai Fu, the other went by a number, Seventy Five. They were also badly hurt, but had luckily survived. On interrogation they both said that since their fight had ended in a death, they would have no complaint if they had to pay with their life.

As to what happened in the dark that night, when they felt someone grappling with them, they grappled back; when they felt somebody hit them, they hit back. They could not tell who was attacking them, or whom they were attacking. As to which blows were heaviest, and by whom they were delivered, not only could the two survivors not tell, even if the dead man had been brought back to life and asked those questions, for sure he could not have told either.

Because there was no need for two lives to pay for one, there would have been no objection if the responsible official had picked one name out of a hat. If the guilt absolutely had to be pinned on one of them, even if the instruments of torture were applied without mercy, all you would have got would be worthless confessions. So in the end the official's hands were tied. The impasse lasted over a month, until Dai Fu happened to die from his injuries, and that opportunity was taken to wrap the case up.

My late father Yao An commented: "In theory this case could have been settled by identifying the instigator of the fighting, but it is clear from the testimonies that the instigator could not be determined. To ascribe guilt on the basis of confession under torture would have been worse than choosing one at random. I have since gone over and over the case in my mind, but still haven't thought of a way of handling it. Let it be said, the job of judge is not an easy one!"

Blood
HXZZ I 12

My great-nephew Ji Shusen contributed this.

A Shanxi merchant entrusted care of the family property to his younger brother when he went to trade in distant parts. On his long travels he took a wife and had a son. A decade or so later this wife took sick and died, whereupon the merchant went back home with his son. The younger brother feared the older brother would reclaim the family property for himself and his descendants, so he alleged that the son was adopted, and being of different family stock was ineligible to inherit. Not being able to resolve this tangled dispute, they took the matter to court.

The magistrate had a one-track mind. Instead of checking out the truthfulness of the merchant's statement, he resorted to the ancient practice of testing a drop of blood from two persons: if the drops merged together, it proved consanguinity. Fortunately the drops did merge together, so the magistrate ordered the younger brother flogged and driven from the court.

This younger brother flatly rejected the validity of the blood test. He had a son himself, and he experimented with mixing a drop of the son's blood with his own: as he had hoped, the drops did not merge together. So he appealed to a higher court, claiming the magistrate's verdict was unsound. His fellow townspeople took unkindly to his unconscionable avarice, and they jointly testified:

"His wife had an affair with so-and-so, and the son is not his son, so of course their blood did not merge together."

His neighbours were confident of their facts, and had evidence to back them up. Finally the accusation of adultery was borne out. The wife's lover was also summoned: he hung his head and confessed. The younger brother wanted to sink into the ground from shame; he went as far as divorcing his wife and disowning his son, then he slunk away himself. Ironically the whole of the family property then came into the elder brother's hands, to general approbation.

We can see from the case of Chen Ye as chronicled in the *Biographies of Good Men of the Runan District* that the "drop of blood" test dates back to the Han dynasty. However, I have heard old hands say: "It is in general true that blood from those of the same kin will merge together. However, if in winter the receptacle is put out in the ice and snow to make it extremely cold, or in summer brushed with brine and vinegar to give the vessel an acid, salty tang, then the blood dripped into it will solidify on contact, and though the drops may come from close family they will not merge together. Therefore the blood test cannot altogether be relied on to deliver a sound verdict."

Nevertheless, if the magistrate had not conducted the blood test, the brother of the merchant would not have appealed, and if he had not appealed, his wife's bearing a bastard child would not have been exposed. Perhaps there was some unseen hand behind that, and the magistrate could be pardoned for taking old recipes on faith.

Success
LYXXL IV 9

In the sixth month of the tenth year of the Yongzheng reign [1732] there was a big storm, and a villager living to the west of the Xian county town was struck by lightning and killed. The local magistrate, named Ming Sheng, went to do an on-site inspection, and ordered the body to be properly encoffined. Two weeks later he unexpectedly had a man arrested, and questioned him as follows:

"What did you buy gunpowder for?"

"To shoot birds."

"One day's shoot with a fowling piece would require anything up from a quarter ounce to a maximum of one ounce of gunpowder. What was the idea of buying as much as twenty or thirty pounds?"

"To stock up for many days' use."

"You bought the gunpowder less than a month ago. You would have used no more than two pounds by now. Where do you store the remainder?"

The man had no answer to that. Ming Sheng questioned him under duress, and as expected he confessed to committing murder because of having an adulterous affair with the victim's wife. They were both sentenced to death.

Ming Sheng was asked how he knew this man was at the bottom of it. He replied:

"You cannot fake the effect of a thunderbolt with less than thirty pounds of gunpowder. Sulphur has to be mixed with the charcoal powder to produce an explosion. It is now high summer, not the New Year when fire crackers are let off, so very few people presently buy sulphur. I sent an undercover agent to the market place to find out who was buying sulphur in large quantities, and the answer came back that it was such-and-such an artisan. Then I had the artisan covertly questioned as to whom he in turn sold his gunpowder, and the finger pointed to this man. That is how he was identified."

He was then asked how he knew that the thunderbolt was faked. He answered:

"When someone is struck by lightning, it comes down from above, and does not split the ground open. Lightning may sometimes bring down a house, but it still strikes from above. In this case the thatched roof and rafters were sent flying up in the air, and the top of the bed platform was also blown off. Thus it was clear that the explosion came from below. For another thing, the village is only a couple of miles from the county town, so the storm conditions were the same there as they were here. Though the storm came fast and furious that night, the lightning was playing in the cloud layer, it did not strike the earth. That convinced me. At the time the victim's wife had gone on a visit to her own parents' home, so I could not take her in for questioning. Therefore I had to apprehend the man first and leave examining the wife till later."

This magistrate can be said to have shown exemplary discernment.

* * *

This event took place when our author was eight years old, and was written about fifty-seven years later: much time had elapsed for reconstruction, both in the way the story had been passed on locally and for the purpose of literary presentation. In the latter respect, the inclusion of directly quoted speech (obviously no longer knowable) need not worry us, because it was ingrained in Chinese historical narrative convention, right from the earliest days. What does worry us is the story itself. It seems remarkable that the perpetrator could have prepared and planted his explosive charge to coincide with a thunderstorm, which could hardly have been so predictable. It also seems very strange, given that this was an agricultural community where everybody would have known what happened when lightning struck, that the perpetrator thought the difference between the effects of lightning and explosives would not be noticed. He might have thought the yamen runners could be persuaded to turn a blind eye: as we so often see, that would not have been an unreasonable presumption. Not so foreseeable was the close inspection of the site by a magistrate who had some practical knowledge. Perhaps it was that which ensured this story would become celebrated.

That a wife might be complicit in the murder of her husband is not thought worth remarking on here (supposing that her absence from home was planned). There were seven counts on which a husband might divorce a wife, but practically none on which a wife could divorce a husband. In extreme circumstances a woman might well have thought of murder.

Failure
LYXXL IV 8

My distant uncle Canchen contributed this.

    A certain magistrate had before him a case of homicide that he could not solve. He procrastinated for days and days, finally resorting to going to the tutelary god's temple to pray for a revelation in a dream. In his dream the god led out a ghost with a big-bellied pot on its head; from the pot sprouted a clump of splendidly green bamboos. On awaking, the magistrate found in the documents pertaining to the case someone called Zhu. Because his name shared the same sound as the word for bamboo, he decided this man must be the man meant, but exhaustive interrogation led nowhere. The magistrate went through the papers again, and found there was a man whose personal name was Jie, which among other things could mean "joint"; he thought to himself, bamboos have joints so that must be the man! He too was exhaustively interrogated, but again with no result. Thus the two men had a narrow escape from death. Deciding nothing further could be gained from this method, the magistrate reported the case as intractable, and proposed that a fresh manhunt for the murderer be made. Still no culprit was brought to book.

Such difficult cases must be approached with an open mind, the evidence sifted and witnesses examined methodically; in that way the truth might emerge. At best the claim to have obtained a revelation through prayer to gods can be used to overawe simpletons and hoodwink them into telling the unvarnished truth. To use pure guesswork based on the figment of a dream to reach a verdict invariably leads to miscarriage of justice. Ancient accounts of cases being solved by recourse to dreams have, I think, been dressed up in the telling.

12

YAMEN STAFF

The government of imperial China was exclusively operated by a centralized bureaucracy, organized as a pyramid, with each level reporting to the one above, and consuming untold reams of paper in the process: each document was drafted, corrected and approved before multiple copies were made, requiring the employment of scores of copyists in a busy county yamen. Only the most trivial business escaped scrutiny by higher authorities.

The magistrate was barred from serving in his native province. When appointed to what could be a very distant post, he took his private secretaries or aides with him to supervise key aspects of his administration, as we have seen. These right-hand men generally enjoyed a reputation for loyalty and honesty, as well as acumen, but a bad egg among them was privy to information that could be used to hold his employer to ransom.

All the routine work had, of course, to be done by local employees, and there were a great many operations to perform: taxing and policing as well as all the local government business that has to be done everywhere. One factor that gave the local staff a lot of latitude was the language gap: the incoming magistrate and his private secretaries would rarely properly understand the local dialect. Furthermore, the magistrate served only a short term, no more than five years as a rule, which meant the familiarization process had to begin anew with each fresh incumbent.

Local staff divided between minor functionaries who might be grouped together under the title of "clerks", and the menial orders, commonly called "runners", who acted as policemen, jailers, doormen, bearers, and so on. Since the orderly conduct of government was done through the transmission of documents, and it was the clerks who prepared, dispatched and received the documents, they had ample opportunity to falsify and conceal. The clerks ran the six departments of government, those of personnel, revenue, rites, military affairs, justice and public works. Oddly enough, they were paid no salaries, which saved the imperial treasury a lot of silver, but made them depend entirely on "customary fees", that is to say, charges for every service performed: even conducting an inquest was included. In practice, a clerk's pickings could be so rewarding that his successor had to pay for taking over the job.

Runners did receive a wage, but the wage was so low that they in turn relied on "squeeze". Policemen were in the best position to exercise squeeze, given their power to detain in very unwholesome jails. One device of theirs, relevant to a following story, was to get an arrested thief to implicate blameless others in the crime, so as to enlarge the pool of clients to squeeze. Though in this case the thief takes the initiative out of spite, the runner concerned would have been equally content.

COUNTRY WOMEN OUTWIT THE LAW OFFICER
GWTZ IV 9

Wang Meishu contributed this.

In Jiaohe county, mid-Hebei province, a simple soul of a villager was wrongfully implicated in a capital crime by a thief. Being unable to prove his innocence, he offered a bribe to a local government law officer. The officer learned that the reason for the villager being framed was that the thief had made sexual advances to the villager's wife and had been beaten up for it, so the officer deduced that this wife must be very attractive. He declined the money, instead hinting broadly to the intermediary: "This matter has to be conducted secretly. His wife will have to visit me on the quiet, so that I can explain my plan to her in person."

The meaning behind the officer's words was clear. The intermediary reported back to the gaoled villager who, unmanned by his fear of death, had his wife's mother called to the gaol, and privately told her how things stood; the mother told her daughter; the daughter indignantly refused to listen.

Some days later, there was a knock at the officer's door in the dead of night. He opened it to see a beggar woman, dressed in ragged clothes and with a kerchief tied over her head. She pushed her way in, ignoring the officer's question, and divested herself of kerchief and outer garment as she walked, to reveal a glamorous woman dressed to kill. The officer asked in surprise where she had come from. The woman's cheeks turned red; she bowed her head and made no reply. She only drew a slip of paper from her sleeve. The officer raised his lantern and read: "A certain person's wife", nothing more. Overjoyed, he led her into the bedroom, where he made a point of having her declare her purpose in coming. Covering the tears in her eyes with her sleeve, the woman said:

"If I hadn't understood your message, would I have come at night? The fact that I am here answers your question. I only beg you not to go back on your word."

The officer volubly vowed to keep his promise, and she yielded to his embrace.

After keeping the woman hidden away for some days, the officer was totally bewitched by her, and was almost driven out of his mind by fear of losing her favour. She then took temporary leave of him, telling him on parting that back home in her village she would surely suffer continual slights and insults, and would not be able to put up with it for very long. If he rented some rooms for her in town, near to his house, then she could enjoy his protection, and be safe from humiliation from hooligans, besides being able to come and go freely. That prospect pleased the officer excessively, and he used every trick in the book to prove the villager's innocence. After the villager was acquitted and released from gaol, however, his manner was cold when he ran across the officer; the latter put that down to embarrassment on account of his debauching his wife.

Some time later the officer's business took him to the couple's village, and he went to their house, but they refused to answer the door to him. He felt extremely bitter at being thrown over. A court case then came up, whereby a man was charged with employing a prostitute to lure people into gambling games. The prostitute was sentenced to being returned under escort to her place of origin. The officer recognized this prostitute as the villager's wife; he went over and spoke to her. The woman explained that because her husband had kept her mewed up, she had had to let the officer down, but she still missed him terribly. By good fortune they had now met again, and in memory of the blissful time they had enjoyed together she implored him to find a way to get her off corporal punishment and deportation. The officer fell under her spell again. He attested to the magistrate:

"The prostitute gave her mother's native place as her own: actually she is the wife of a villager in this county. The responsibility of the husband for her conduct should be looked into."

His plan was to persuade the magistrate to have the woman put up for auction, at which point he would buy her himself. Runners were then sent to bring the villager to court. He arrived accompanied by his wife, only this was another woman altogether. His fellow villagers all confirmed when questioned that this was no deception. The law officer could not explain why he had pointed the finger at the villager. He could only offer the excuse that it was word that he had picked up. When asked from whom, he could not name anybody.

The prostitute was then summoned. She explained that it had all started with the officer plotting to enjoy the villager's wife. The wife was put in a quandary: if she complied she would lose her honour; if she did not comply her husband would lose his life. So when this new prostitute turned up, the wife gave her all her jewellery to make the assignation in her stead. That was how she had become so intimate with the officer. Now when she was about to be flogged for her involvement in the gambling case, they ran into each other again. She had continued to pretend to be the villager's wife in the hope of getting out of the flogging. She had not foreseen that the officer would cook up a little scheme of his own, which in fact brought about both of them being exposed.

The magistrate then re-examined the crime the villager had originally been tried for, and found that he had indeed been falsely implicated. As for his later assenting to his wife's sacrifice of her chastity, it was taken into account that his life was on the line, and the ensuing subterfuge was of his wife's devising, so all further charges were dropped. The officer, for his part, was severely punished.

The most cunning rogues and worst malefactors in society are found among local government officers, yet this one was hoodwinked by a common village woman, toyed with like a baby. Now ignorant people are normally at the mercy of intelligent people, yet according to the principle that excessive confidence will turn against itself, it often happens that what the intelligent do not contemplate is that someone cleverer than them will suddenly come forth and worst them. Nature does not allow that traffic should be in just one direction. If the intelligent class comes out tops at every turn, then only the intelligent will survive and the ignorant will die out. How could that be?

A Snake in the Grass
RSWW I 61

The true identity of personal aides to district officials is hard to be sure of. They disguise their origins in order to escape being traced and apprehended should their peculations be exposed one day. My late father came across an aide in the employ of Mr Shi Changchen, an examiner of his; this aide called himself Zhu Wen, and said he was from Shandong province. Later on he saw the same man in the service of the magistrate of Gaochun county in Jiangsu province, Mr Liang Runtang; this time he went under the name of Li Ding, and was supposed to come from

Henan province. Liang relied heavily on this man. Liang was then due to be transferred to another post, and on the eve of his departure, this Li Ding went down with a mysterious illness. So Liang temporarily entrusted Li Ding to my father's care, on the understanding that Li would rejoin him when he recovered. That never happened, for starting from his toes, Li's flesh festered, the contagion spreading upwards inch by inch; when it reached his chest, his pleural membranes ruptured, and he died.

After Li Ding's death, his personal effects were examined, and a notebook filled with tiny characters was found. Li served seventeen officials in all, and for each one he noted the business they had conducted behind closed doors, scrupulously recording the time and place, who abetted, who observed, together with details of letters exchanged and files for cases tried: nothing was left out. A colleague who knew the inside story stated:

"This fellow had a number of officials under his thumb. His wife had been a maid owned by one of them; he took her off with him when he did a flit, impudently leaving a farewell note on the table. The official concerned did not dare to go after them. That this man should have fallen foul of a disease shows there is justice in heaven!"

The venerable Huo Yishu commented:

"Their ilk attach themselves to people in authority with the intention of exploiting weaknesses. To engage them is like keeping a hawk, and it would be fatuous to expect hawks to feed on birdseed. The key is to keep them on a short tether. If because of their sharpness you trust them to be your eyes and ears, you will inevitably find the tables turned on you, and place yourself at their mercy. I personally think the blame lies with the seventeen officials who employed this man, rather than with the man himself."

My father's view was:

"I don't think this talk gets to the heart of the matter. Supposing these seventeen officials did nothing that had to be hidden from view, this man would have prepared paper and ink in vain, for he would have had nothing to write about!"

Excessive Clemency
RSWW III 11

A certain man named Yu had seen long service in a governor's tribunal as a clerk of court. For forty years he had been in charge of recording court proceedings. Some time after his retirement he lay sick in bed, his life ebbing away. By the faint light shed by his bedside lamp and the moon above, he thought he could see the shapes of ghosts lurking menacingly in the shadows. He indignantly burst out:

"I have always aspired to behave honourably and mercifully. I swear I have never lent myself to the execution of innocent defendants. What do these stupid ghosts think they are up to!"

That same night he dreamt of a gaggle of men all covered in blood standing before him. They said:

"You, sir, are aware that extreme harshness can build up vengefulness in its victim; you don't realize that good and kind intentions can have the same effect. When the weak and friendless are brutally murdered, they die a death of indescribable pain. In the nether regions their lonely ghosts weep silent tears and nurse their grievance, craving the execution of their murderer, which alone can appease them. Yet you see only the pitiable state of the living, not the wretchedness of the dead. So you get to work with your nimble writing brush, distorting facts to mitigate the crime. Accordingly the cutthroat slips through the net, and the victim is denied justice.

"Try to put yourself in the place of others. Suppose you, innocent and blameless, are cut to pieces by another, and in the afterlife observe those in charge of your case changing deep wounds to superficial wounds, many wounds to few wounds, a feeble defendant's case to a strong one, and altering deliberate to unintentional, so that your abominated enemy is by this connivance let off the hook and is free to terrorize again—would you be bitter, or not?

"Yet you put aside such thoughts, and instead congratulate yourself on having performed a secret act of virtue in letting an evil-doer go free. Who do you expect his guiltless victim to hate, if not you?"

Yu woke up in a sweat. He told his sons gathered round him all that had come to pass in his dream, and slapped himself round the face, crying: "I have been deluded, I have all along been deluded!" Hardly had he settled back on his pillow than he breathed his last.

SERVANTS

The Manchus who conquered China in the middle of the seventeenth century had a history of making slaves of their captives. In border raids south of the Great Wall prior to their conquest they transported Chinese farmers north to work their fields, effectively as slaves, in the process freeing themselves to assume a purely military role. Under the system codified by the first Manchu emperor to rule the whole of China, the Manchu bannermen (their armies were organized under divisions called "banners") were in fact forbidden to engage in any occupation except a fighting one. For that they received a stipend from the treasury, which continued to the end of the empire, though by then it was a paltry sum.

Once the transition to rule over all the Han people was made, outright slavery obviously could not be maintained, but it left a legacy: the element "nu" (slave) incorporated in the names for classes of servants was widely taken literally. Servants had virtually no legal rights, except the right to life. Given sufficient influence, unnatural deaths, including suicides, could be hushed up, but they properly occasioned an inquest, and were best avoided. While there were no bars to inflicting violence on servants, any resistance on their part was punishable by law. Those striking their master faced decapitation, and open abuse of a master merited strangulation.

The mildest form of servitude was indenture for a number of years. The alternative was being sold for life, when servants simply became the property of their employers, to do with as they pleased. Female servants could be freely used for sex by their masters until they were married, which they regularly were, to male servants within the same household; thereafter a certain amount of discretion had to be observed.

Given the vagaries of agriculture and commerce, indigent parents were often driven to sell their children into service; the supply being plentiful, the price was cheap. If their master or mistress was a martinet, as exampled in our first item below, servants lived in constant fear. On the other hand, when they were fortunate enough to be employed by a civilized person, the balance of power within a household could be tipped in the servants' favour. An official, for instance, would have had no time, or probably even ability, to attend to the purchase of goods and services, so such responsibilities had to be delegated to servants: some degree of dependency was thus created. It also seems that there was some social obstacle to dismissing family retainers; Ji Xiaolan himself writes of some very obnoxious individuals whom he kept on in his service, despite giving the impression that he would have been glad to see the back of them. And when the body of servants was large enough for them to close ranks, they could apparently thwart their master's wishes with relative impunity.

Our author was by no means a social rebel. He did not question the authority of employers over servants, or of husbands over wives—if servants were low, servants' wives were the lowest of the low. What did exercise him, indeed horrified him, was wanton cruelty. He goes so far as to more or less endorse unlawful revenge for cruelty when it could be taken by the victims or their family members, and when it could not be so had, he comforts himself with signs of divine retribution.

Inhuman
HXZZ II 25

After the wife of a certain vice-minister died and was sealed in her coffin, and just when the sacrificial offerings were being laid out, a white dove flew into the curtained-off area, and immediately disappeared from sight. While a panicky search for it was going on, smoke started to belch from the coffin and flames licked up from its sides. Soon the roof beams were ablaze, and in no time the whole wing was reduced to ashes.

This matron, as it turned out, had ruled her servants with a rod of iron. Whenever a new maidservant was engaged, the bill of sale signed, and the girl admitted to the house, she was bidden to kneel before her mistress, who first delivered a long harangue about the dos and don'ts in her household: this was called "indoctrination". After this preliminary, the girl was stripped of her clothes and had her hands tied behind her. In that position she was given a hundred lashes: that was called the "corporal punishment test". If the girl squirmed about or cried out in pain, the lashes fell heavier. Not until she neither moved nor uttered, and the whipping made only the hollow sound of impacting on wood or stone, was she deemed to have "learned what to expect", and was ready to be ordered about. My great-aunt had visited this matron's establishment, and said that the men and women servants trooped in and out in better order than soldiers drilled before their general.

In a similar connection, I used to pay frequent visits to an older relative. I saw two whips, one hanging either side of the door to his inner apartment; their thongs were stained with blood, and their handles were so shiny from constant use that you could see your face in them. I understood that before retiring to bed, his practice was to tie all his maids down to benches before covering them with quilts for the night, in order to prevent them from absconding or killing themselves. As his death approached, the flesh on his thighs became gangrenous, exposing the bones, just as if his legs were split open by a cut of a whip.

The Ingrained Habits of Faithless Servants
GWTZ I 53

There is a couplet in a Song dynasty poem entitled "The Crab" which reads:

In spring waters its pincers grow black with greed
With autumn's age its shell turns red through boiling.

This refers by analogy to the infamously avaricious Zhu Mian [favourite of emperors at the end of the Northern Song dynasty].

With other creatures that supply our kitchens, death comes of an instant; only the crab is thrown alive into pot or steamer, scalded and slowly cooked. The shortest time from the water coming to a boil to its meat being done is over an hour, so it must long in vain for death to come to relieve its intense torture. A person's sins in a previous life must be heinous indeed for him or her to be reborn as a crab.

The story is told that when Zhao Hongxie was Governor of Zhili province (at that time Zhili had no governor-general) he dreamed that dozens of deceased servants, male and female both, knelt in a semi-circle at the foot of the steps, kowtowing and begging for mercy. They said:

"In our lifetime we servants were beholden to you for taking us in and feeding us, yet we colluded to hoodwink you, our master, and in the course of time cemented a coalition so entrenched that its defences were impregnable. Even if some misdemeanour did come to light, we presented a united front and made artful excuses for the culprit. Though you, master, may have seen through our game, there was nothing you could do. As further time went on, we tacitly put obstacles in your way, so that you could take no measure that did not suit us. Because of our sins we were relegated to rebirth as aquatic creatures, and lifetime after lifetime suffer the pain of being boiled and steamed. Tomorrow you are to be served crabs at your meal—and the crabs will be us! We beg you to grant us pardon."

The governor was a humane and kindly man. First thing the following morning he told his chef of the dream. He ordered the crabs to be released into the river and a Buddhist service for the salvation of those repentant souls to be arranged. Now at this time of the autumn the crabs were at their most fleshy, and those provided to the governor's kitchen were particularly choice and succulent. The governor's current servants had a good laugh behind his back, saying:

"The old man is very sly—ten to one he made up that story to put the wind up us. If he thinks he can pull the wool over our eyes, he'd better think again!"

So in fact they cooked and ate the crabs (though they reported they had been released), and pocketed the fee for the priestly service (though they reported it had been duly performed). Governor Zhao never found out.

The duplicity of the servants was habitual to them; at the same time the pattern for their behaviour was set by the previous generation of servants, who now fell victim to their own bad practice. The expression "paid back in your own coin" seems to sum the thing up.

Servants Mistreat Their Wives
HXZZ III 2

My bondservant Song Yu had three wives in all. The first wife did not share his bed after they took their vows, and was later cast off. The second wife's pregnancies always resulted in twin births. Song detested the trouble of looking after them, besides which his wife's milk was not enough to suckle them, so he looked for a drug to sterilize her. Foolishly he followed old Mother Wang's advice and ground gravel to powder for his wife to swallow. The stone powder hardened in her stomach and killed her. Years later he fell dangerously ill, and in his delirious state muttered and grumbled as if arguing with somebody. On coming to his senses he confided to his third wife:

"When I put away my first wife, my parents accepted another proposal of marriage for her, and had fixed a day for the new husband's party to come and fetch her. My wife was kept in the dark about all this. The night before she was due to leave I enticed her into sleeping with me. She thought I had changed my mind about divorcing her, so gladly played along. We were still in bed together when daylight came and the wedding procession rolled up with its drums and horns. She was filled with hatred for me when she was taken away. The trouble was, the matchmaker had assured her new husband that she was still a virgin, and my parents and brother had backed the matchmaker up. When they found out she was in fact damaged goods, she came in for a lot of abuse and mistrust, and finally died from misery.

"My second wife, to tell the truth, resisted taking the powdered stone, and I had to beat her soundly to get her to swallow it down. When she died I was afraid she would come back and haunt me, so I paid a shaman to make a spell to keep off malignant ghosts. Just now when I was woozy I came face to face with the two of them. I'm not long for this world!"

Indeed, Song Yu soon breathed his last.

Another servant of mine was called Wang Cheng. He was very odd: in the middle of sharing a laugh with his wife he would suddenly bellow at her, commanding her to lie flat on the floor and receive a whipping. The whipping over, he would continue joshing with her. Alternatively, he might interrupt his whipping, raise his wife to her feet and jest with her, then say, "I can finish off the whipping now," and as before repeat the performance. In the space of a day and night his capricious alternation of mood might occur several times.

His wife went in fear and trembling of him: when he was merry she had to force a smile and appear cheerful; when he was angry she had to docilely endure. One day she complained in tears to my late mother, who called Wang Cheng to explain his conduct. He knelt before her and said: "I can't tell the reason, neither can I control myself. It's just that I feel she is lovable this minute, and the next minute feel she is hateful."

My mother replied: "That is simply irrational. Probably it is retribution for a wrong done in a previous existence, what the Buddhists call karma."

Worried that the wife might commit suicide under her roof, she sent them both away. Later on we heard that Wang Cheng had died, whereupon his wife dressed in the red colours of rejoicing.

Now, that the husband should have authority over the wife is a law of nature. Yet the honour the wife owes the husband is less than that owed by the subject to the ruler, and the emotional bond is not as strong as that between son and father, which is why the word for wife [*qi*] is cognate with "equal" [*qi*], implying that there should be parity between husband and wife. In their life together, husband and wife should rightly and properly treat each other on the same footing.

Song Yu did not intentionally kill his second wife, his crime was only in using brute force. As to his first wife, since she had already been set aside and the betrothal gifts accepted, the marital bond had already been severed: they could not be considered to be married any more. Therefore Song Yu was plainly guilty of seducing another man's intended, which led to her death. He got his just deserts in paying with his own life.

Wang Cheng was cruel and violent, but not to the extent of procuring his wife's death. All the while she lived under his roof, he was her master. When he expired she did not wear mourning, instead treating his death as a festive occasion. In thus flying in the face of decency and accepted principles she merits no sympathy on account of being mistreated.

Maid Gets Own Back on Mistress
GWTZ III 22

My senior Zhou Huang contributed this.

A certain grandee was on his way to take up office. The boats carrying his family and retinue made up a convoy. They moored for the night in the middle reaches of the Yangtze River. A big junk soon came to moor alongside the leading boat. Judging by the lantern over the cabin door and the pennants flown from the mast, it too was a government vessel. At sundown a score of men streamed out of this junk's cabin and boarded the grandee's boat with swords drawn. They drove all his women out onto the deck. A richly attired woman on the junk pointed through her cabin window at a young wife in the grandee's party, saying "That's her!" At this word the bandits dragged her off. One of the bandits shouted to the grandee:

"I am the father of such-and-such a maid in your household. Your daughter tortured my daughter, subjecting her to inhuman flogging, beating and burning. She took a lucky chance to slip away and join up with me, since when we have evaded your attempts to recapture her. You have earned our undying hatred, and now we are taking our revenge."

With that the junk set sail downstream, and was out of sight in an instant. Pursuit proved fruitless. What befell the kidnapped woman was never known, but her lot can be imagined.

If a man is so destitute that he has to sell his daughter, the assumption will be that he is powerless: the possibility that he might turn outlaw is never entertained. When a maid is cruelly used, it seems inconceivable that she can retaliate: the possibility of *her father* resorting to outlawry to avenge her is never entertained. As they say, the wasp and scorpion may be small, but they have a deadly sting in their tail!

Li Shougong chimed in with this:

A man's wife who maltreated her maidservant shut her up in a bare side room for some accidental fault, and she died from cold and hunger. There being no visible injuries on her body, the girl's father found no redress in the courts: instead he got a flogging for vexatious litigation. Having no outlet for his outrage, he scaled the man's wall at night and stabbed to death both his wife and daughter. An all-points warrant for his arrest was in force for many years, but he slipped through the net. This showed that revenge could be exacted without turning outlaw.

Li Shougong also told of a house in the capital catching fire and burning to death husband, wife and children. The fire was the concerted work of maidservants whose hatred of the family had overflowed the measure. With no concrete evidence against the maidservants, there was no prosecution to bring. This showed that revenge could be exacted without the intervention of fathers.

I myself had a relative who took flogging a maid or concubine as a kind of child's game; some actually died from the flogging. One night a mass of vapour as round as a cartwheel descended from the house eaves and swirled around as if driven by a wind, soughing mournfully; then it made straight for the bedroom and disappeared. The next day an ulcer developed on this relative's neck, as small as a grain of millet. It gradually spread and festered until the head was as if severed from the body by the executioner's axe. In this case humankind could not exact revenge, but unearthly powers could.

Other people love their children no less than we love ours. Strong fathers nurse their grievance in silence until with the denial of justice their pent-up fury breaks its banks. Such an outcome is inevitable. The weak carry their bitterness to the underworld with them, where their sorrows will surely move the gods and spirits to take up their cause. The malefactors will get their deserts, if not from the hands of mortals, then from the powers that rule the universe. Such is the nature of things.

ADDENDUM: Family letter to sister Lin (*Family Letters*, FLP 2012 edition, p. 232)

Maidservants are also daughters loved by their parents; it is only because families are on the verge of starvation that parents can bring themselves to sell their daughters into service. As young as six or seven or as old as ten or eleven, these girls have long been at their mother's knee. When the day comes for them to be separated, truly words cannot express their heartache. Their mistress should pity them, care for them, and gradually wean them from their pining for home; then they will naturally perform their tasks conscientiously.

[...]

Yesterday your eldest son arrived in the capital, and I had him stay with me. As we conversed in the evening, he mentioned in passing that you treated your maids too severely. Last year one absconded and another died, so now only one remains. Since you have enough servants to see to your needs, there is no point in acquiring new ones. I will tell you some true facts that will shock you into taking notice.

The first concerns a grandee from Yangzhou (I keep back his name because he still holds high office). He was on his way to take up a new post; the boats carrying his family and retinue made up a convoy. They moored for the night in the middle reaches of the Yangtze River. A big junk soon came to moor alongside his leading boat. By the lantern over the cabin door and the pennants flown from the mast, it proclaimed itself a government vessel. Almost immediately a score or more of strapping men leapt onto the grandee's boat with swords drawn and drove all his women onto the deck. A richly attired woman put her head out of the junk's window and pointed to the wife of the grandee, saying "That's her!" At this word, the bandits dragged her off. One of the bandits shouted to the grandee:

"My daughter was the maid who ran away from your household. I had to sell her into service because I was destitute. That she should do your bidding was only right, but you had no call to torture her. She was flogged and burnt till not an inch of her flesh was unscathed! Luckily she got away and met up with me. She is now married to a bandit chieftain, and has evaded all your attempts to capture her. You have earned our undying hatred, and now we are taking our revenge. We'll take your wife and give her a full taste of the flogging and burning my daughter suffered. After that, we'll let her go."

The junk set sail as soon as he had had his say. The grandee put up a large reward for their arrest, but they had disappeared without trace.

Now, if a man is so destitute that he has to sell his daughter, what recourse could he be expected to have? The possibility that he might turn outlaw is overlooked. If a maid, for her part, is treated inhumanly, how could she take her revenge? The possibility that she might marry a bandit would not be considered. As they say, the wasp and scorpion may be small, but they have a sting in the tail. Does it not pay to be cautious?

To give another example, the wife of a certain plutocrat ruled her servants with a rod of iron. Because a maid committed a minor fault, she was stripped of her clothes and shut up in a bare side room—this was in the depths of winter. The next day she was found frozen to death. Her father sought redress in the magistrate's court, but as the coroner detected no visible injuries on her body, his charge was not upheld; instead he got a flogging for his trouble. Having no outlet for his outrage, he armed himself with a knife, scaled the wall of the plutocrat's house and stabbed both his wife and daughter to death. A warrant for his arrest was in force for many years, but he was never caught. This was a case personally handled by Li Shougong while he held office, not something I have made up to give you a fright.

Yet another example, this time of maltreated maids who were fatherless: it led to an even greater loss of life. This spring a fire broke out in the house of a man called Lu in the outer Qianmen district. Husband, wife, and their children, five persons in all, were burnt to death. Only their two maids escaped the conflagration. Again it was an instance of the mistress's excessively callous treatment. Having no outlet for their grievances, the maids resorted to arson. Since there was no concrete evidence against them, no prosecution could be brought.

Furthermore, there may be retribution on behalf of maltreated maids who have already died. The wife of a board under-secretary made a daily sport of whipping maids; one of them died from this cruelty. About two weeks later a mass of black vapour descended from the house eaves and spun round like a whirlwind, soughing mournfully; then it made straight for the women's apartments. The next day an ulcer the size of a grain of millet formed on the mistress's back. It gradually spread and festered, until her head was severed from her body, as if by an executioner's axe. This is an example of revenge taken by ghostly intervention where revenge by human agency was impossible.

To sum up, if harm by human hand is ruled out, punishment will surely come from Heaven. Please do not dismiss these words as empty make-believe. I cannot urge you more strongly!

Crossing the Class Barrier
GWTZ III 47

My tenant farmer Shao Renwo contributed this.

A band of robbers raided a rambling mansion at night, and broke down the door. Torches and swords in hand, they threatened the occupants:

"We'll kill anyone who calls for help! Anyway, in this strong wind nobody will hear if you shout, so your death would be pointless!"

Those inside did not dare make a sound.

A fifteen-year-old scullery maid was sleeping in the kitchen. She quietly got a shovelful of live cinders from the cooking range and crawled on her stomach through the darkness to the back yard, where helped by the wind she blew a flame from the cinders and set a stack of firewood alight. Thick smoke and tongues of fire shot high in the air, arousing the whole village. People from other villages nearby also rushed to put out the fire. By the time these masses of people gathered round the mansion, the scene was lit as bright as day. The robbers failed to break out of this cordon, and despite resisting fiercely were overcome and arrested.

The head of the house was deeply grateful to this maid, and expressed his inclination to marry her to his son. The son nodded his agreement, saying:

"Seeing she is so quick-witted and resourceful, there's no doubt she will be able to make a good home. She may be a scullery maid, but that makes no odds."

His father was delighted. He lost no time in ordering the wedding dress and ornaments, and had the marriage ceremony performed the same night. He explained:

"If we put it off till later, there will be debate about social status, well bred and low bred, and suchlike. Some will be for, some against, and I fear there might be second thoughts."

There's no denying it, this was a remarkable young woman!

Part III
Family and Friends

14

HEARTH AND HOME

If it is true that the family forms the first and most lasting unit of cohesion in human societies, China must have been hard to match in elevating the family as the model for governance of the state, and promoting "filial piety", that is the duty to care for, honour and obey parents, as the bedrock of all morality. In the state structure the emperor was of course the father figure. Russian peasants formerly called their tsar "Little Father", but Russians did not have the Chinese genius for systematization and love of formulas, a relevant example being the Five Cardinal Relationships, namely: sovereign and subject, father and son, husband and wife, elder and younger brother, and friend and friend. Since sovereign-subject is simply an upgrading of father-son, and friends were commonly family friends, we see that these Cardinal Relationships were essentially family-based. The matching formula was the Three Bonds, which were the obligations between ruler and ruled, the love between father and child, and the harmony between husband and wife. These principles were embedded in school books like the San zi jing (Three Character Classic), compiled in the thirteenth century for primary education, and had the same status as the Ten Commandments in Christendom.

An extended family was indeed a kind of state in miniature, and not all that much easier to keep in order. As most of our author's contributors came from the same class of scholar-officials, the locus of his domestic stories favoured big houses with a full complement of husband, wife, concubines, sons and step-sons, and a bevy of male and female servants who could well look after their own interests. The authority of the patriarch had few limitations, his chief constraint being his obligation to honour the good example of his ancestors in order to preserve their spectral protection; what those good deeds were was fully recorded in family genealogies that went back to the year dot. In second position was the eldest son, but his priority among siblings was not guaranteed: he had to contend in performance with brothers and half-brothers. Since an adult's hold on life was uncertain even in affluent families, remarriage after a wife's death produced sons of different mothers, and that complicated matters further. Sons of concubines had also to be reckoned with. Potentially all these sons were heirs to the family fortune, and few, if any, willingly let slip their chance to inherit. At the highest level of society, history presents us with many examples of the sons of emperors turning the palace precincts into a battleground.

Concubines are a subject in themselves. The most honourable motive for taking a concubine was stated by the great sage Mencius: "Of the three sins against filial piety, lack of progeny is the greatest." That almost required the husband of an infertile wife to take a concubine to produce sons in her stead. Men without that excuse also took concubines to satisfy their libido, if their means allowed. Wives were often content with such an arrangement, especially if that afforded sexual relief. Ji Xiaolan himself had six concubines (not all at once), and his favourite among them was found by his wife. Concubines were usually bought at puberty or soon after, and as a chattel could be dismissed without ceremony.

Given the separation of the sexes (which could be from as young as six years old), the wife was in charge of the distaff side, and that included concubines. Inevitably there could be jealousy if the wife felt deprived of her husband's affections, and that jealousy immediately be made manifest in cruel chastisement of the concubine and discrimination against her sons. Ideally the saintly and submissive wife would manage her establishment serenely, secure in the knowledge that legally and ritually she was the mother of all sons born to her husband, entitled to their support in life and their worship after death. Human nature being what it is, that pattern sometimes held, sometimes did not. The popularity of harridans rather than saints and of dominant rather than submissive women in Chinese literature must have had some basis in reality. A wife's sense of authority could be bolstered by the fact that in high society they would have contributed substantially to the family's wealth by bringing with them a handsome dowry. Though her son became head of the family on his father's death, a widowed mother would have had some claim to communal property.

Among the lower orders different customs and practices prevailed. Women necessarily had more freedom of movement and association, and consequently adultery was more common. The position of wives was also more insecure: if a husband was in financial difficulties he was able to sell his wife, and parents-in-law could sell their son's widow. On the other hand, widows frequently asserted themselves by remarrying of their own free will, not being under the heavier obligation of respectable women to remain "chaste", which as we shall see elsewhere, rated so highly in the moral code that a woman distinguished for that virtue could earn for herself an inscribed archway and for her sons exemption from corvee labour.

CONCUBINES HAD BETTER WATCH OUT
RSWW I 10

Guan Panpan and Yuxiao mentioned below were faithful concubines of the Tang dynasty, much celebrated in poetry.

* * *

Jin Mengao of Suzhou, a fellow graduate of mine, once moored his boat at the confluence of the Huai and Yangtze Rivers. At night he observed two old men meeting on the bank and going to sit in a thatched arbour at the water's edge. One of the old men asked: "What have you been up to lately?" The other replied:

"The master of the house has camped out in the grounds to get relief from the summer heat. I have been slipping into his gazebo every day to spectate on a living illustrated sex manual: the female form in all its glory, a sight for sore eyes. His fifth concubine is particularly voluptuous. I saw her cut off a tress to swear an oath to her master, vowing that in time to come she would shut herself up in a Swallow Tower and stay faithful to his memory like Guan Panpan, and again like a second Yuxiao return to serve him in a life to come. The master was moved to tears. Yet I overheard the same girl say in a private talk with her mother that the master was already advanced in years, and she had better start putting money and valuables by in readiness for remarriage. Do you think such women are to be trusted?"

The two old men lapsed into long sighs.

The first man resumed: "I have heard that his lady wife is good and kind. Is that true?"

The other turned aside in disbelief, exclaiming:

"She's the most jealous woman in the world! Good and kind is pure nonsense. She knows that to get into brawls through jealousy is to hand the advantage to your opponent. This wife has different strategies to deal with new concubines. The weak she smothers with kindness, lets them come and go and flaunt themselves without hindrance, and allows them to slip into licentiousness, with the result that her husband sends them away out of shame. The strong-minded she treats with great courtesy, on the surface respecting them as equals, but behind the scenes inducing them to take issue with the husband, so that they become imperious and overbearing, with the result that the husband gets rid of them when his tolerance runs out.

"With concubines who do not fall into either trap, she will set one against the other by spreading underhand gossip, with the aim of bringing down both antagonists. If they are lucky enough to temporarily retain their position, mutual insults and backbiting constantly disturb the domestic peace, with the result that the husband is met with complaints and long faces in the concubines' quarters, in contrast to dulcet tones and glad welcome in his wife's chamber. It is obvious which he would find more to his taste. I say again, this is the most jealous woman in the world; good and kind is sheer nonsense."

Mengao eavesdropped on this conversation with growing respect for the old man's astute analysis, but was puzzled by the reference to slipping into the gazebo every day. He was still mulling this over when an official junk approached with beating drums and furled its sails in preparation to tying up. In a flash the old men vanished; Mengao then realized they were not of human kind.

The Son and His Stepmother
LYXL IV 22

The peculiar situation described here derives from the not unheard-of circumstance of a widower buying a married woman as a second wife, and the consequent antagonism between that wife and the widower's existing son or sons. Extreme poverty or indebtedness might compel a man to (quite lawfully) sell wife or children.

* * *

Given the vastness of China, adultery and theft occur in every place and on every day. What is remarkable is theft which is not normal theft, yet cannot be called by any other name; and adultery which is not common adultery, but still must be classed as adultery. Even more remarkable is for that same theft and adultery to be both condoned. Most remarkable of all is for the two to coincide and on coinciding be immediately exposed, yet because of the link between them, cancel each other out: the exposure being like the boiling over of a pot, and the cancelling being like the extinction of a flash of lightning.

My uncle An Wuchang told me the following story.

A man lost his wife in middle age, and though he had a grown-up son, bought a married woman to be his second wife. Fortunately he was able to keep this second wife in check, and their domestic life was peaceful. The man soon died, and all his life's savings came into the hands of this wife. His son heard unsavoury rumours, and demanded possession of the money, but he could not substantiate the rumours, and the wife refused to admit any truth to them. By and by the son found out where she kept the hoard, so one night he bored through a partition wall into her bedroom. He had just opened the chest and was about to make off with the contents when his stepmother woke up and raised the alarm. Her shout of "Burglars!" aroused the servants, who armed themselves and rushed to the bedroom. The son fled in panic through the hole he had made, but was struck unconscious as he emerged on the outside. The servants then squirmed through the hole to look for any of the burglar's accomplices who might still be inside. They heard heavy breathing coming from under the bed, and shouted that they had discovered another burglar. They dragged the man out and trussed him up. When lanterns were brought and the burglars inspected, it turned out that the one with the broken crown was the son of the house, and the one under the bed was the former husband of the second wife.

After the son regained consciousness, he and his stepmother locked horns in argument. The son contended: "A son who takes possession of his father's fortune is not a thief." The stepmother argued: "A wife who takes up with a former husband is not an adulteress." The son said: "That applies only to a legitimate reunion, not to improper assignations." The stepmother said: "And you have the right to petition for your father's fortune, but not to seize it by theft." So they went on trading accusations, neither being willing to yield an inch.

The next day the clan met in closed session. They took the view that both parties would suffer if the matter was taken to court, and the family's good name would be sullied for nothing. So behind the scenes they patched up a compromise, whereby the father's entire savings would pass to the son, and the stepmother would be free to revert to her former husband. In this way the storm spent itself. However, as the *Book of Songs* says: "When the great bell in the palace is struck, the sound is heard beyond the walls."

My late uncle Yinan commented:

"It was the will of heaven that the theft and adultery should coincide, but what brought both things about was human doing. If the father had not taken this married woman to wife, what motive would the son have had to turn to theft, or the woman to adultery? The father relied on his ability to keep both of them under control; what he did not take into account was that he could exercise control while he lived, but not when he was dead."

Ranking of Progeny
RSWW II 43

A scion of a distinguished family had before him a career to be crowned by high honours, according to the predictions of fortune tellers. However, at the onset of old age his official placing was merely the sixth rank. One day he consulted a planchette to ask why his career had proved so uphill. The presiding spirit made reply:

"The fortune tellers were not deluding you. Your late mother's partiality towards you curtailed your rise in office, simply that."

He responded: "Partiality is hard to avoid, I grant you, but how could its consequences extend to reducing one's career prospects?"

"It is prescribed in the *Rites of Zhou* that a stepmother be like a birth mother, in which case she should look upon the sons of a former wife as her own sons. It is also prescribed that the sons of a concubine should observe three years' mourning for their legal mother, in which case the legal mother should likewise look upon the sons of a concubine as her own sons. But human feelings are perverse: mothers draw lines, dividing the children she has borne from the children she has not borne as sharply as fire is distinct from water. Once the mind to show favour takes over, her machinations know no end. Both in small matters like diet and daily routine and in big matters like possessions and property, it is her own children who are treated generously and those who are not her own children who are treated shabbily. This already goes against behaviour approved by the Creator. Yet it does not end there: sowing dissension by flattery and disparagement, hatching closet plots, raging and reviling, disregarding propriety—all these follow. Those who have been traduced have to bite back their protests, those who look on grind their teeth, while she rants on about her own children being done down.

"The gods look down in anger, the spirits of the ancestors are embittered and fearful of the consequences. How else is the justice of Heaven to be demonstrated, if not by making her sons pay a price? You have to understand: there is a limit to the advantages one can enjoy in one's lifetime, so it follows that a surfeit on one side will be offset by a deficit on the other. If you unduly benefit from your superior position within the family, naturally there will be an unseen reduction in your career prospects. You were privileged in comparison with your half-brothers, and you can't have it both ways. Why grumble about your frustrations?"

Severely chastened, the man retired in confusion. But when a married woman among my relatives heard this story she exclaimed:

"That spirit was talking absolute rubbish! Each and every son of a former wife exploits his seniority to swallow up his younger brothers, that's true. It's also true that each and every son of a concubine tries to undermine his older brothers, relying on his mother being doted on. If their mother did not take their side, wouldn't they all be lambs for the slaughter?"

My late father judged:

"Though she speaks from personal envy, one cannot deny that such things do happen. People change, the world never stands still, but if the master of the house manages his domestic affairs with an even hand, things can go on reasonably well."

Mending Ways
GWTZ III 53

Confucius said: "There are five ways of remonstrance; I follow the mode of implication." That shows the Sage's profound understanding of human nature.

Among my relatives there was a matron who had no sons of her own, and secretly resented the sons of her husband's concubines. Her nephew and son-in-law busily fomented discord and spread slanders, joining together to conspire against the sons. There seemed to be no way the matron could be brought to see the dangers inherent in the situation.

The matron had an ancient nursemaid, over eighty years old. Learning of this state of affairs, she humbly requested an interview with the matron. Once she had made her obeisance, she burst into tears, saying: "Your servant has not eaten for three days."

The matron asked: "Why did you not turn to your nephew for support?"

"To begin with, when I had my savings, my nephew waited on me as if I was his mother. Now he has tricked me out of all my money, he treats me like a stranger. He won't even grant me a bowl of rice."

"Why don't you turn to your daughter and son-in-law?"

"Like my nephew, my son-in-law fleeced me and cast me aside. What my daughter thinks makes no odds, she has no say in the matter."

"In a case like this when close family turn their backs on you, you can go to the magistrate for redress."

"I have done so. The magistrate says that after my marriage I ceased to be a member of my birth family; my daughter is also married, and likewise belongs to a different family. If they took care of me, it would be as a special act of charity; if they did not take care of me, they would break no law, so the magistrate could not intervene on my behalf."

"What are you going to do in future?"

"My late husband took a concubine when he was serving with an official in another province, and they had a son, who has now grown up. When I took my complaint to the magistrate, he pointed out that this son was obliged to look after me, his legal mother. If he didn't step up to the mark, he would be severely punished. His honour has already issued a warrant to summon him, but I can't tell when he will arrive."

The matron was disconcerted by the nursemaid's story, and gradually mended her ways. So, as we see, her own relations could talk themselves hoarse without persuading her, yet this old woman could change her mind with a few words. Proving a point by using one's own experience as an example attracts no blame for the speaker, yet gives effective warning to the hearer.

[...]

A Whipping Too Far
LYXXL II 2

My great-uncle Ji Jingxing was appointed garrison commander in Zhenfan, Gansu province. He told of the wife of an imperial academician named Li who habitually mistreated her husband's concubine. When angry with her, she had the concubine stripped of her lower garments and given a whipping. Hardly a day passed without this happening. There was an old woman in their neighbourhood who had admittance to the underworld to carry out a certain duty there. This old woman remonstrated with the academician's wife so:

"I have learned that you, madam, were wronged by this concubine in a former life, but her penance was set at two hundred lashes, no more than that. In your jealous rages you have whipped her so frequently that the number of lashes given her exceeds that total more than tenfold; now the tables are turned, you are in her debt. Besides that, when physical punishment is meted out to respectable women, they are not divested of their lower garments even when the punishment is ordered by a court. Yet you, madam, insist on humiliating her by baring her buttocks. You take such great pleasure and satisfaction in doing so that you break the taboos recognized by the gods and spirits. Because you have been kind to me, I sneaked a look at the underworld dossiers for you, and I can't keep from you what I found."

The wife scoffed: "You rascally old crone, with these wild slanders you want to get me to pray for absolution at some shrine, and take your commission!"

At this time the Wu Sangui Rebellion spawned widespread mutinies, and Academician Li was killed in the turmoil. His concubine passed into the hands of Lieutenant General Han. Impressed by her intelligence and good sense, Han made her his favourite. Since he had no wife, she was given control of his household administration.

As for Li's wife, she was carried off by the rebels. When these rebels were put down, she was made captive by the government forces, and was among those women awarded as a prize to the victors. By coincidence she was allotted to General Han, and the concubine retained her as a serving maid. She had her former mistress kneel before her in the ceremonial hall and addressed her thus:

"Your life will be spared if you accept my terms, which are: to kneel down before my dressing table every morning, take off your trousers yourself, and suffer five lashes of the whip; and afterwards carry out such chores as you are assigned. If not, as wife to rebels, there is no bar to killing you. I can have the flesh sliced from your body and fed to our dogs and pigs."

Fear of death demoralized the wife: she kowtowed and vowed to conform. Still, the concubine did not want her to succumb too quickly, so the whippings were not too vicious, just enough to be painful. After a year or so, the wife died of an unrelated illness. When the lashes she had received were totalled up, they numbered the same as those she herself had unduly meted out. This woman was truly pigheaded and brazen. Even the gods in the underworld could not abide her behaviour, so they took away her will to live.

General Han made no secret of this affair, in fact he paraded it as an example of the workings of karma. That is how the ins and outs of it came to be common knowledge.

[...]

15

PIETY AND PARAGONS

Filial Piety

The lengths to which children were invited to go to comfort and succour their parents were truly extraordinary. One of the most spectacular and certainly the most widely known of those was the son's or daughter's resort to slicing a piece of his or her own flesh to make a curative broth to treat a parent's critical illness. Less lurid and more thoughtful was the idea of a child preceding the parents to bed so that the mosquitoes could drink their fill of blood, and so have no appetite to feed on the parents when they in turn retired. In the Yuan dynasty a collection entitled Ershisi xiao *(Twenty-four Paragons of Piety) was compiled to illustrate such morals and maxims, and it remained prescribed nourishment for the young mind right up to the end of empire. The contents are extremely diverse, ranging from effecting miracles to emptying chamber pots; some strike one as grotesque, like a daughter-in-law feeding her frail mother-in-law with her breast milk. To suit the purpose of a reading primer, entries are very short.*

Of much higher status was the Xiao jing *(Classic of Filial Piety), probably compiled in the early Han dynasty, which purported to be a dialogue between Confucius and his disciple Zengzi. It presented filial piety as the basic model for all personal and societal relationships and the fountainhead of all moral values. These relationships were all conceived of as stratified, the lower being obedient to the higher, but also as reciprocal, the higher having the duty of care for the lower. If the precepts were observed, then something like peace on earth and goodwill to all men would follow. The premise was that everyone from highest to lowest should know their place, and the status quo should be permanently preserved.*

Though the pattern was said to have been set by the legendary first kings, always lurking in the shadows behind this doctrine were the ancestors: indeed, ancestor worship could well have been the rootstock for the outgrowth of filial piety. By their exemplary behaviour, descendants brought pleasure to their ancestors in the spirit world, who in return protected them. If an individual went on to achieve distinction, the ancestors enjoyed reflected glory. In fact, the Classic only brought together and amplified strands of long-held belief. Those are found embedded in the Book of History, the earliest recorded dynastic annals; that book states in one section that unfilial acts are worse than robbery and murder.

In the established imperial order, filial piety was institutionalized at least for the upper classes as a period of mourning to be observed on the death of parents, in which event no office could be held, no examination could be taken, no marriage entered upon. The length of that period was prescribed as twenty-seven months.

Chastity

Lu Xun, later to become the most celebrated Chinese writer of the twentieth century, published in 1918 an essay mocking the imposition by men on women of the virtue of chastity, which had been reasserted as an obligation in 1914 by the then President of the Republic, and exemplars of which were still being lauded in the press. Lu Xun split the binom jielie, which we translate as "chastity", into its two constituent parts: "constancy", meaning cleaving to the one husband even after death parted them, and "fervency", meaning steadfastly defending her sexual purity, even at the expense of her life. He wrote that the moralists' view was this:

"Constancy absolutely rules out remarrying or taking a lover after her husband dies; the earlier the husband dies, and the poorer the family, the more admirable the constancy. Fervency is manifest in two ways: the first is for the woman, whether married or betrothed, to take her own life on the death of her husband or husband-to-be; the second is, when she is faced with forcible rape, to either forestall the rape by killing herself, or to be killed in resisting the rape; the more cruel and agonizing her death, the more admirable her fervency. If she is taken too unawares to prevent being ravished, and only commits suicide after the event, there is bound to be talk. Should her case be examined by generous minded moralists who have been known to take mitigating circumstances into account, they could allow her the recognition of 'chaste'. Even so, our men of letters would be reluctant to pen her obituary, and if pressed would be sure to conclude with the words 'sadly' and 'regrettably' repeated several times over.

"To sum up, if a woman loses her husband she should remain faithful to his memory, or die. If she is violated, she should die. And if such a person is generally acclaimed, it shows that the state of the nation's morals is sound, and China is saved."

Though this presentation is evidently satirical, it was firmly rooted in practice. The virtue of chastity in women had indeed been placed on an altar and sanctified by a body of literature, and too come to be regarded as a symbol of the superior morality of Chinese civilization. It is also a fact that women themselves did internalize the notion to the extent of voluntary self-immolation. It seems odd, though, that the prospect of rape loomed so large in the calculations. That danger from bandits and rebels was a historical reality, but the recommendation of rules to follow in the event of rape is so unusual as to point to the possibility of rape in the course of everyday life; that is, as it happens, the presumption on which some of the tales in this collection are based.

A Termagant Spared

LYXXL V 35

The wife of our tenant farmer Second Brother Cao was very fierce: at every turn she would rail against her troubles and curse the gods up hill and down dale. On the slightest provocation from her neighbours, she would roll up her sleeves to bare her arms, and flailing two laundry paddles, would jump about roaring like an angry tiger. One day she took advantage of a wet-weather break from work to slip out and steal some grain. A sudden storm blew up, hurling down hailstones as big as goose eggs with such force that they flattened her. But then out of nowhere a gust of wind whirled a wicker basket through the air to land in front of her. The basket was a big one, of five bushel size, and by putting it over her head she was able to avoid being pounded to death. Could it be that even Heaven Above feared her temper?

A witness commented: "Though she was violent and perverse, she served her mother-in-law very diligently. If she got into a fight and her mother-in-law took her to task, she would docilely desist. If her mother-in-law went so far as to slap her face, she would still submit on her knees to that punishment. Bearing that in mind, there was some justice in her surviving the peril."

Confucius said, "Filial piety is the unchanging law of Heaven and code of Earth." Does not this story go to show that?

* * *

The above quotation is not found in the Lun yu *(Confucian Analects), but such a formulation does occur in the* Classic of Filial Piety.

Prodigious Piety

GWTZ II 5

When I was about eleven years old, I heard my father's cousin Canruo tell this story.

A local man named Qi had been exiled for criminality to the northern frontier province of Heilongjiang, where he had died. Several years later his son, now grown up, wanted to fetch his remains home, but was too poor to undertake the journey. He wore a perpetual frown, as if something was deeply troubling him. Eventually he got hold of a small sack of beans, ground them into flour, mixed in water, and moulded the dough into pills, which he coated with a mixture of red clay. He then set off in the guise of a hawker of remedies, hoping to con enough small change out of people to save from starving on his journey. However, some of his customers immediately recovered from even acute illnesses, and the word went round. He then got a very good price for his pills, which was more than enough to see him all the way to the frontier outpost. There he collected his father's bones, loaded them into a wicker basket, and set off home, basket on back.

When he got to the ancient forest on the border of Heilongjiang and Jilin, he ran into three outlaws. He abandoned his money belt to them and fled with his basket. The outlaws caught up with him, opened the basket, and in their surprise asked him what he was about. He tearfully told them his story. The outlaws took pity on him and released him, giving him some of their own silver into the bargain. As he knelt on the ground to express his thanks, one of the outlaws pounded his chest and stamped his feet in an agony of remorse, saying:

"A puny weakling like him can come thousands of miles to retrieve his father's bones. Do you suppose a big strong man like me, who thinks himself a hero, can't measure up to him? You two make out as best you can; for me, I'm off now to Gansu."

So saying, he gave a wave and headed west, towards where his own father's bones lay. His fellows called after him that he should first say goodbye to his wife, but he did not look back, such was the strength of his feeling.

Sadly, when this faithful son passed on, his death made few ripples, and his deed has not been celebrated. When I put together my previous collections, I had forgotten about him. On the third day of the third month in the fifty-eighth year of the Qianlong reign [1793], when I was on duty in the Haidian district, he happened to come to mind, and so I here fill this gap in local history. It might be that his shade was not at rest because his private act of virtue had not been acknowledged, and it subtly activated my subconscious mind!

A Martyr to Chastity Pleas for Justice
RSWW I 2

My childhood tutor Mr Xu Nanjin contributed this.

In the fifty-fourth year of the Kangxi reign [1715], I crossed the river Man in Fucheng county. The going was heavy because of summer rain, and my horse was on its last legs. I rested under a tree by the roadside, and found myself nodding off. I was dimly aware of a woman approaching and making herself known:

"I am the wife of Huang Baoning, née Tang. I was set upon in this place by a gang of vicious brutes. I fought against them to my last breath, but died from my many stab wounds. Although the authorities caught and executed the villains, I was not honoured for my defence of my virtue because my body had been defiled. In consideration of my martyrdom, the courts of the dead allowed me to stay here and head a band of lost souls who had died a violent death. That was all of forty years ago.

"Imagine a poor beggar woman, driven by poverty from her home, and all alone on the road, suddenly face to face with three strong men who grabbed hold of her, tied her to a tree, and raped and lacerated her. What could she do, beyond cursing those beasts and praying to die? My submission to debauch was due to my strength being unequal, not to my defence of my chastity being faint-hearted. Yet the investigating magistrate condemned me out of hand, a gross injustice!

"You, sir, appear to be a learned gentleman, so should know right from wrong. I beg you to clear my name."

I was about to ask the woman's native place, but my dream abruptly ended at that point. Afterwards I enquired of the local gentry if they knew of this incident, but none had heard of it. Then I asked some old clerks in the yamen, but they could find no mention of it in their files. Probably she was not regarded as a martyr to chastity, so her memory had been obliterated.

* * *

In fact Ji Xiaolan at the very end of his life made a successful recommendation to the throne for virtuous women who died in such circumstances to be honoured along with those who killed themselves before they were raped. His old tutor's implied wish was granted.

A Widow Woman
HXZZ IV 61

Old Mrs Ni of Wuqing county near Tianjin was widowed before the age of thirty. Her parents-in-law wanted to marry her off, but she swore she would rather kill herself. In their anger they drove her out, and let her fend for herself. Despite being in dire straits and without a home of her own, she managed to bring up two sons and one daughter, but none of them amounted to much. Forlorn and forsaken, she had only a grand-daughter who had become a nun to turn to, and she depended on the convent's charity to keep body and soul together. This year she is seventy-eight years old. She is a classic example of a woman making a vow of constancy in her youth and maintaining that vow into ripe old age. I sympathized with her steadfastness, and often helped her out. My lady wife once asked me in passing, "You are President of the Board of Rites, in charge of honouring chaste women, yet you overlook this old lady who is in front of your nose. Why is that, I wonder?"

I replied: "The state institutions all have their rules and procedures. In the case of faithful wives and chaste women, colleges jointly put forward names to the local authorities, the local authorities draw up a list to submit to the province, the provincial administration presents a memorial to the throne for approval, and this is passed down to the Board of Rites, where each case is judged on its merits. The board may scrutinize, accept and reject, but may not seek out and introduce candidates on its own behalf, in order to prevent partiality and inflating of numbers. It is similar to the state examinations, where the supervisors have the authority to pass or fail candidates on the basis of their scripts, but cannot confer a degree on persons of talent who have not taken the examination.

"This old lady left her home district ages ago, so no one there would propose her. Neither would anyone know of this lone widow lost in the floating population of this teeming capital. That would be the explanation for this 'pearl lying undiscovered in the bosom of the sea'. If I had been able to do so, how could I have failed to recommend her?"

From time immemorial it has been the tellers of tales who have brought to notice remarkable persons whom history's annals have neglected. So I have sketched in an outline of her life, and included it in this miscellany. Though my basic intention was to record paranormal happenings, and to include it breaks the pattern, yet it does not deviate from my overall purpose of promoting moral edification.

Martyrs for Their Men
RSWW II 30

The marvels of female virtue and self-sacrifice performed by unknown and unsung women are surely uncountable! The Honourable Geng Zhongmin told my late father of one such.

"In the turmoil of the last days of the Ming dynasty, a cutthroat saw that the husband of a couple fleeing the disorder seemed to be carrying a heavy purse, and pursued them with drawn weapon. All of a sudden the wife turned round and stood stock still, waiting for the cutthroat to catch up, when she clasped him in a tight embrace. He hacked at her with his blade; her blood gushed out in a torrent, but she did not loosen her grip. By the time her strength gave out and she dropped dead, her husband had got clean away. Regrettably, I did not learn her name."

The Honourable Liu Wuyuan gave another example:

"The famine in the five provinces north of the Yellow River at the end of the Ming dynasty was so bad that people were killed and sold for their flesh; the authorities were powerless to prevent it. A traveller stopped for a midday meal at a hostelry on the border of Shandong and Hebei. A naked woman was stretched out on a chopping board, her hands and feet bound. Water was just being fetched to wash her down. The sight of her trembling in terror was unbearable. The traveller was moved to pity, and redeemed her for twice her body price. He released her bonds, and while helping her to dress his hand touched her breast. The young woman turned on him in fury, saying: 'You have given my life back to me, sir, and I would not object to serving you in the most menial of tasks. But while I am willing to be a drudge, to be your concubine is out of the question. It was because I refused to remarry that I was sold to this place. Why should you take it into your head to demean me so?'

"Thereupon she threw off her clothes again, and once more stretched out naked on the chopping board, closing her eyes as she prepared to be butchered. The butcher had taken against her, and carved a slice of the living flesh from her thigh. She cried out in pain, but to the bitter end gave no sign of regretting her resolve. Likewise, I am sorry I did not learn her name."

* * *

Another item in Perceptions *also tells of a "human flesh market" at the end of Ming, this time narrated by a Ji family servant. In this case the rescued woman does become the rescuer's concubine, and lives happily ever after: different class, different focus.*

In a letter to his wife (Family Letters, FLP *edition, p. 28), Ji gives a different slant to the story of the naked woman on the butcher's slab: she says she sold herself to provide for her mother-in-law. He also makes the traveller "feel" instead of "touch" the woman's breast, making it clear that the contact was not accidental. In the other story, the cutthroat stays his hand when he sees how pretty the wife is, intending to possess her. She promises to let him have his way with her if he lets her husband get away, which he does. The woman then seizes his knife and cuts her own throat.*

16

LOVE PLEDGED AND BLIGHTED

The ancient book on ritual, the Li ji, set a ground plan for religious services, social behaviour, and the proper channelling of emotions, with the object of perpetuating the way of life of a race of people. The channelling of the sexual urge was naturally into the institution of marriage, and the purpose of marriage in turn was procreation. As the link between present and future, marriages called for deliberation rather than whim: they were to be arranged by family elders, following lengthy procedures. Mutual attraction was in any case ruled out by the segregation of the sexes. This conception of marriage was sustained till the end of empire, its essence being captured in the expression qu xifu (marry [a woman as] a daughter-in-law [for parents]), rather than wife for oneself.

Among respectable people, prospective brides and grooms rarely caught more than a glimpse of their intended before the wedding ceremony. On the other hand, among the working classes where segregation was impractical, most young men and women would have been familiar with their intended before and after betrothal, allowing for affection to be stronger and the bond to be firmer. Allied to married love was the sense of commitment for life, graphically expressed in the woman's saying "Marry a chicken, stick with the chicken; marry a dog, stick with the dog", in Cantonese extended by "marry a monkey, rove all over the mountains".

That does not mean that romantic love did not get a look-in. On the contrary, Chinese opera and prose fiction were full of possibly dangerous liaisons between "brilliant men and beautiful women", where the rule was yi jian zhong qing (*enamoured on first sight*). And in real life men of great distinction made no secret of their affairs with courtesans. It is not, however, with the level of elegant dalliance that the episodes here are concerned, but with the often grim reality of life on the ground.

Broken-Hearted Young Lovers
GWTZ I 7

Ding Jin, a tenant farmer on the Dong estate, had a son to whom he had given the name of Second Ox. He also had a daughter who married a man called Cao Ning, who moved in to live with the Ding family. The two junior families worked together, and got on well together, too. Second Ox had a son named Third Treasure, his sister had a daughter whom they named Fourth Treasure, the numbers being sequential because they lived under the same roof. Those two children were born in the same year and month, only a few days separating them. The two sisters-in-law took turns in nursing and breastfeeding the boy and girl, and they were betrothed to each other while still in swaddling clothes. Besides that, Third Treasure and Fourth Treasure were very fond of one another, and as toddlers were never parted. Among these simple folk nothing was known about avoidance between the sexes, and when the children played together the grown-ups would point to one or the other and say "That's your husband, that's your wife". Though the children did not know what those words meant, they got to so think of themselves.

From the age of seven or eight the children became somewhat more knowing, but they both slept alongside their grandmother, and in no way shunned each other's company. By ill chance, successive harvests failed at the turn of the Kangxi and Yongzheng reigns [1721–1723], and Ding Jin and his wife died. Left destitute, Cao Ning drifted to Peking, but being unable to support himself there he indentured his daughter Fourth Treasure in the service of a high-placed civil servant named Chen (I don't know Chen's personal name, I only know he was a southerner). Second Ox later drifted to Peking in turn. By coincidence the Chens were looking for a houseboy also, so he too pledged his son Third Treasure to that family, at the same time forbidding him to mention that he and Fourth Treasure were betrothed.

This Mr Chen was a strict disciplinarian. He noticed that whenever Fourth Treasure was beaten, Third Treasure silently wept, and vice-versa. His suspicions thus aroused, he passed on the girl's indenture to a person named Zheng; the boy he simply dismissed. Third Treasure found another job as houseboy through the old woman who had placed him in his first job. Eventually he tracked Fourth Treasure down, and contrived to be taken on by the Zhengs. When after some days he came face to face with her, they wept in each other's arms. By this time they were in their early teens.

Mr Zheng was taken aback by this behaviour. They pretended to be brother and sister, now reunited. In view of their names being in family order, Zheng accepted that explanation. However, since the women's and men's worlds were strictly segregated in his household, they still could only exchange looks as they came and went.

With the return of good harvests, Second Ox and Cao Ning set out again to the capital to redeem their children, and after some time traced them to the Zhengs. Only then did Mr Zheng find out they were in fact engaged to be married. He was very sympathetic, and was willing to help them tie the knot; in the meantime he would continue to employ them. Unfortunately the Zheng family tutor, a certain Yan, was a doctrinaire Confucian who would not allow that times had changed. He vehemently opposed their union, saying:

"Marriage between first cousins is forbidden by the rules of propriety and also by the law of the land: Heaven will punish contravention. Although the master's intentions are good, we men of education must take on the duty of maintaining social and ethical standards. Not to stand in the way of incest and indecency is to be complicit in sin, and is conduct unbecoming to a gentleman."

He reinforced his opposition by threatening to resign. Mr Zheng was basically a mild and timid person, while the two fathers were both ignorant yokels, so to them the talk of illicit liaisons and dire punishment was alarming. Hence they backed down. Subsequently Fourth Treasure was sold as concubine to an official up in the capital awaiting appointment. Before many months passed she took ill and died. Third Treasure went out of his mind, and ran off: nobody knew how he ended up.

My informant told me, "Though Fourth Treasure was forced into marriage, I understand she disfigured herself and cried her heart out; she never had sexual relations with the intendant official. Unfortunately the details cannot be known." If that was indeed the case, then this pair of lovers will meet again, either in heaven or in a future life. They won't have closed their eyes never to see each other again. As to that fellow Yan, I can't say what prompted him to create such mischief, or what happened to him later, but the eye of Heaven is all-seeing, and no good would have come to him. The same person added: "I don't believe he really was a stickler for tradition, or that he sought good repute for his high standards. I suspect he had designs on Fourth Treasure, and wanted to possess her himself."

If so, hell was created precisely for such a person.

* * *

The letter to his younger cousin Ciliang (Family Letters, FLP edition, p. 191) telling the same story of Third Treasure and Fourth Treasure was occasioned by a similar objection to marriage between cousins in Ciliang's family, that time overridden. The bigoted tutor Yan Ziqing (his full name is given) is said in the letter to have died of a festering sore, and Third Treasure drowned himself.

The Maid Liu Qing
LYXL I 8

The rights and wrongs of any question on earth can be decided by applying the rules of propriety and the statutes of the law. Yet we have examples of persons who stay resolutely true to their own lights in defiance of propriety and law.

There was a serving maid in the household of a gentleman belonging to my own circle. Her name was Liu Qing. At the age of only seven or eight her master promised her in marriage to a boy servant named Yishou. When she reached her mid-teens and preparations for the formal engagement were being made, Yishou suddenly absconded because he was saddled with a gambling debt he could not pay. For a long time nothing was heard of him. Liu Qing's master then proposed to match her with another servant. She adamantly refused.

Now, Liu Qing was a very comely maid. Her master saw his chance to make advances to her, offering to make her his concubine. Again she adamantly refused. Nothing daunted, he instructed an old woman to win her round. She used the following argument:

"Since you won't give up Yishou, why don't you fall in with your master's wishes for the time being? Meanwhile the master will make every effort to trace Yishou, and when he is found he can marry you as intended. On the other hand, if you don't comply he will sell you to a buyer in some faraway place, and you will never have the chance of seeing Yishou again."

Liu Qing cried to herself for days on end before she finally submitted and agreed to sleep with her master, though she constantly urged him to continue searching for Yishou. After three or four years passed, Yishou came back of his own accord, and true to his word, her master had them married. She then resumed her former duties as a serving maid, but never spoke a word to her master. Whenever he sidled up to her she took evading action. He tried whipping her and bribing Yishou to put pressure on her, but to the last she stood fast against him. Seeing that he would get nowhere with her, he granted the couple an honourable discharge from his service.

On the eve of her departure Liu Qing presented her mistress with a casket, kowtowed, and left. The casket contained all the personal gifts her master had made her, each and every one.

Afterwards Yishou turned hawker, while Liu Qing took in sewing. It was a hard life they had together, but she never repented or repined. In the thirtieth year of the Qianlong reign [1765], when I was staying back home, Yishou called on me, still peddling brass and china ware. His hair was already white. I asked after his wife; he said she was long dead.

This was a strange case: The serving maid was neither chaste nor loose, yet at the same time both chaste and loose. I can't think how to place her, and in the end have recorded her story for enlightened men to pass judgement.

The Frustration of Married Love in Troubled Times
GWTZ I 41

Li Bo has some lines that read:

> I linger to catch the flash of the singer's fan
> Like a moon seen through clouds
> Better not to have met
> Than to meet without closeness

That is written from the point of view of a frequenter of houses of ill repute. In fact separation and estrangement can take place between ordinary husband and wife meeting on a daily basis, goodness knows by the working of what karma.

Guo Shizhou contributed this:

The mother of a certain gentleman in Henan province named Li fell sick less than two weeks after he married. He and his wife took turns looking after her. For seven or eight months they did not even take off their clothes to go to bed. After the mother died they observed strict mourning ritual, the husband not sharing the marital bed for three years.

Reduced then to poverty, the couple had to throw themselves on the mercy of the wife's family. Li's father-in-law was also only barely able to put food on the table, and his house was quite small. A back room had to be cleared out for them. Before a month was out, the mother-in-law's younger brother got a tutoring job in a distant place, and confided their mother who lived with him to his elder sister's care. The enlarged family had no spare rooms, so the only thing was for Li's wife to share a bedroom with her mother, while Li himself bedded down in the study. They came together only at the breakfast and dinner table.

After two years like this, Li went to the capital in the hope of advancing his career, while his father-in-law took his family south to Jiangxi, where he had found a post as assistant to a magistrate. Some time later, Li got a letter saying his wife had died. Li was devastated by this news, his situation went from bad to worse, and he got to the point of not being able to support himself. He then took a boat to go south in search of his father-in-law, but the latter had already moved on elsewhere in the service of a new employer. Left with no one to turn to, Li resorted to setting up a stall as a scrivener to eke out a living.

One day a burly man of masterly mien came to Li's stall in the market place, picked up a specimen of Li's writing, and said: "You write a very good hand. Would you be willing to take a job as secretary for thirty or forty ounces of silver a year?" Li was overjoyed, and immediately joined the man on his boat. They traversed mist-shrouded rivers and lakes, where Li lost all sense of direction. On arrival at his employer's island home, Li was very generously provided for, but when he saw the correspondence he had to deal with he realized his employer was an outlaw of the greenwoods. There was nothing he could do about it, so for the time being he settled down in his role. However, as a precaution against possible future trouble, he falsified his name and native place.

Li's employer was outgoing in personality and extravagant in lifestyle. He kept a harem of singing girls, who were allowed to mix rather freely with male guests. Whenever they put on a musical entertainment, Li was free to attend. One of the girls was so strikingly like his wife that he thought he must be seeing a ghost. The singing girl also shot frequent looks at Li, as if he reminded her too of somebody, but they did not venture to speak to each other.

What had happened was this: As he was in transit to his new post, Li's father-in-law's boat was boarded by this same outlaw; the outlaw noticed that Li's wife was attractive, and so took her away as part of his booty. The father-in-law thought this abduction was a great disgrace, so he hastily bought a coffin of thin plank wood, pretended that his daughter had been killed in the melee, wept false tears over the empty coffin, and took it with him on the rest of his journey. For her part, Li's wife had preferred dishonour to death, and was already established as the outlaw's concubine, which is how the two met again in this place. But Li believed his wife was dead, while his wife was unaware that he had changed his name and thought the resemblance must be a chance one: hence they were like passing strangers. As a rule they would come across each other every few days, but when that became routine they ceased to eye one another.

This state of affairs went on for six or seven years, until one day Li's employer summoned him to say:

"My activities have been uncovered. You are a bookman, and don't need to be caught up in my downfall. Here are fifty ounces of gold, my gift to you. Hide it away somewhere in the reed beds. When the soldiers withdraw, find a fishing boat as quick as you can to take you home. The people around here all know you, so you need have no fear they will turn you away."

So saying, he gestured for Li to go and hide himself. Shortly afterwards Li heard the clamour of battle raging. When it died down, he heard the order shouted: "The outlaws have all fled. Now we can impound all the valuables they have left behind, their women too."

By this time it was dark. In the light of the soldiers' torches he espied a gaggle of singing girls, half naked and with hair hanging loose, hands tied and necks roped together, being lashed to hurry them along. Among them was that particular woman; she was shaking with terror, a sight to make anyone's heart bleed.

The next day the island was deserted. Li stood in a daze at the water's edge. For a long while all was still, then a man rowing a small boat called out to him: "You're Mr X, aren't you? Our chief is safe, and he's told me to ferry you back home."

After travelling for a day and night, they got back to Li's starting point in Jiangxi. Li did not linger: afraid he might be pursued, he took off north with his gold. As it turned out, his father-in-law had preceded him, and Li stayed with him as before. He exchanged his gold for cash, and his circumstances gradually improved. He reflected sorrowfully that he and his wife had been deeply in love, yet over their ten years of marriage, from first to last they had slept together for not one whole month. Now that he was more comfortably off, he could not bear the thought of her being buried in a flimsy coffin, and he resolved to replace it with a hardwood one. Besides, he wanted to take a last look at her remains, as an act of remembrance.

His father-in-law did his utmost to dissuade him and only came out with the truth when his arguments failed. Li then repaired with all dispatch to Nanchang in Jiangxi in the hope of being reunited with his beloved wife, but the captured singing girls had long since been allocated as prizes to the victors, and there was no telling where she had ended up. Whenever he recalled that number of years on the island, when they were so near yet so far away, he was chagrined; and when he pictured her a captive tied up and being whipped along, and imagined what further suffering she was subjected to, his heart broke.

Li did not remarry; he was said to have ended his life as a monk.

My senior Ge Jiezhou commented:

"A play could be made of this man's experience. The only

pity is that there is no finale, rather like *The Peach Blossom Fan*. Though it has been said: 'When the song ends the persons fade away, but along the river the peaks stay resolutely green', yet the sad mood lingers on and on, as if one is caught up in a boundless haze. It has to be admitted, hearing this does make the world feel a bleaker place."

Love in a Penal Colony
RSWW II 57

The convict Peng Qi, transported to Changji in the wilds of the Western Regions, had a daughter of sixteen who like her mother suffered from consumption. The mother passed away first, and the daughter was in the terminal stage of the disease. Peng had to plough government land, and could not look after his daughter. He therefore abandoned her in a wood, and left her to her fate. The girl's whimpering was harrowing: no one who saw her was not moved to pity. A fellow transportee named Yang Xi said to Peng:

"You are so heartless, I can hardly believe it! I'm willing to carry her back to my hut and nurse her. If she dies I will bury her, if she lives I will take her to wife."

Peng replied: "That's fine by me," and signed a note of consent on the spot.

Half a year went by, and all hope of recovery was lost. On her deathbed the young woman said to Yang:

"I am deeply grateful for your noble deed. Because my father freely gave consent to our union, we have shared the greatest intimacy without fear of disrepute, and you have massaged and caressed my body free from inhibition. But weak and wasted by illness as I am, you have never been able to enjoy your conjugal rights, and that weighs on my conscience. If there is no afterlife, there is nothing more to say. If there is awareness after death, I will certainly find a way to repay your kindness."

She gave a sob and expired. Yang Xi tearfully buried her.

Afterwards he dreamed every night of her coming to his bed, amorous and playful, just like a living woman, though when he woke up there was no trace of her presence. When he lay awake at night and called her, she never came; but as soon as his eyes closed in sleep, she appeared, stripped off her clothes and offered herself to him. This went on for some time, and Yang Xi was aware while he dreamed that he was in fact dreaming, so he questioned her as to why she would not make herself manifest. She replied:

"I learned from the other ghosts that living beings belong to the yang element and ghosts to the yin. If the yin trespasses on the yang, the living will be harmed. It is only when living beings hold in their yang and enter into the sphere of yin in sleep that they can meet with ghosts. As long as this is an encounter of spirits and not a joining of flesh, no harm will come of it."

This took place in the thirty-second year of the Qianlong reign [1767], and four years had passed by the spring of the thirty-sixth year, when I was recalled to the capital. I lost touch then, and don't know how the story ended. Gan Bao's *In Search of Spirits* [fourth century AD] records how Lu Chong's brief union with a maiden in the nether world resulted in a son being born, while much farther back Song Yu wrote in his prose-poem that the King of Chu just the once had congress with the goddess of Mount Wu. As for a couple coming together every day, but only in dreams, that has rarely if ever been recorded in our literature.

So Near Yet So Far
HXZZ II 17

I heard this story from one of my clerks when I was Director of Education for Fujian province.

During the Yongzheng reign [1723–1736] a concubine of the then director died from a fall from a tower. In the absence of any other known cause, it was assumed that she had simply lost her balance. It was only a long time later that the true story came out. Apparently the concubine came from Shandong province. She married a boy from a poor family around the age of fourteen. They soon found they were very compatible, and became inseparable. Then a famine came, the family were unable to support themselves and her mother-in-law sold her to a trafficker in women. The girl clung to her young husband and wept the whole night long. When the time came for her to leave, the couple bit their arms to mark their bond in blood.

The husband could not bear being parted, and set off to follow the trafficker, begging as he went. By walking day and night he managed to catch up with them, and shadowed their cart all the way to the capital. From time to time they came within sight of each other, their eyes met, but being young and timid, and fearful of being cursed and shouted at, the husband did not dare approach: they could only gaze at one another and wipe away their tears. After the girl was installed in the house of a professional matchmaker, the boy stationed himself at her gate. Once he was lucky enough to talk to her: together they vowed not to take their own lives, hoping against hope that one day they might be reunited.

Later on the boy learned that his wife had been bought by the said Director of Education to be his concubine. He then engaged himself as bondservant to one of the director's private secretaries. In this way they both arrived in Fujian. But the women's quarters in the yamen being strictly segregated, they had no contact with each other, and the wife did not even know her husband was there.

Eventually the young husband fell ill and died. His wife heard from the women servants' gossip the name, age, native place and appearance of the dead man: she realized then that it was her husband they were talking about. At the time she was sitting at the top of one of the twin towers flanking the yamen; she stood up and for what seemed ages stayed rooted to the spot. All of a sudden she blurted out her whole story to those around her. At its end she uttered some long wailing sounds, and leapt to her death. The director ordered the matter hushed up, so no news of what had happened got out.

Actually the director had nothing to be ashamed of. Generally speaking, there are two causes for a woman to kill herself in order to keep faith with her husband. The first is to uphold the social contract, preferring death over shame: that is based on the ethical code. The second is to drag out an ignoble existence, clinging to the last breath of life in the hope of at long last being reunited. Only when hope dies and the sands run out does she kill herself in order to show where her heart lies. That derives from emotional attachment.

In this case, the woman did not die while in the hands of the trafficker, nor in the house of the matchmaker; she died on hearing of her former husband's demise, namely after her body was sullied and her virtue tarnished, which one could say was late in the day. But her resolve to die had long since been taken, it was just that her love lingered on, and she could not bring herself to call quits. She did not look on her clinging to life in defiance of convention as a slight to her husband's love; her only thought was that to give up on even the slimmest chance of reunion would be to let him down. To sigh over her misfortune, to pity her resolve, to regret her surrender to her feelings, would be admissible; to take the moralizing high ground and censure these unlettered young people, would show a deplorable lack of charity.

A Potential Opera?
RSWW III 14

In the fourth and fifth years of the Yongzheng reign [1726–1727] refugees from famine begged their way to Cui Village, where my family live. A husband and wife among them came down with an epidemic disease. As their death approached they held up a deed of sale in the marketplace, pleading to sell their daughter as a maidservant for the price of their two coffins. My late grandmother took the girl in so that her parents could get a decent burial. She named the girl Liangui. The deed named the father as Zhang Li and gave the mother's maiden name as Huang, but their place of origin was not stated; by the time they were asked for it they were already incapable of speech. Liangui herself said they came from Shandong province, and their house was on a post road along which passed the carriages of high officials, but could not name the county. All she could say was they had been on the road for a month or more. She added that the previous year she had been betrothed to a boy named Hu who lived opposite them; the Hu family had also taken to the road, and she did not know where they had ended up.

Over a decade passed without any relatives coming to ask after Liangui, so she was married off to a stable boy named Liu Deng. Deng's own story was that he was from Xintai county in Shandong, and was originally surnamed Hu. He was taken in by a family called Liu on the death of his parents, and had adopted their name. When he was small he had heard that his parents had betrothed him to a girl, but he did not know what her family name was. Since Liu Deng was originally a Hu, and there was a post road that passed through Xintai county, and also the time it would have taken refugees to beg their way to Cui Village was about a month, his story tallied with Liangui's. So there were strong grounds for suspecting that fate had first parted then reunited this young couple, as in the fable a broken mirror is made whole again, though there was no clear proof.

My late uncle Lifu commented:

"With some slight ornamentation their story could actually have made a good play. The trouble is, this girl is as dumb as an ox; her horizons don't go beyond good meals and sound sleep. It's a pity, but she's just not up to ornamenting."

The distinguished private scholar Bian Lianbao was present. He responded by citing past examples of distortion of true personalities in literature, and concluded:

"Even our historical works are not free from embroidery, let alone our operas. Yuan Yuling's opera *West Tower*, for instance, portrays the courtesan Mu Suhui as of unearthly beauty, but Wu Lintang claims his grandfather saw her when he was a boy, and reckoned she was squat and plump, a very common looking woman. From that we can infer that the raving beauties of operas are mostly products of the imagination. So though this servant girl may be lumpish, if some busybody writes the right words to the right tunes, the orchestra strikes up and the arias performed, who can tell if on the stage she won't be acclaimed as a gorgeous and seductive female? I'm afraid your trouble, sir, is that you believe what you read in books is true."

17

FRIENDS AND FALSE FRIENDS

Friendship has not been neglected as a topic for essayists in the West, but not as highly honoured as it was in China, where it was elevated to a place among the Five Cardinal Relationships. Confucius, not a man to use words lightly, is quoted in the Analects *as saying: "Is it not a great pleasure to greet friends from afar?", to which his disciple Mencius later added: "The mark of friendship is trustfulness." Loyalty to friends is a major theme in Chinese history and literature; when sanctified by the oath of blood brotherhood it overrides obligations to family, as most famously exemplified in the classic novel* Sanguozhi yanyi *(Romance of the Three Kingdoms). It is, however, a more qualified statement of Confucius that Ji Xiaolan quotes in a letter to his eldest son, one which warns that friendship with the upright, reliable and knowledgeable is beneficial, but friendship with the devious, sycophantic and empty-headed is harmful. The former kinds are not much in evidence in* Perceptions.

Friends

GWTZ III 27

Mr Zhang Shilin was my father's old friend and fellow graduate. In character he was blunt and outspoken, given to criticizing people to their face. On the other hand he set great store by keeping faith: he stood up for his friends, being willing to take trouble and risk hostility on their behalf. He once dreamt of a deceased friend angrily accusing him thus:

"You served two terms as prefect, during which time you provided for all the sons and grandsons of old friends who had come down in the world. Yet when my son travelled a thousand miles to appeal to you for help, you treated him as a stranger. How can you justify that?"

Mr Zhang was both angered and amused. He replied:

"You have a bad memory. How can friendship be about attaching yourself to people to promote your interests, or fraternizing out of a taste for roistering? Friendship is about standing by one another in a crisis, and sticking together through thick and thin. I remind you of the time my bondsmen leagued together to suck me dry; their solidarity was so impregnable I was helpless against them. I looked upon you as a brother, and privately asked you to investigate a certain person. You personally observed his skulduggery, but out of fear of attracting suspicion and incurring a grudge you kept from me what you had found out. When that person brought about his own downfall by his excessive greed, you sought to win a name for magnanimity by pleading for clemency. You gave no thought to whether or not my career was ruined or my fortune dissipated, you just sought to earn the gratitude of those slaves and make them look up to you as their patron. Was that not to show generosity to exactly the wrong parties? You treated me as a stranger then, yet you now blame me for the same fault. You do have a bad memory, don't you?"

Mr Zhang's accuser withdrew, deflated.

This happened all of fifty years ago. To generalize, there is a deplorable convention among the cultured elite to think that not to speak ill of others makes you a gentleman, regardless of the ties of friendship or degree of harm to the persons involved. To draw on my own experience, I saw Hu Muting so exploited by his gang of servants that he could barely keep himself in food and clothing. His Hanlin colleague Zhu Zhujun boldly took matters into his own hands and drove away those servants, so managing to restore some stability to Muting's existence.

On another occasion, after Chen Yuzhai died, his widowed concubine and orphans were cruelly used by his son-in-law. Cao

Mutang, the Vice-Director of the Imperial Clan Court and fellow graduate with Chen, rounded up their old friends, drove out the son-in-law, and the children were given back their lives. In the general opinion of the time, those who thought Chen's friends acted in the best tradition numbered not more than one or two in a hundred, while those who thought they unnecessarily interfered made up eight or nine out of ten.

To cite another case, Cui Yingjie, President of the Censorate, had a grandson who was about to be married, and wanted to hire a decorated palanquin to deliver the bride to the family house. His household servants connived to set the cost at 300 taels: they were adamant that nothing less would secure one. One or two days before the ceremony, the asking price was doubled. Mr Cui was furious, and besought his friends to hire one for him, bypassing his servants. To avoid getting into the servants' bad books, none of them complied. They even alleged there was no fixed price for hire of decorated palanquins: it could go up or down according to the wealth and standing of the hirer; and furthermore the palanquins were not allowed to be rented in someone else's name. That excuse was the friends' ingenious way of holding to the middle ground. In the end Cui had no alternative but to have his own sedan chair decorated and used for the occasion. In the public opinion of the time, those who thought it was wrong to sit tight and look on were again not more than one or two in a hundred, while those who thought his friends fairly judged his servants' interests again numbered eight or nine out of ten.

So we have two opposing standards of right and wrong. Which side should we come down on?

Blowing Hot and Cold
LYXL III 16

A pupil of mine was appointed county magistrate in Yunnan province. His means being very slender, he made the long and arduous journey with only a younger son and one manservant. After reaching the provincial capital, he had a long wait before a post became vacant. This was in central Yunnan, actually a very fertile region, but very distant from the provincial seat. Moreover, his family back home lived in a village off the beaten track, which made the exchange of letters very difficult. Occasionally he found someone to carry a letter for him, but inevitably such letters were unlikely to reach their destination, so he was practically cut off from his wife and children. It was only from the annual gazetteer of serving officials that they learned he had been appointed to a certain county.

This magistrate discovered in the course of his duties that a crafty yamen servant had been feathering his own nest. He had him beaten and dismissed, thus incurring the servant's bitter hatred. This servant knew all there was to know about the magistrate's family affairs; he proceeded to fake a letter from the magistrate's manservant telling those back home that his master had died, followed by his son, and their coffins temporarily rested in a Buddhist temple; the family were asked to take out a loan to have the coffins shipped back home. At the same time he concocted a will whose provisions showed convincing knowledge of the magistrate's family affairs.

To begin with, the magistrate's circle of relatives and friends thought that because of his plain and hesitant way of speaking a vacancy would not come his way, and if it did, it would be a bad one. Only when they heard he got this plum posting did they become more pleasant and accommodating, some helping the family out in time of need, some offering gifts and kind regards. Were the son of the house to request a loan, there would be willing suppliers, and sons and daughters were betrothed to the magistrate's family members. His sons never failed to receive invitations to local banquets.

However, when news of the magistrate's death came in this letter, expectations were dashed. Some people expressed their condolences, others did not. By and by debts were called in, people started passing as strangers in the street, household servants left one after another. Before many months passed, no one was calling at their door.

At that point, a colleague of the magistrate was returning to the capital to report on his tour of duty, and the magistrate entrusted to him a sum of 1,200 taels to pay for his family to join him in Yunnan. Not until then was the previous letter known to be a forgery. The family's tears turned to laughter, and they felt they were in dreamland. The circle of relatives and friends to some extent regrouped, though quite a number did not dare show their face again.

In a later letter to his circle, the magistrate observed:

"It is a common experience for one's standing to fall from high to low, and one's condition to rise from poor to rich. But I am probably the first person to go from perfectly well to suddenly dead, from being dead for the best part of a year to return to life, and learn the fickleness of favour in the process!"

ADDENDUM: Ji Xiaolan's letter to his wife (*Family Letters*, FLP edition, p. 143)

It is better for the master of a house to treat his servants leniently, rather than lord it over them. The servant class are not educated in what is right and proper: when reprimanded they think of getting their own back, and because they lack a sense of proportion, their victims may find themselves in terrible trouble. Our children have now assumed the manner of the spoilt brats of official stock, bossing the servants about as if they were workhorses. If the servants are a little dilatory, they are immediately hauled up and castigated unmercifully. Generally speaking, if at home one constantly hears the sound of both men and women servants being cursed, it will bode ill for that family's prospects; besides that, as the servants' resentment builds up, they are bound to plot revenge.

Take the case of my student Li Xiaomei. He was assigned a magistrate's post in Yunnan province. Being of humble origin, he took only one son and one servant with him. After a long wait in the provincial capital a vacancy finally came up, and his circumstances gradually improved. The only thing was, his family home was in a backwoods village in the southeast, so letters hardly got through, and eventually he practically lost contact with his wife.

His servant started swindling expenses. Li's son found out and accused him to his face, and when the servant stubbornly denied he was at fault, the son was even more angered. He rushed to tell his father, and the upshot was the servant was beaten and dismissed, thus engendering his bitter hate.

The servant knew all there was to know about his master's affairs. He forged a letter announcing the death of father and son in an epidemic, saying that their coffins were temporarily lodged in a Buddhist temple: funds should be raised to have them transported home. He added exact details of Li's last words on how family dispositions were to be made. Li's wife wept copiously on receiving this dread news, and urgently set about raising the money to go to Yunnan to bring back the coffins. However, social favour blows hot and cold: despite being hard up, she normally could still borrow from relatives to tide her over, but after her husband's death was known, let alone lending to her, her creditors actually pressed for repayment. When she went the round of relatives, she was treated with nothing but disdain. Every day her tears served only to wash her face.

By coincidence a colleague and fellow provincial with Xiaomei was returning home to observe mourning for a parent, so Xiaomei entrusted him with delivering 1,500 taels of silver to his wife. Only then did she discover that the letter had been a deception; naturally her tears turned to smiles.

I got a letter from Xiaomei the year before last, remarking that there are many cases of the mighty being abruptly humbled and of men suddenly going from rags to riches, but he alone had gone from being alive to suddenly being dead, and then reappearing to his wife like one reborn.

It was that fit of anger on the part of Li's son which led to his mother's unwarranted distress: indeed, if that colleague had not gone home, even her life would have been in the balance. Though it is true that the servant deserved to be punished, the son also cannot be absolved from blame. Please have the children read this letter, so that they can learn from the younger Li's mistake. If a servant is caught embezzling, he should simply be dismissed, not thrashed. This is fundamental to family governance!

18

PERSONAL

A Very Personal Obituary
HXZZ II 12

Possibly originating in Ji Xiaolan's own references to his concubines in his writings, apocryphal stories later accrued about his sexual appetite and prowess. In any case, a literary man with some claim to genius and afflatus was quite expected to have his due share of sensual pleasure (significantly, the term fengliu, *applied to such charismatic persons, included amorousness in its range of meaning). One oft-quoted story had the emperor himself presenting Ji with two girls from his own harem in recognition of this side of his make-up. While that story cannot be granted credence, it is true that Ji's acquisition of concubines started early and finished late in his life. He had six concubines in all, and seems not to have denied himself the enjoyment of maids. However, he did form a bond of genuinely matrimonial trust and affection for the two of his concubines about whom much is known. They were his second concubine Guo Caifu, taken in 1748, when he was twenty-four, and his fourth concubine Shen, whom he named Minggan (Bright Gem), the subject of the obituary that follows. She was taken when Ji was aged fifty.*

Guo Caifu came from a Shanxi family that had washed up in Tianjin. She entered the Ji household at the age of thirteen. Her only surviving child was a daughter. It was this daughter who married a grandson of Lu Jianzeng, the family connection which led to Ji being exiled to Chinese Turkestan, as described in the Introduction to this book. During Ji's exile, when Guo Caifu shared the household management with Madam Ma, she went down with a debilitating illness; she survived to rejoice in his return in early 1771, but died in the autumn of that year, aged thirty-six. Ji wrote a wistful poem mourning her demise.

* * *

I gave the name Bright Gem to my concubine Shen. Her forebears came from Changzhou in Jiangsu province, and had drifted north to my home region of Hejian, where her father raised his family, she being the second of his two daughters. She was bright and clear-minded, quite unlike the typical common girl. She confided to her elder sister, "I couldn't marry a farm hand. Of course I would never be considered a suitable wife for the high and mighty, but do you think I might suit as a concubine for some distinguished person?" Her mother got wind of her idea, and finally agreed to let her have her way.

Being natively sensitive and discreet, she never crossed anyone. When first wedded to me, she paid her respects to my lady wife, Madam Ma. Madam Ma said, "I understand it was your own wish to be a concubine. I should advise you, though, that is not an easy thing to be."

Bright Gem bobbed a curtsey, replying, "It is only difficult to be a concubine if one is unwilling. Since I *am* willing, I can't imagine any difficulty." Consequently Madam Ma treated her from first to last as a favourite daughter.

Bright Gem once said to me, "Women ought to die before the age of forty, when people will still mourn their passing. I don't want to hang on till I wear black dress and have white hair, a nobody who people don't want to be around." In the end she got her wish: she passed away on the twenty-fifth day of the fourth month of the fifty-sixth year of the Qianlong reign [1791], at the age of only thirty.

To begin with she was barely literate, but as she accompanied me while I sorted through books and papers, by and by she got a rough idea of what they said, and also could compose simple poems. Shortly before her death she gave her daughter a little portrait of herself, at the same time reciting a poem which she asked me to write down for her. It ran:

> Thirty years have passed like a dream
> I hand my likeness to my daughter to keep
> When they speak of my life in time to come
> She can trace the features of Miss Shen from old Suzhou.

Then she quietly passed away.

Just when her illness became critical, I was serving in the Yuanmingyuan, and slept at my Acacia Lodge in the Haidian district. One night I saw Bright Gem twice in muddled dreams, and thought it was simply due to my missing her. It was not until later that I learned she had swooned away the same night, and only regained consciousness after about four hours. She said then to her mother: "Just now I was transported in dream to that villa in Haidian. I was woken up by a crash like a thunderclap." Thinking back on that night, it actually happened that the string of a copper pitcher hanging from a hook on the wall broke, and it fell with a crash. So it was true that her living soul had made the journey there.

I inscribed two little poems on her portrait to commemorate this event:

> In some ways like, in some ways not
> Was that your sweet soul rejoining me that night?
> One glimpse caught of fond times gone
> Dimmed was the shape that drew me most.

And:

> The dying silkworm still has thread to spin
> The maiden need not doubt her soul had taken wing
> A sudden noise jolts her from lulling dream
> Just when I hear the copper pitcher drop.

My Faithful Dog

LYXXL V 40

I kept a number of dogs when I was in Urumqi. In the thirty-sixth year of the Qianlong reign [1771] I was graciously recalled from banishment, and set out on my journey back east. A black dog I called Quattro tagged along after me, refusing to be driven away. In the end he stayed with me all the way to Peking. Quattro guarded my trunks very closely, not allowing even my servants to open them unless I was on the spot. If anyone approached them, his hackles would rise and he would growl threateningly. During our crossing of the Bizhan Mountains (this range, with its seven ridges, twisting trails and sheer cliffs, forms a natural bulwark), two of my carts had got over a ridge when darkness fell, leaving the other two stranded on the other side. This dog took his stand on the crest of the ridge, keeping a watchful eye on the carts in both directions. When he caught any movement, he would rush over and investigate.

I composed two verses for him:

> Now relieved of the job of taking my letters
> You share the rigours of life on the road
> While servants snore at dead of night
> You stay alert to guard our wagons.

And:

> Crossing bare mountains has worn you thin
> Nothing but icy rock-strewn tracks
> What have I to offer, out of office?
> Your trouble is, you're too dumbly devoted.

One dark night a year after we were back in the capital, Quattro died of poisoning. Someone opined: "The servants resented the dog keeping too strict a night watch, and used a lure of poisoned meat to kill it, putting the blame on burglars." I thought that must be the answer. I had the dog buried, intending to raise a mound over its grave with the headstone to read "Here lies the faithful dog Quattro", and alongside it have stone figures carved to represent the four servants who had accompanied me in exile, kneeling before the grave, with their names incised on their chests, to wit: Zhao Changming, Yu Lu, Liu Chenggong and Qi Laiwang. But the same person objected, "I fear the dog would disdain the company of those four slaves!" So I desisted, contenting myself with hanging a board over the gate of the servant quarters that read: "A pack fit to take lessons from a dog".

To backtrack to the occasion when Mr Zhai, holder of the master's degree, made a present of the dog to me, I had dreamt the previous night of my servant Song Yu, then deceased, kowtowing to me, saying, "Considering that you, my master, have been seconded to the army a thousand miles away, I have come to enlist." Since I got this dog the very next day, I am quite sure he was a reincarnation of Song Yu. The strange thing was, Song Yu was first and foremost among my servants in deceit and connivance, so how come he was loyal and honest as a dog? Could it be that he was conscious of having been demoted to a canine existence because of his many sins, and had reformed out of contrition? If so, I would have to concede his good deeds more than made up for his previous faults.

The End of an End
RSWW I 25

The bibliophile Qian Zeng noted in the catalogue of his books that the descendants of Chao Qimei, another famous book collector, sold off his rare volumes when he died, a sacrilege which provoked the spirits of his native Wukang Mountain to wail in broad daylight. Seeing that whatever is assembled must be dispersed, why not take a more philosophical view?

After the death of Zhang Luan, father of the consort of the Ming dynasty Emperor Xiaozong, his estate in Hebei province was broken up, leaving only its main hall standing. Eventually my late grandfather bought the building for its timbers. On the day it was demolished, the workmen heard weeping coming from the pillars. So it seems that down the ages the sentimental spirits all take after each other.

I observed to Dong Qujiang:

"The Buddhists consider that even the mountains and rivers of the great earth are figments of the imagination, so of what consequence are we puny humans? After my life is done, if my books, curios and antiques are scattered, and come into the hands of connoisseurs who fondle them and say, 'This once belonged to Ji Xiaolan,' that would make a good story. I'd have no regrets at all!"*

Qujiang replied, "What you say shows that you still care about your name carrying on. I take the view that indeed one has to turn to such things as you mention to beguile one's leisure time, but when you yourself cease to exist, what else is left to lose? Let those things go to fill the stomachs of bookworms and rodents, or sink into the soil. Therefore I stamp no seals on my books, carve no inscriptions on my inkstones. To draw a parallel, when I come upon fine flowers and bright moons, grand mountains and living waters, I own them; when they pass out of my vision, I do not ask who they belong to. Similarly there is no point in engraving my name or writing my signature with the object of being remembered later."

His view is still less encumbered than my own.

---

* For the kind of "curios and antiques" that scholars like Ji Yun would have collected, see Figure 7 on p. xxxix.

Part IV
A Mirror on Society

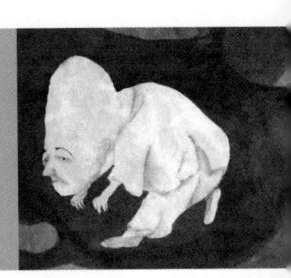

19

DOGMA AND DOGMATISTS

It must have been coincidental that an intellectual sea change occurred in China at roughly the same time as one occurred in Europe, yet it did happen. In China it took the form of a shift from "Song Learning" to "Han Learning"; in Europe it was called the Reformation. The nature of the change was similar, too: a reversion from the sophistication, scholasticism and abstract dogma of latter-day authorities and theologians to the simple truths and plain talk of prophets and core texts: in Europe the Bible, in China the Confucian classics.

To turn to Chinese specifics, Song Learning refers to the Neo-Confucian philosophers who accounted for the origin and nature of the world by devising a scheme which appealed to the rational mind, namely one of universal patterning principles (li) ordering the inchoate stuff of the material world (qi). The superior principles derived from Heaven and were incontestably good; lodged in the mind, they guided proper thought and conduct. The stuff of physical matter derived from Earth and was responsible for human passions and base instincts, and therefore had to be guarded against. Perception of and accordance with the higher moral principles depended on disciplined introspection, which went along with the suppression of desires: in a word, there was seen to be a potential conflict between mind and body.

Song Learning continued to dominate the succeeding Ming dynasty. It was the decline and fall of the Ming which prompted a number of intellectuals whose life spanned the transition to the Qing dynasty to seek an alternative. In their view, the head-in-air intellectual climate created by Song Learning had greatly contributed to the downfall, the focus having been on what should be rather than what was, to the detriment of attention to practical matters. The answer was to return to the down-to-earth concerns and simple ethical principles of early Confucianism, as summed up in the historically-oriented scholarship of the Han dynasty—hence the "Han Learning" tag.

Now Ji Xiaolan lived in the middle of the Qing dynasty, and quite early in their occupation the Manchu rulers had sought to establish their cultural legitimacy by reaffirming the supremacy of Song Learning: the Song philosopher Zhu Xi was enthroned as the supreme arbiter of ethical and intellectual matters. Nevertheless, Han Learning remained as a powerful undercurrent. By pursuing its ends through historical, philological and scientific channels it subtly undermined many of the claims and pretensions of Song Learning. The scorn for Song astronomy expressed by Ji's former teacher below is an example. The robustly down-to-earth attitude of looking facts in the face taken by Ji's father, as exemplified in his many appearances in this collection, must also have been a strong influence on our author. But perhaps the most influential of all in fostering Ji's doubt that Neo-Confucianism had all the answers was his friendship with the extraordinary polymath Dai Zhen (1724–1777), whom Ji appointed tutor to his children in 1755 and who later joined him in editing the imperial Compendium in 1773. Dai Zhen dispensed with the duality of "principle" and "matter", and denied the conflict between mind and body. Indeed he embraced the fundamental instincts represented by the desire for food, sexual pleasure and procreation as the natural order of things; to him the higher propensities towards sympathy, justice, decency and the like were in fact extensions of those fundamental instincts, developed from recognizing the same rights to those things in others. When desires are wrong and harmful, it is because of selfishness.

That is the conceptual background for the pieces that follow. Ji Xiaolan was no ideological rebel. He subscribed to conventional social values and practices, accepted class distinctions, had a limited view of human rights. But he also had a store of sympathy and recognized injustice where it occurred. In his old age, when this collection was compiled, he could also look back with some independence, and express his frustrations, his impatience with the folly of pointless factionalism, and his distaste for the bigotry and evils of religious intolerance endemic in his competitive society. We conclude with the sad story of how such bigotry destroyed the lives of two innocent youths.

ON THE THREE TEACHINGS
LYXXL IV 44

This is one of Ji Xiaolan's many explorations of belief. It probably reflects the consensus among liberal intellectuals regarding the relative merits of Confucianism, Buddhism and Taoism.

* * *

One hot summer night Ma Dahuan of Dongguang slept naked in the library of the Zisheng Monastery, where the sutras were kept. He was awoken by someone jogging his arm and saying, "Get up, get up! Do not defile the sutras!"

An old man was standing beside him. Ma asked, "Who are you?"

"I am the custodian god of the sutras."

Ma Dahuan was a bluff and downright sort of person, not easily frightened. Outside the moon was shining as bright as day; he invited the old man to sit down and discuss the matter. He asked, "For what reason, good sir, do you guard the sutras?"

"At the order of Heaven."

"Our bookshelves groan under the weight of Confucian works, yet I have not heard of gods guarding them. Could it be that Heaven favours Buddhist sutras?"

"The Buddha's teachings belong to the divine sphere. The common man may disbelieve as well as believe, so there is a divinity to protect Buddhist scriptures. The Confucian teachings belong to the human sphere; mankind in general should respect them, and indeed knows they should be respected, hence there is no call for the agency of a god. It is not a matter of favour being shown to the Buddhist scriptures."

"Should I take it then that Heaven regards the Three Teachings as on a par?"

"Confucianism has self-improvement as its core, and governance as its practical function. Taoism has quietude as its core, and passive influence as its practical function. Buddhism has meditation as its core, and compassion as its practical function. Their purposes are divergent, so they cannot be seen as one. Yet in teaching people to do good they do not differ. Neither do they differ in providing sustenance to all living beings. Given this similarity in end result, Heaven truly must allow all three to coexist. However, Confucianists aim to create a good life for the people, and exemplify their philosophy in their own conduct. Buddhism and Taoism are self-motivated schools of thought, and their adherents only secondarily extend their energies to others. Therefore, preaching the way of humanity takes precedence, and preaching the way of the spirit plays a supporting role. It would not do for Buddhism and Taoism to hold sole sway on the world. In this way, the Three Teachings, though different, are yet as one; though as one, yet are different.

"Let me put it this way. Confucianism is like the staple grains: hunger follows if we don't eat them for one day, death must ensue if we don't eat them for several days. Buddhism and Taoism are like tonics: taken at times of crisis or when in emotional turmoil, they can relieve our frustrations or grievances and dispel melancholia, bringing results more speedily than Confucianism can. Also, their doctrines of good and bad fortune flowing from one's own deeds are more easily impressed on the ignorant masses than the Confucian morality. Nevertheless, this good medicine should be limited to treating sickness: it must not be taken regularly or by itself, for that would risk the peril of bigotry.

"By engaging in empty talk about the inner man, some Confucianists join the camp of the Buddha and Laozi, while other Confucianists abominate both of them, as if defending themselves against bandits or sworn enemies. Both views are narrow-minded."

"But," Ma objected, "the yellow-capped Taoist priests and the black-robed Buddhist monks meddle in sorcery and indulge in chicanery. If they are not vigorously attacked, will they not cause great harm to society?"

"We are speaking here only of their fountainheads. If we extend the discussion to the latter-day, it is not only Buddhism and Taoism that have left a harmful legacy, Confucianism too has fallen on bad times. Even your example, good sir, of sleeping naked after drinking too much is, I fear, hardly consonant with the etiquette of the Duke of Zhou and Confucius."

Suitably chastened, Ma Dahuan begged pardon. They continued to discourse freely until dawn broke, when the old man took his leave. In the end it was unclear what god exactly the old man was. Some said he was a fox spirit.

The Dead Hand of Dogma
LYXXL IV 36

As Zhuangzi remarked, "The sages refrained from discussing matters beyond the visible world." Yet there are also matters within the visible world which are also not amenable to discussion—death, for instance. All the Confucianists have to say is that the ethereal soul ascends and the corporeal soul descends. Even Buddhist doctrine holds that ghosts are registered by the bureaucracy in the underworld and cannot reappear in the world above. Yet there is a widespread belief in baleful souls returning to the body after death. Popular divines have produced a manual that predicts the date and time of these revenants' return, and the direction they will take when they leave, which is, one admits, the height of absurdity. All the same, I personally have seen one depart from an upstairs window of a neighbouring residence: it was like a puff of smoke from a kitchen chimney, and it trailed off in a south-easterly direction; remarkably, the time and direction of departure were exactly as predicted. In addition, I twice opened the locked door of the room in which the corpse lay and carefully examined the places where the dust had settled; the hand and foot prints perfectly matched those made by the deceased person when alive, as verified by his family members. What theory can account for that?

Good and ill fortune are fated, one's life span is predetermined; even sages cannot pit themselves against the Creator in these respects. Nevertheless there are current in our world the black arts of poisoning without trace and putting a jinx on people, which in fact receive specific mention in the penal statutes. I have never witnessed such poisoning, but I have encountered several cases of jinxing. Those who practise these black arts are mere blind men, shamans and masons, but they truly can affect fortune and life span, as is constantly borne out. In this way they flagrantly usurp the authority of the gods. Again, what theory can explain this?

There must be some kind of natural laws or principles to account for such things, but they are beyond human ken. The Neo-Confucians of the Song dynasty declared that anything which "principles" could not explain simply did not exist: that, alas, would seem to be too stubborn a denial. My teacher Mr Li Youdan offered this opinion:

"The Song Confucians conceived the heavens in terms of principles, and considered that they had penetrated to the root of the interaction between the primal positive and negative forces. They claimed there was no iota of doubt about their calculations of the movement of sun, moon and planets: they were as plain as day. Nevertheless, the Song calendar went through ten revisions and ended up more defective than ever. After the work of the Yuan dynasty astronomer Guo Shoujing, a new calendar was tested using actual measurements of the orbits of heavenly bodies, and the results confirmed by the eclipses of sun and moon. Only then was it realized that all four schools of Song learning had totally failed to get a grasp of the subject. Even the eminent Song mathematician Shao Yong used only the fundamentals of odd and even numbers and basic geometry to deduce the passage of heavenly bodies; he did not arrive at his conclusions by astronomical observation.

"Hence the more elevated the theory, the harder it is to avoid error being compounded in transmission. The orbits of sun, moon and planets have tracks that can be followed: if even those cannot be conjectured on the basis of principles, how much less, given their formlessness, can such things as the First Cause and Inherent Nature be apprehended? The Great Sage had a saying: 'On matters of which they have no knowledge, enlightened men are best advised to keep silence'."

Rights and Wrongs of Confucianism and Buddhism
HXZZ IV 25

Xu Wenmu contributed this.

The old monk Cheng Zhi was very strict in his religious observances. As he lay dying, he addressed his pupils in these words:

"I have adhered to Buddhist law in every particular and progressed far; I thought I was destined for the fourth Dhyana Heaven. But the World Honoured Sakyamuni Buddha has reproached me for exalting Buddhism over Confucianism in the lectures I have given in the course of my life: I have not transcended my sense of self, so I cannot escape return to the wheel of transmigration."

His pupils said: "Do you mean to say that the World Honoured One blames you for extolling him?"

"That is why the World Honoured One is world honoured. If he sided with his own adherents and campaigned against dissenters, promoted himself and humbled others, how could he be honoured by the whole world? I have now seen the light, while you are still off track."

That reminded me of something Yang Guiting told me. Apparently, in the tenth year of the Qianlong reign [1745], graduates from the provinces were assembling in the capital to take the highest examination, and Yang was on his way there with a group of his contemporaries. He happened to fall into conversation with a monk who was putting up at the same inn. One of his fellow graduates gave him a disapproving look, and said: "What business have you to consort with those of alien faith?" The monk objected, saying: "Buddhism and Confucianism are indeed different, but they both have their hierarchy. Confucius himself would be in a position to gainsay Buddha, but his chief disciples Yan Hui and Zengzi would not enjoy that status. Yan Hui and Zengzi in turn would be in a position to gainsay the bodhisattvas, while the Han dynasty ideologues Zheng Xuan and Jia Kui would be debarred. Zheng Xuan and Jia Kui could gainsay the arhats, while the Song dynasty Neo-Confucians Cheng Hao, Cheng Yi and Zhu Xi could not. Zhu Xi and the two Chengs could gainsay various gurus, but their hangers-on and self-professed interpreters of the doctrine could not. Why? Because they don't measure up. That you, sir, should gainsay the Buddha is to pretend to too high a position, is it not?"

Yang's confrere was angered. He smiled sarcastically: "It is precisely because there are hierarchies that Confucians of my standing can gainsay monks of your standing." They almost came to blows before breaking off the argument.

To put the fundamentals of each teaching in proper perspective, I propose the analogy of a domestic establishment. The supremacy of the Confucian persuasion stretches way back to antiquity, and even if a new sage were to emerge, it would not change anything. In that sense, Confucianism can be compared to the master of the house. Buddhism came from the Western Regions. Its doctrine of vacuity and purity can make those who recklessly pursue fame and fortune relinquish their scheming and self-seeking, and enable those who are plunged into doubt and despair to obtain relief. Its doctrine of karma, of reward and retribution, also suffices to make the base and benighted come round and lead a good life. In that way the doctrine contributed in some degree to the general well-being, hence it was accepted in China. We can compare its role to that of a retainer with special abilities. The problems of Buddhism arise when the retainer does not stick to his last, but instead aspires to reform the domestic regime, aims to have the master yield his position and convert to his way of thinking.

To turn now to the decadent stage of each teaching, one can adopt the analogy of farming, with Confucians being those who do the ploughing and weeding. What happens is, the Buddhists neglect their primary purpose, and instead of making good and evil deeds the root cause of bliss and torment, put in their place the giving or withholding of alms, which has led to the rampancy of deluding the masses in order to amass wealth. This is like invading people's fields and stealing their crops.

The Confucians, for their part, abandon their ploughs and ploughshares, let their fields grow rank with weeds, and rush to take up cudgels and pikes to seek out those who would steal their crops, and do battle with them. Even if they achieve total victory, what will become of their crops? Is this not lunacy on the part of Confucians?

Buddhism has spread all over the empire since its introduction in the reign of Emperor Ming of the Eastern Han dynasty, two thousand years ago. Even if the founding fathers of our civilization were to come again, they could not banish it. On the other hand, if the Confucian precepts ordering the relation between father and son, ruler and subject, and the institutions of army, law, ritual and music were all put aside, there would be no means of governing the empire. Though Sakyamuni himself were to appear in the world, he would not be able to make his writ run in China.

In point of fact, there is no need for strife. The trouble is, the Buddhist clergy cannot overcome their cupidity: they foolishly hope that Confucianism will shrink and Buddhism expand, whereby the converts to Buddhism will further enrich the monasteries with their donations. The Confucians, to speak of them, cannot overcome their thirst for fame: if in their works there are not numerous rebuttals of Buddhism, they think their gallantry in defending the Way will not receive due regard. Hence the discourses on both sides are like bubbles in water: once they form, they burst; once they burst, they form again. They never cease trading insults. They do not realize that after hundreds of years of protracted warfare, they will still coexist as ever was; and the same would be true after an equal period of truce. They would be better occupied if both cultivated their own garden.

Back to Basics
LYXXL III 29

My teacher He Li'an contributed this.

Legend has it that towards the end of the Ming dynasty a certain scholar was walking by himself in the wilderness when he heard voices raised in chanting. Surprised to hear this going on miles from anywhere, he traced the sound to its source. An old man was sitting in the midst of grave mounds with a circle of a dozen foxes round him, each fox squatting on its heels and holding a book in its paws. The old man rose to greet him, and the foxes too stood erect, still holding their books. Seeing that the foxes could read, the scholar calculated that they presented no danger to him. Polite greetings having been exchanged, the scholar joined them in sitting on the ground. He asked what the purpose of their studying was. The old man replied:

"We are preparing ourselves to achieve immortality. There are two paths for foxes to reach that goal. The first is to draw on the primal cosmic energies, to worship the constellations, and gradually acquire supernatural powers; then proceed to acquire spirituality through long tempering. This is to seek immortality by occult means. However, it is possible to stray into heterodoxy, in contravention of the rules of Heaven. This path is direct but dangerous.

"The second path for foxes is to first acquire human form, and then go on to nurture the divine spark within themselves. This is to seek immortality by temporal means. Although the breathing exercises and physical disciplines required are not learned overnight, persistence will bear fruit. This path is roundabout but safe.

However, bodily form does not change by itself, only along with an alteration of mentality. That is why a precondition is to study the books of the sages in order to understand the principles of the Three Bonds and Five Moral Constants. The idea is that bodily transformation will follow mental transformation."

The scholar asked to look at the books they were studying. They were all Confucian classics, such as the Five Books, the *Analects*, *Classic of Filial Piety* and *Mencius*. They contained only the bare text, without commentaries. He asked how they could get the meaning of the classics if they left out the explications. The old man replied:

"Our aim in studying is simply to understand the principles. The language of the sages is actually not abstruse. Verbal instruction can clarify the sense and gloss archaic words, which suffices for students to discern the purport. What is the point of having commentaries?"

This eccentric view nonplussed the scholar. Not being able to think of a response, he resorted to asking the old man's age.

"I really don't remember," was the reply. "I only recall that wood-block printed books hadn't come in when I did my pupillage on the classics."

"Having lived through several dynasties then, what would you say has stayed the same, and what has changed?"

"In general there hasn't been a great difference between the dynasties. The only slight change I would mention is that before the Tang dynasty there were simply learned men, while after the Northern Song I was always hearing of certain people being placed on a par with the sages."

The scholar did not know what to make of that comment. He made an abrupt bow and took his leave. Afterwards he ran into the old man again, and wished to resume their conversation, but the old man averted his eyes and went on his way.

I suspect that my teacher made this up as a parable. He had previously stated the following:

"Using exposition of the Confucian classics as the path to

success in the imperial examinations resulted in fragmentation and over-elaboration: the finer the writing of the expositions, the greater the neglect of the original text. Then scholars using an interpretation of the classics to set up their own schools of thought resulted in argument and rival argument: the more sophisticated their theses, the greater the distance from the source."

In my opinion, that gets to the nub of the matter. Mr He Li'an has also remarked: "Any ingenious scheme will carry inherent risks. If you proceed step by steady step, you may go slightly off track, but you won't end up falling on your face." That also has a bearing on the two paths to immortality which he spoke of.

Dogma Blights Young Lives
LYXL V 2

The *Book of Rites* states that food, drink and sex are the great drives in human lives. Granted, to offend against the moral code, to profane social order, and to corrupt customs are all behaviour proscribed by imperial law, but calf love between infatuated youths, as long as it does not greatly exceed the bounds of decency, need not be harshly treated according to the letter of the scriptures.

When I was young I heard tell of a board secretary in the capital who prided himself on his strict moral probity. He pledged one of his maidservants to a young manservant as his future wife. More than a year passed in this state of expectancy, during which they were not obliged to avoid each other in their comings and goings. One day they met each other in the courtyard, where their master surprised them before they could wipe their smiles from their faces. He was outraged, and said: "This is a clear case of licentiousness! The law prescribes the penalty of bastinado for seducing a fiancée!" He immediately called for an attendant to administer the beating.

Those around him protested: "That was just playfulness

between boy and girl, it doesn't mean he has disgraced her. If she were no longer a virgin, there would be physical signs to prove it." The board secretary's reply was: "The law decrees that if a crime is plotted but not carried out, the punishment is only reduced by one grade. A lighter sentence is admissible, but pardon cannot be countenanced." In the event he had both servants beaten to within an inch of their lives. He was confident his household governance was in no way inferior to that of Liu Gongzhuo, the model disciplinarian of the Tang dynasty.

Out of disgust for what he thought was the boy and girl's improper behaviour, he deliberately put back the date of their marriage. When the two of them worked together, they felt hampered and hesitant; when they had free time, they avoided coming within sight of each other. Put in an impossible position, their life wasn't worth living. This stifling of natural impulses led to sickness, and in less than half a year both were dead.

The grief stricken-parents of the young couple begged their master that they be buried together. He responded angrily as before: "It is improper to bury immature youths as if they were married, don't you know that?", and he brushed their plea aside. Later on, when this man was near to dying, he muttered as if talking to someone. His words were unclear; only the two phrases, "Nothing happens without my permission" and "forbidden by the rules of propriety", were distinct because they were repeated a dozen times. It was thought he was experiencing some confrontation in his delirium.

By long accepted convention, young persons do not know who their marriage partner will be until the go-between performs her office. This man betrothed his servants while they were scarcely more than children, making them fully aware that they were destined to be husband and wife. To have them dwell under the same roof and not have feelings for each other is to ask the impossible.

It has also been the long accepted rule, stated in the *Book of Rites*, that "the inner female quarters and the outer male quarters should not communicate". This man employed few maids and manservants, and they could not be completely separated in their tasks. Given that they frequently came into close contact, to expect them to not exchange a word was again to ask the impossible.

If the root is not sound, the branches will not grow straight: the pair's indiscretions were brought about by their master. On top of that, the impetuous way he handled the matter and the excessiveness of his punishment would have surely been resented by his victims. When their aggrieved ghosts came back to haunt him, he still pleaded: "forbidden by the rules of propriety". Was that the basis of his claim to be a moral authority?

20

MORALITY

All ordered societies reduce conflict and promote harmony, otherwise they cannot remain ordered. Those desirables are realized on the level of government by deference to authority and compliance with laws; on the personal level by the sharing of moral values. While on the governmental level there may be disparity between peoples in the character of authority and laws, on the personal level there is broad convergence in morality. The virtues of such qualities as honesty, sincerity, trustworthiness, respect, gratitude, kindness and sympathy are more or less common to the moral codes of all advanced societies, and are well represented in traditional Chinese discourse. The Confucian classics gave prominence to ren (benevolence, or humanity), shu (consideration for others, on the basis of do as you would be done by) and zhongyong (moderation or "the golden mean"), while Buddhism emphasized charity and compassion for all living creatures (hence the ban on eating meat).

Since the trend of Ji Xiaolan's stories and parables is towards warning against transgression, the items that follow show those virtues being more honoured in the breach rather than the observance. Significantly, those who do set a good example are mostly plain and simple people.

Words Not to Be Trusted
GWTZ III 51

Wang Qingshi contributed this.

A younger brother plotted to usurp his elder brother's property rights. He summoned an advocate to his private study. Lamps were lit and the intrigue began. The advocate designed ruses and set snares, every step being exactly thought out. The tactic of sowing discord and planting informers in the opposite camp was also described in its every intricacy. The plot having been laid, the advocate stroked his whiskers and said:

"Had your brother the strength and ferocity of a tiger, he would not be able to break through this mesh of steel. Now let us talk about my reward."

The younger brother expressed his gratitude:

"We are the closest of allies, our bond is as firm as that of the same flesh and blood: how could I forget your inestimable service?"

They sat facing each other at a square table. Suddenly a man emerged from under the table and did a hopping dance all round the room. His eyes blazed like a torch, his body hair was long and straggly, like stalks of a straw cape. He pointed at the advocate:

"Dwell on this thought, sir! If this gentleman looks upon you as his own flesh and blood, you had better look out for yourself!"

He continued his dance, laughing all the while, before leaping to the overhang of the roof and disappearing. The two men and the pageboy attending them collapsed in fright. Having heard strange sounds coming from the room, the other servants collected at the door, raised an alarm, and went in to see what was happening. Those inside were all dead to the world. Ministrations to revive them restored the boy to his senses around midnight; he divulged all he had seen and heard. It took until dawn for the two men to stir. By that time their secret was out, and in face of the scandal it created, the younger brother had to abandon his scheme. For some months he did not dare venture out of the house.

The story is also told of a man who consorted with a courtesan. They fell deeply in love, yet when he proposed to redeem her from prostitution, she turned down his offer. When he promised to set her up in a house of her own and grant her all the courtesies of a legal wife, she refused even more vehemently. Perplexed, the man pressed her for an explanation. She told him with a sigh:

"You abandon your rightful wife to take up with me. How can I trust my future to such a man as you?"

You could say she took more or less the same line as the aforementioned demon.

* * *

From letters written to brother Qinghu (Family Letters, FLP edition, p. 66) and nephew Qifan (ibid., p. 217) it can be seen that Ji Xiaolan was greatly exercised over the practice of educated men to act as legal sharks whose job is to draw up indictments for their clients that distort facts and falsely incriminate their adversaries. Ji warns his relatives that if they do take on that work they will reap the punishment of Heaven.

A Hypocrite Undone

LYXL VI 17

My uncle An Shizhai contributed this.

Our Neo-Confucian ideologues assert that there are no ghosts. I have never seen a ghost, but I have heard words spoken by a ghost. In the tenth year of the Yongzheng reign [1732], when I was on my way home from taking the provincial examination, I put up at a hostelry in Baigouhe. The hostelry had three rooms; I occupied the west room, and a scholar from the south was installed in the east room. After we became acquainted we bought some wine and stayed chatting into the night. The southerner told me how he came to be there:

"This boyhood friend of mine was dirt poor, and I often

helped him out with money and food. In later years he came north to take the metropolitan examination, at which time I was acting as private secretary for a top mandarin. I felt sorry for my friend's homelessness and invited him to stay with me. In time he got into my employer's good books. He then pried into my domestic affairs, and spread malicious rumours behind my back. In that way he squeezed me out and took over my position. Now I'm headed for Shandong to scrape a living there. To think that people could be such blackguards!"

I sighed in sympathy. Then suddenly there came the sound of plaintive weeping from outside the window. It went on for a long time before a voice spoke:

"You have the gall to call another a blackguard? You already had a wife, yet when you approached me as I was buying cosmetics from a hawker at my door you lied that you were unmarried, and deceived my parents into accepting you into the family as their son-in-law. Did that not make *you* a blackguard?

"My mother and father died in an epidemic, and since we had no other relatives, you took over their house and gained control of their wealth. Yet their coffins, burial clothes and funeral were all skimped and niggardly, no different from the way you would bury a servant. Did that not make *you* a blackguard?

"Your wife got passage on a grain boat to come north to find you, and kicked up a terrible row with you as soon as she got in the door, demanding that I be sent packing. Only when she learned that the house had been my family's and we had kept you in food and clothing did she come round to letting me stay for a while. With your wiles and guiles you got me to agree to being demoted to concubine. Longing only for some peace and quiet, I unwillingly and tearfully submitted. Did that not make *you* a blackguard?

"Having become mistress of my house, and spending my family's substance, your wife still ordered me about and mistreated me, demeaning me by using my childhood name, and on the slightest excuse making me lie flat on the floor and be whipped. You aided and abetted her, pinning me down and bellowing at me to keep still. Did that not make *you* a blackguard?

"After a year or so of that, after I had been robbed of my inheritance, my jewels and finery, and left with nothing, you sold me to a Shanxi merchant. When he came to inspect my looks, and I refused to show myself, you caned me unmercifully, driving me beyond endurance and leaving me no option but to kill myself. Did that not make *you* a blackguard?

"After my death, you furnished me no respectable coffin, you burned no paper money, you even stripped me of my worn garments, leaving only my trousers, rolled me up in a reed mat, and buried me in a paupers' graveyard. Did that not make *you* a blackguard?

"I have appealed to the gods, and now come to take your life. Do you still have the gall to condemn others as blackguards?"

Her voice was plangent and shrill, quite audible to our servants. The southerner trembled and cringed in fear, unable to utter a word. All of a sudden he let out a cry and fell to the ground. I was afraid of being implicated, and left before dawn. I do not know what ensued, but assume he was unlikely to have lived. In this case the link between sin and retribution is as plain as day, and the facts are clear. I wonder what evasions our Neo-Confucian ideologues would resort to if confronted with it!

Gossip

RSWW IV 5

A blind musician in Cangzhou named Cai was invited by an old man to sing and play every time he passed the Nanshan Tower, following which they relaxed over a drink. They gradually became quite close, and the old man often accompanied Cai home to share a bottle. The old man had said his name was Pu, he was born in Jiangxi, and had come to Cangzhou as a trader in china ware. In due course it dawned on Cai that the old man must be a fox spirit, but as the bond between them was firmly established, and the fox spirit made no bones about his identity, Cai had no fear of him.

At that time a court case blew up over libellous rumours spread about someone's marital problems, and that provoked great controversy. Cai happened to mention this to the fox spirit, saying, "Given your supernatural powers, you must know the truth of the matter." The fox angrily replied:

"Would I and those like me who are dedicated to the pursuit of the Way intrude in other people's petty matters? The bedchamber being a private world, and lovers' trysts being held behind closed doors, their obscurity breeds suspicions: one dog barks at a shadow, and a hundred dogs bark at the first dog's bark. Even if the suspicions are true, what concern is it to outsiders? For the passing satisfaction of broadcasting their opinions, the rumour mongers cause a family to live under a cloud for generations: that already disturbs the harmony of heaven and earth, and incites the disgust of the gods and spirits. What makes it worse is that people make bricks without straw, embroider and elaborate on mere surmises, and tell their tales as vividly as if they had been eyewitnesses. The upshot is, the persons involved are put under intolerable pressure, yet have no means of defending themselves, so more often than not are locked in depression and end their lives nursing a grievance. The pall of injustice will take untold ages to dissipate. If there are spirits of the departed, will they not seek redress? I am afraid a place in the most painful of hells will be reserved for those gossip mongers.

"I have always found you to be a sound and sensible person, and would have expected you to close your ears to this scandal. Instead you want to know the ins and outs of the matter. What could have got into you? Do you mean to say that not being content with losing your sight, you also want your tongue cut out?"

So saying, the fox spirit threw down his wine cup and left in a huff. He never consorted with Cai again. For his part, Cai was ashamed and contrite. He slapped his own face, and at every opportunity thereafter told his story as a warning to others, not concealing the shabby part he had played.

A Stickler for Principle
RSWW III 71

Wu Huishu contributed this.

There was a certain doctor who was always circumspect and law-abiding. One night an old woman brought a pair of gold bracelets to buy from him a potion to induce abortion. The doctor was horrified, and sternly rejected her request. The next day she brought two pearl hair clasps as well. The doctor was even more affronted, and brusquely chased her away.

Over half a year passed. Out of nowhere the doctor had a dream of being summoned to the court of the dead to answer a charge of homicide. There he was confronted with a woman whose hair hung loose and around whose neck was wound a red silk sash. In tears she told of how the doctor had refused to provide the drug she needed. The doctor said in his defence:

"Our potions are for saving people's lives: how would I dare to take a life for the sake of ill-gotten gain? Your downfall came from your adultery being exposed—how can I be to blame?"

The woman replied:

"When I asked for the potion the foetus had not yet been formed. If I had been able to abort the embryo I could have stayed alive. By destroying an unfeeling lump of flesh, a life threatened with extinction could have been saved. Since I could not get the potion, I had to give birth, with the result that the child suffered the agony of strangulation, while I was forced to hang myself. So to preserve one life you ended up killing two lives. If you are not to blame, who is?"

The underworld judge sighed and said:

"The gist of your argument is that you have to judge each case on its merits, while what he stuck to was principle. Would he have been the only one since the Song dynasty who has stuck rigidly to a principle in disregard of the good or ill consequences? You had better let the matter drop!"

There came the sound of the judge's ruler hitting his desk, which startled the doctor from his dream.

* * *

The Hippocratic creed developed in ancient Greece also expressly forbade physicians from dispensing pessaries for inducing abortions.

Virtue Rewarded
RSWW I 62

That which reason will not allow to exist, experience sometimes proves does exist. In such cases there is indeed an explanation, but rationalists simply hold too obstinately to their views to recognize it.

In recent years there have been two incidents in my home county of Xian. The first one concerned the wife of Han Shouli, née Yu. She served her husband's grandmother most devotedly. When in the twenty-fifth year of the Qianlong reign [1760] this grandmother lost her sight, she tried everything in the way of cures and prayers, all to no effect. Some trickster or other spun her the tale that if she sliced off a piece of her flesh, melted its fat to fuel a lamp, and prayed for divine intervention, a cure would quickly come about. The woman did not realize she was being taken in, so she went ahead with slicing her flesh and burning the lamp. Two weeks later the grandmother's sight was actually restored.

Now, the woman was stupid to believe that tall story, but it was precisely through her stupidity that she proved her sincerity, and it was precisely through her sincerity that the gods were moved to compassion. So from this unreason there emerged a higher order of reason.

The other incident concerned the beggar Wang Xisheng. Due to his feet being twisted he had to use his knees as his feet and propel himself along propped on his wrists. One day he found on a path a bag containing two hundred taels of silver that someone had dropped. He hid the bag in a clump of grass and kept guard over it, waiting for the owner to come looking for it. He did not have to wait long before the shopkeeper Zhang Jifei came along, searching the ground in great agitation. Beggar Wang stopped and questioned him, and when Zhang accurately described the bag and its contents, Wang returned it to him. Zhang offered him a percentage of the silver as a reward, but Wang refused. Zhang then invited him home, and proposed to keep him in bed and board for the rest of his life. Wang replied:

"My being crippled is the punishment of Heaven. If I flout Heaven's will by enjoying a life of idleness, I am sure to bring greater calamity down on my head."

He left without saying another word.

Later on, Beggar Wang was lying tired out in the shelter of the temple to the Blessed Pei (there is no information about Pei in the local records, but he is said to have prayed successfully for rain), when some drunken fellow started pulling and tugging at his feet, causing him terrible pain. After the drunkard went away, Wang saw that his feet had been straightened. Gradually he gained the ability to walk. He died in the twenty-fourth year of the Qianlong reign [1759].

The shopkeeper Zhang Jifei enjoyed the patronage of my late grandfather, and I got to hear him tell this story in graphic detail. It seems the beggar Wang merited being rewarded for his good deed, but he was contented with his fate and turned down Zhang's offer, so the gods were moved to reward him in man's place. Surely this is also an example of a higher order of reason emerging from seeming unreason!

My senior Ge Jiezhou included these two incidents in the Xian county gazetteer, and was severely taken to task by the intellectual establishment for introducing the supernatural. In my opinion, Ge's editing of the gazetteer … conformed meticulously to proper historiographic principles. These two accounts were included to show that humble men and women are capable of performing such acts as may move the gods, and thereby kindle the will to do good and strengthen public morality. Ge Jiezhou was not uncritically giving space to the stock in trade of storytellers. The fact that he excluded from his gazetteer two well-known anecdotes connected with Xian county that feature in classic collections of the supernatural surely attests to his discrimination!

* * *

In a letter to his second son (Family Letters, FLP edition, p. 230) Ji commends this son's wife for her devoted care of her mother-in-law (i.e. Ji's wife) in her recent critical illness, which saved her life. Crucial to the cure was the slicing of a piece of flesh to mix in the medicine. Similar to the story above, this act of piety prevented the minions of the underworld from seizing the good lady's soul. No scepticism is expressed here.

Good Nun, Good Monk
LYXL IV 21

In Sweetwater Well, Cangzhou county, there was an old Buddhist nun known as Mother Hui. I don't know if "Hui" was her given name or her religious name, and my choice of a character to write the name is also guesswork, but anyway "Hui" is what she had always been called. When I was little I often saw her going in and out of my maternal grandfather's house. She was extremely fastidious in observing religious discipline. She did not eat candies, saying they were impregnated with lard. She did not wear fur, saying wearing animal skins was as bad as eating meat. Neither did she wear silk, saying one foot of silk cost the lives of a thousand silkworms to spin. She herself made the cereal gluten offered to Buddha, saying the stuff you bought in the market had all been trodden out. She always used a flint stone to light a joss stick, saying tapers from a kitchen stove were unclean. She existed on one plain vegetarian meal a day, and was self-supporting, never badgering people to give alms.

One of the older woman servants in my maternal grandfather's house offered her a donation of a roll of cloth. The nun examined the cloth closely and recognized it for what it was. She said:

"When you give alms you have to use your own belongings for it to count as a pious deed. Because this roll of cloth went missing in your household, several junior maids were beaten. How could the Buddha accept such an object?"

The servant explained:

"My idea was that since they had dozens of rolls of cloth, they would not check them one by one, so just this once I decided to help myself to this one. I hadn't realized that other people might be suspected of stealing and get a flogging. I came in for a lot of badmouthing, and really had a guilty conscience, which is why I thought to offer it now to atone for my sin."

The nun threw it back at her, saying:

"If that's the case, you should put it back where it came from. That way the others would be cleared, and you wouldn't feel so bad."

The nun's disciples divulged these details some years after the servant's death, otherwise they would never have been known. In the nineteenth or twentieth year of the Qianlong reign [1754–1755], when the nun was in her seventies or eighties, she turned up unexpectedly at my house, saying she was on her way to the Tanzhe Temple near Peking to take part in a service to induct novice nuns. In the course of conversation, I mentioned this incident to her. She shook her head:

"That never happened: just the gossip of mischievous nuns."

We were all impressed by her candour and lack of pretention. Before she left she asked me to inscribe a votive tablet for the Buddha's Hall. I had Zhao Chunjian do the calligraphy for me. She brought her palms together and said:

"Whoever did the writing should sign with his own name. There should be no falsity before the Buddha."

Not until the signature was changed to Zhao's did she accept the tablet. She never came again. I recently asked some people from Cangzhou about her, but she was unknown to them.

A monk from the Tianqi Temple in my home town of Jincheng, the third disciple of the abbot Guocheng, was held in high regard by the scholar class. He was always referred to as Third Father, and his personal name fell into disuse. Generally speaking, the abbot's pupils were a great disappointment, mostly scattering to the four quarters with their begging bowls: he was the only one who did not bring discredit on his master. He had none of the mercantile manners of the hospitality priests of the grand monasteries or the arrogance of high priests on the podium. He meticulously followed monastic discipline. Even for a journey of hundreds of miles he did up his bundle and went on foot, never travelling by cart or on horse. My late brother Qinghu once passed him on the road and pressed him to share his carriage, but he would not be persuaded.

When officials visited the temple he accorded them no extra ceremony; when farmhands or yokels visited the temple, he accorded them no lesser ceremony. Big donors, small donors, non-donors, were all greeted with the same courtesy. When not chanting the sutras he would sit bolt upright in his cell, and you wouldn't know the temple was not deserted. That was what he did and what he was, nothing more. Yet the common folk from miles around all spoke with one voice, commending him as a good and honourable priest. But if you asked them what his spiritual heights were, in what way he was good and honourable, they were nonplussed, unable to put their finger on anything. He touched people's hearts precisely because they could not figure out how he had that effect. I once put that question to my father. He said:

"From what you have seen, was there any way he was not good and honourable? If not, then he *was* good and honourable. Would you have a monk perform miracles like riding the clouds on his staff and crossing a river in a wooden cup before you would call him enlightened?"

In following their calling, this nun and this monk stayed true to their own lights.

Token Piety
RSWW IV 30

My teacher Dai Suitang contributed this.

A grandee attended a temple on the eighth day of the fourth month to perform the rituals of repenting sins and releasing living creatures. Taking a walk in the gardens afterwards, he ran into an itinerant monk. The monk saluted him respectfully, and asked,

"What brought you here today, sir?"

"To do a good deed."

"Why choose today to do a good deed?"

"It is the Buddha's birthday."

"You do a good deed on the occasion of the Buddha's birthday: should you not do good deeds on the other days of the year? That you should release living creatures on this day, sir, is a virtue performed in the public gaze. I just wonder if the living creatures slaughtered year after year in your kitchen match the number released today?"

The grandee was stumped for an answer. The priest in charge of hospitality reprimanded the itinerant monk:

"His eminence lends prestige to our order by supporting our rules and observances. How dare a ragged monk like you say such outrageous things!"

The itinerant monk said mockingly as he walked away:

"Since the purple-robed bonze does not raise the question, this ragged monk is obliged to."

He dismissed them with a wave of his arm and went on his way, his destination unknown. An old monk who was listening sighed to himself: "That brother is too unworldly, but to our community his words were a warning—like hearing a sudden lion's roar!"

I once heard Ming Yu, a resident priest on Mount Wutai, speak on this subject. He said:

"If you constantly and sincerely repeat the name of Buddha, evil thoughts will be kept at bay. To simply say the Buddha's name a few times a day is not a virtue. If you hold to vegetarian diet every day, the sin of slaughter will be excluded. Abstinence for a few days hardly counts. If to stuff yourself with fat and juicy roasts at every meal but abstain from meat on certain days of the month is considered principled behaviour, in that case for a government officer to give way to venality when corruption is openly practised, but mark out certain days of the month when he does not pocket bribes, should qualify him as law-abiding."

This opinion seems to chime with what the itinerant monk said. The censor Li Shou disagreed with Ming Yu, however:

"He was only being spokesman for his religion. Given the circumstances of those in public life, it would be impossible for them to be lifelong vegetarians. If an individual abstains from meat on some days in a month, then for those days slaughter will decrease; if numbers of people together abstain, then even more creatures will be saved from slaughter. Is that not better than not abstaining at all?"

So different people have different perspectives, each has a point to make. If Ming Yu is still alive, I just wonder if he would have a countervailing argument to propose?

A Moral in the Tail

HXZZ I 30

My senior Huo Yishu said he had heard this story from Hai Wang, President of the Board of Revenue.

A scion of an old established family was doing some studying in a park of remembrance. Dozens of grave attendants for grand houses lived outside the park with their families. One day this young man caught a glimpse of a beautiful girl peeking through a breach in the perimeter wall, but there was no sign of her when he went over to get a closer look. Some days later he saw her picking wild flowers beyond the wall, but at the same time constantly casting glances inside the park; she even went as far as stepping into the breach and allowing a good look at her figure. The young man was reminded of the ravishing beauty who showed herself to Song Yu in his famous poem, and his imagination ran riot. But he was held up by the thought that those living roundabout were all plain commoners, unlikely to possess such pulchritude, and besides, their women were all poorly dressed, which made the girl's fine attire abnormal, too: he suspected she might be a fox fairy or pixie. So though they made eyes at each other, not a word passed between them.

Some nights later, as the young man stood by himself under a tree, he heard two girls whispering on the other side of the wall. One said, "Your beau is just now taking a midnight stroll. Why don't you go to him?" The other said, "He thinks I might be a fox fairy or pixie. Why should I give him an unnecessary fright?" The first girl said, "How could foxes and pixies appear in broad daylight? He'd have to be a simpleton to believe that!"

The young man was secretly delighted to hear this. He was tucking up his robe to climb out when he suddenly thought: "Since they deny they are foxes or pixies, that's exactly what they must be! No mean-minded men will admit they are mean-minded; not only that, they will go out of their way to denigrate mean-minded men to prove that they themselves are not so. This pixie is using the same tactic."

The next day he made enquiries, and found that indeed no such females as them lived in the neighbourhood. Nor did they trouble him again.

THE SLIPPERY PATH TO PERDITION
HXZZ IV 60

Bridges in the north only have handrails to prevent you falling, whereas in Fujian province, due to frequent rain, they have huts on the bridges where walkers can take shelter in a downpour.

Qiu Ertian told this story.

One night a man ran into a shower of rain, and made a beeline for the hut on a bridge. It was already occupied by a clerk holding a sheaf of files and soldiers and bailiffs guarding a number of people. Hearing the clanking of chains, the man realized that the clerk was checking convicts' particulars. He shrank back into a corner, keeping as far from them as possible. One of the convicts was crying his eyes out. The clerk angrily rebuked him:

"It's too late now to get in a funk, you shouldn't have done what you did in the first place!"

The convict sobbed: "I was led astray by my teacher. He was always preaching rational Confucianism to us, denouncing all talk of retribution from on high as a lot of rubbish put about by the Buddhists. I believed what he said and thought to myself, if my devices are cunning enough, and I cover my tracks skilfully enough, I can get away with anything I want to, and my misdeeds will not be exposed as long as I live. When I pass away, my breath of life will return to the Great Void, where all is dark and featureless, and I will be deaf to praise and blame. So why should I not give my every lust its head! Alas, I have discovered that hell is no lie, and there really is a king of the underworld to judge me. Not till now did I realize that my teacher sold me down the river. It is because I repent my folly that I am so sorry for myself."

Another convict spoke up:

"Your fall was due to believing in Confucianism, while I was ruined by Buddhism. The Buddhists preach that any evil deeds you commit can be cancelled out by performing good deeds, and even if you land in hell your repentance can bring you deliverance. I reckoned that burning joss sticks in my lifetime and paying for monks to hold services for me after I died was something well within my means. So with the dharma as my shield and protector I could get up to all sorts of things, and even the courts of the underworld would be unable to punish me. Alas, the bliss or torment that Buddhism professes turns out to be based on the good and evil things you do, not on how much you spend on revering the Buddha. My money has been wasted, my torture in hell is sure and certain. If I hadn't trusted the Buddhists, I'd never have been such a reprobate!"

He let out a long wail, and the rest of the convicts fell to weeping. The man then knew they were not of the mundane world.

The Confucian Six Classics are there for us all to read: nowhere do they deny the existence of gods and spirits. The Buddhist Tripitaka nowhere speaks to the purpose of amassing worldly wealth. It is since the Confucianists started fishing for fame and the Buddhists started trawling for gain that their malpractices have grown to the proportions here described. Buddhism is a religion imported from alien lands, and its bonzes cannot be too severely blamed for resorting to such means in order to survive. But why should Confucianism have come to this sorry pass?

TRAVESTIES
HXZZ III 22

Li Yudian contributed this.

The scion of an eminent family lost his way while hiking in the hills at night. Coming upon a cave, he decided to rest in it, but when he saw it was occupied by a deceased family elder he took fright and hung back. His forebear, however, invited him in most solicitously, which reassured him, and so he went forward and made his bows. After the usual pleasantries were exchanged, the conversation turned to family matters, and both shook their heads in sorrow.

The young man asked: "Your grave is in such-and-such a place, how is it that you have strayed so far out here?"

The elder replied with a sigh: "I led a blameless life, but as a scholar I just followed convention, as an administrator I only kept to the beaten track: that is to say, I did nothing creative, had no achievements to boast of. But some years after I was buried, to my surprise a massive headstone was erected over my grave, the upper margin carved with dragon motifs and carrying my name and office in ancient seal script. The inscription below told for the most part of accomplishments of which I had no knowledge, while those which had some slight foundation were all exaggerated. I have always been a plain and unpretentious person, so this already unsettled me. Worse was to come: trippers who passed by generally made derisory remarks, and the souls of the departed gathered round to scoff more openly. I moved out here because I could not put up with their babble. It is only at festival times when my descendants come to sacrifice and sweep my grave that I go back to see them."

The young man gently comforted him: "Honourable and filial sons are obliged to glorify their ancestors in this way. Such an exalted scholar as Cai Yong of the Eastern Han admitted to composing epitaphs he was ashamed of, and the great Han Yu of the Tang also knowingly wrote flattering epitaphs. History is full of such examples. Why should you take this to heart so, sir?"

The elder's face set in a stern expression: "We all know in our hearts the difference between right and wrong. Even if one succeeds in fooling others, it still goes against one's conscience. Deception is even more pointless if public opinion is against you. Ancestors should be exalted for their undisputed merit—why invite contumely by making false report? I hadn't thought that the bearer of a noble name would sink to that level!"

With that, he stood up and strode off in a huff. The young man did not know what to do with himself.

I said this was a parable made up by Yudian. His father-in-law Tian Baiyan commented: "This encounter did not necessarily happen, but the viewpoint expressed cannot be dismissed."

A Gentleman of the Old School
HXZZ I 21

Mr Shen Qianju graduated in the same year as my father [1713]. He was by nature mild-mannered and pacific, not having ever been known to give way to anger. At the same time he was aloof and independent, beholden to no man. He took after the austere and untouchable men of old.

He never dressed in anything other than a thin hemp gown, and always ate the plainest food. Were a student of his to bring him a share of sacrificial meat, he would exchange it at the market for bean curd, saying: "It's not that I try to be contrary, I simply don't eat that sort of thing."

On his way back from one of his tours of the province to test first degree holders, his pageboy led the donkey he rode on; when the boy tired, he had him ride the donkey and took over leading it himself. It started raining as dusk fell, so they found shelter in a disused shrine. The shrine consisted only of one empty room space, and the floor was so dirty they could not sit on it. Mr Shen resorted to taking off a leaf of the door, which he placed outside the threshold to lie down on.

He woke up in the middle of the night to hear a soft voice say: "I wish to get out in order to avoid you, sir, but you are lying across the doorway, blocking my exit."

"You are inside and I am outside," Shen replied, "neither of us is trespassing on the other's space, so what is the need for avoidance?"

After a long pause the soft voice resumed: "According to the rule that male and female should keep separate, you are obliged to let me go out."

"You inside and I outside are already separated, whereas if you came out we would cease to be so."

He turned over and continued his sound sleep.

When local people came across him the next morning, they were taken aback. "This shrine is occupied by a fox pixie," they said. "It comes out to seduce young men. Anyone who dares to go in there is met by a barrage of brickbats. How come you were left in peace?"

Later on, Mr Shen happened to refer to this incident in conversation with my father. Stroking his beard, he smiled: "The idea that a fox should wish to seduce me, Shen Qianju, boggles the imagination." My father joked: "Even if the fox seduced the whole of mankind, there's no chance it would get round to you! It surely would never have seen your like, and would have wondered what weird creature you were. It was sheer fright that made it desperate to flee from you."

From this one can see what sort of a man Mr Shen was.

Immoral Earnings

HXZZ III 79

In olden days the organizers of gambling games were called "bag men", because they took a cut of the winnings. The practice was described by Li Zhao in the Tang dynasty, and it has been carried on to the present day. As for keeping bawdy houses in order to pocket a slice of the girls' nightly earnings, that was not known before the Ming dynasty, the reason being that before then the rich houses had their own corps of female entertainers, and there were government-run brothels for the public. But when official supervision of the urban entertainment quarters ceased, private bawdy houses spread and flourished, becoming both a source of profit for racketeers and a snare for the heedless and unwary. Laws and statutes were passed to ban them, but failed to stamp the business out.

However, the word for "profit" has the graph for "knife" as one of its components, and greed will in the end lead to self-destruction. I once knew a man who engaged in this trade. With enticing young females living under the same roof, he could not make his juniors follow the example of Ruan Ji, whose libertarian excesses were limited to drinking himself to sleep. His two sons both contracted venereal disease, and went on to infect their whole family. This vile malady proved incurable, and his family line was cut off. Eventually his spirit would go hungry, there being no one left to offer sacrifice.

* * *

Various symptoms of unspecified venereal diseases were described in medical treatises as early as the Han dynasty, but it was not until the late Ming that syphilis, which is what seems to be referred to here, was identified. It was thought to have originated along the southern littoral, and was attributed to the fetid airs there, but modern speculation puts the blame on Portuguese sailors who got a foothold in Guangdong in the mid-sixteenth century.

21

PEDANTS

Lives Lost through Pedantry
LYXL III 14

My late father Yao An told me this.

"Apart from academic study, the younger generation should understand something of family management, and of the outside world. Only then will they be ready to head a household and play a part in society. Towards the end of the Ming dynasty, Neo-Confucian doctrine enjoyed increasing prestige, and examination success gained in importance. Hence devious and calculating men professed the 'primacy of mind' in order to enhance their reputation and win acclaim, while the plain and stolid types stuck to the textbooks to advance their career. The result was that fewer than two or three out of ten had any practical knowledge.

"In the fifteenth year of the Chongzhen reign [1642], great-great-grandfather Houzhai moved the family to Hejian City to escape from the banditry rife around Meng Village. After Houzhai died warning came that Hejian was to become a battleground, so it was decided to take to the countryside again. They were loading up, all ready to leave when the old man who was their next door neighbour pointed to the guardian gods on either side of the gate, and said: 'If those two great generals of the Tang dynasty, Yuchi Gong and Qiu Qiong, were alive today, we wouldn't be in such a fix.'

"At that moment your two great-uncles Jingxing and Jingchen, both scholars of some repute, were securing their baggage to the wagons outside the gate. When they heard what he said, they riposted: 'These are the images of the gods Shen Tu and Yu Lei, not the generals you speak of.'

"The old man stuck to his guns, and fetched a copy of the Taoist master Qiu Chuji's *Journey to the West* to prove his point. Your great-uncles dismissed that book as popular fiction, so nothing to go on, and went indoors to get Dongfang Zhuo's Han dynasty work *Classic of Marvels* to controvert his view. By that time night was already falling, and the finding of places in books and the arguments that followed took up a lot of time. While all this was going on, the city gate was shut, so they could not leave. The next day the city was besieged, and they were stuck inside. When the city fell, the whole family was wiped out, with the only exception of your great-grandfather Guanglu and your great-uncles Zhenfan and Yuntai. Now I ask you, with life hanging in the balance, not a second to be lost, even then to go into the authenticity of old books—was that not down to only knowing book learning, and not engaging with the world outside?"

I did not include this discourse of my father's in my previous publications because it concerns two great-uncles of mine. On reconsideration, though I would grant that bookishness has something to say for it, yet not a few eminent scholars down the ages have suffered from the same shortcoming, so I have found room for it here.

Fatal Consequences
GWTZ IV 45

My bondservant Fu Xian was keen on reading. He took in a lot of book learning as well as a bit about doctoring. He was slow to react, and in general gave the impression of a doddering old scholar. One day he meandered through the market place, asking every man he met, "Have you seen Wei Zao?" (Wei being another servant of mine.) Eventually someone told him where to find Wei, and he resumed his perambulation in that direction. When he caught up with Wei, he took a long time recovering his breath. Wei asked him what the matter was. He replied:

"Just now I came across your wife by the well. She had dozed off under a tree while she was doing her sewing. Your little boy was playing next to the well, only a few feet from it, in fact, and that seemed to be a cause for concern. But since we are told, 'men and women should keep their distance', it was not proper for me to wake her up, so I came to find you."

Wei was greatly alarmed, and rushed to the place, only to find his wife already bent over the well, lamenting the loss of her son.

Now it is a good thing for servants to get an education, but the purpose of education is to make sense of things, and the purpose of gaining such understanding is to put it to practical use. To swallow without digesting, to pick up some precepts and follow them blindly, is both perverted and benighted, and can have terrible consequences. What price such learning!

Self-Assertion

GWTZ III 28

Some of the instances of self-assertion here decried seem less to be blamed than the snobbery of the speakers in predicating that deference should be paid to fame or social superiority. Egalitarianism is an unknown concept to them.

* * *

Zhu Qinglei offered this:

"I once visited a temple dedicated to Yang Jisheng, the Ming dynasty official martyred for his devotion to justice. I saw a group of men enter. They all kowtowed, except for one who only bowed from the waist. When asked why, he replied: 'The honourable Yang held the post of board secretary; I am also a board secretary, so we are equal in rank. There is no occasion to make ceremonial salutation.' When it was pointed out that Yang was venerated as a loyal official, the man retorted indignantly: 'Are you implying that I am a treacherous official?'"

Yu Dayu had a story to match that. It was about the erudite Nie Jimao, who was acclaimed as the greatest carver of seal script of his generation. Nie was riding his donkey along a narrow path when he came up with a hewer of millstones, and was annoyed that this man would not make way for him to pass. The millstone hewer said: "We are both workers in stone. There is no reason why one should make way for another."

I chimed in with a story of my own. It concerned Zhang Ruo'ai, son of the Grand Councillor Zhang Tingyu. A family tutor from Jiaohe county got into a discussion with Zhang over stylistics, and their disagreement became heated. The tutor angrily said: "We took our first degree in the same year, and so far neither of us has taken the second degree. In what way are you better than me?"

These three cases are similar: the most eloquent debater would get nowhere with these people. Tian Baiyan commented: "In the wide world you will find all sorts and conditions of men. With the kind you speak of, the only way of dealing with them is to ignore them, and no harm will come of it. If you persist in trying to make them see sense, it will only lead to endless entanglement. I once met with two pedants staying in a Buddhist monastery. One of them cursed the rationalism of Zhu Xi, the other cursed the idealism of Lu Jiuyuan. Their altercation went on till midnight, when a monk attempted to mediate. Thereupon those two united in condemning Buddhism as a heresy which was destructive of Confucian orthodoxy, and joined forces to attack the monk. By the next day all three had bloody heads, and ended up suing each other. Is that not a case of silly people bringing trouble down on their own heads, when actually there is nothing to fuss about?"

WOMEN

If there was not much to praise in the way Confucian society treated women in late imperial times, neither, in comparison with contemporaneous societies in the West and Middle East, was there much to blame. The Chinese fondness for dicta and formulae makes bad seem worse. For instance, the commonplace saying that "for females to be without talent is a virtue", meaning that women should not shine, or get above themselves, did not differ greatly in sense from "a woman's place is in the home", which was a widely stated view in the West before the female emancipation movement. More coercive was the code originally formulated in the Han dynasty of *san cong si de* (three obediences and four virtues), the three persons to be obeyed being the father before marriage, the husband after marriage, and the son in widowhood; the four virtues had to do with modesty, decorum and diligence in the domestic setting. The articulation of that and other formulae as orthodox ideology caged women in, and at the same time prescribed for them an ideal of purity and selflessness of which not only they themselves but also the nation could be proud: since men rarely could claim such virtue, it was a good thing that women should be able to.

In practice the seclusion of respectable women precluded any public function, and the inferior schooling given to the female sex limited their intellectual development. Needless to say, there were prominent exceptions to the latter rule, and humankind being as diverse as it is, some women ruled the roost, but probably most women willingly aspired to be "a helpful wife and wise mother".

The male assumption that respectable women should be passive and non-assertive is reflected in the following anecdotes, an attitude that our author does not challenge. Yet it is also clear that he admires boldness in women when boldness is called for. Generally speaking, it is men who come out as the bad lot.

Feisty Women
HXZZ III 3

Wu Huishu contributed this.

A family who fished in the waters of the huge Lake Tai were ferrying their daughter over the lake to get married. When their boat reached the middle of the lake a sudden storm blew up. The helmsman was overcome by panic, the boat pitched and yawed, and was about to sink under the waves. Everyone clung together, weeping and wailing. At that point the bride burst out of her cabin, took hold of the rudder in one hand and the sail rope in the other, and sent the boat scudding into the head wind. They still managed to get to the bridegroom's home before the propitious time for the ceremony had elapsed. The people of Dongting Island celebrated their salvation as a miracle, though some derided the bride's actions as immodest and improper.

Huishu commented: "The girl was a fisherman's daughter, after all, thoroughly used to manning the oars. She cannot be blamed for not following the example of the fine lady Song Boji, who when her house caught fire famously preferred to be burned alive rather than to venture out at night without her governess."

I also heard the tale of a woman named Jiao from my home region, I forget which county, who was betrothed and waiting to get married. Some man who fancied taking her as a concubine for himself spread malicious rumours about her morals, making the bridegroom's family determined to break off the marriage contract. The girl's father took the matter to court, but the schemer had laid a deep plot: not only was firm circumstantial evidence produced, but a man came forward to claim he had been the girl's paramour. She saw that desperate measures were called for. She prevailed on an old woman neighbour to take her to the house of her intended, where she presented herself to her prospective mother-in-law, saying:

"A maiden is not the same as a married woman, her virginity can be tested. Rather than expose myself to the court-appointed matchmaker and risk being further traduced, I prefer to expose myself to you, my mother-to-be."

Thereupon she closed the door and took her clothes off for her future mother to verify her maidenhood. The case was immediately resolved.

This young woman's actions were more of an affront to etiquette than the bride's taking charge of her boat, but when life or future is at stake there may be no other choice. Our dogmatists are quick to declare martyrdom obligatory in such circumstances, but that would surely fly in the face of good sense.

ADDENDUM: Letter to wife (*Family Letters*, FLP edition, p. 36)

This letter gives a painful domestic context for a blandly told story above.

* * *

So Yugu, the eldest daughter of my distant cousin Guishan, has gone so far as to hang herself out of indignation at slanders spread about her. How foolish of her!

Though she was a girl of unblemished virtue, she attracted the attention of a certain lecher who lusted after her. On learning she was promised in marriage to the Xie family, his hopes of getting her for himself were set back. He proceeded to spread unsavoury rumours about her conduct, and when they reached the ears of the Xie family, they were stupid enough to be taken in by his treacherous scheme. They demanded that the matchmaker negotiate an annulment of the marriage, but when that did not work out they appealed to the authorities. Magistrate Zhao, I'm afraid, turned out to be extremely muddle-headed: given the fact that nothing is more important to a young woman than her virtue, how could he have taken the tittle-tattle of teahouses and wine shops as evidence for dissolving a marriage contract? The result was to leave a stain on Yugu's purity, and in her fury she put a noose round her neck, believing that her suicide would prove she had been defamed. On the contrary, the Xie family made out that she killed herself because her immoral conduct had been exposed. What a terrible injustice!

Only you and I continue to believe in Yugu's chastity. I vow to write her life story and have it inscribed on her tombstone, so that all will know that she died unjustly. Hopefully that will comfort her wronged soul. A person's length of life is written in their fate. If I had been at home at the time of the divorce proceedings, I would have been able to solve her situation, knowing as I do of a precedent.

When I was young there was in my prefecture a beautiful and intelligent daughter of a poor family named Jiao Yu'e; she was quick-witted and resourceful to boot. She caught the eye of a local despot who planned to make her his concubine. But Yu'e was already betrothed to her cousin Wang Tongsheng. Faced with this impediment, the despot did the same as the lecher did with regard to Yugu: he fabricated slanderous rumours in order to break up her marriage. The man's family were duly deceived, and they appealed to the magistrate for an annulment. Knowing that reason was not on their side, they colluded with the matchmaker to fake supporting evidence that would deviously entrap Yu'e.

Just before the case was heard, Yu'e got wind of their machinations. She realized she would be shamed in public and that would lead to her rejection, so she hurried along with her mother to the house of her fiancé, where she declared to her prospective mother-in-law:

"It can easily be proved whether an unmarried young woman

is a virgin or not. I do not wish to expose myself to the government matchmaker and be traduced by the man who wants me for a concubine, but I am willing to make an object of myself before you. Please examine me closely."

After the attendants were excluded and the door closed, she took off her clothes. Her mother-in-law's examination completed and her virginity proved, the charge was withdrawn and an auspicious date set at once for the nuptials. Yu'e's quickness of wit was truly unmatched. If I had instructed Yugu in this strategy, her marriage would have gone through and her life preserved.

A Geisha to the Rescue
GWTZ IV 5

The prefect Zhang Mogu contributed this.

A rich man residing on the borders of Shandong and Hebei provinces invested his wealth in cereals rather than silver, in order to forestall robbery. At the transition of the Kangxi and Yongzheng reigns there was a succession of bad harvests, and the price of rice rocketed. Anticipating that the price would continue to rise, he sealed his granary and refused to sell even a pint of rice. The local people murmured against him, but there was not much they could do about it. A geisha whose professional name was White Fox said: "No problem. Just get your money ready and bide your time."

She presented herself at the rich man's house and said:

"Though I am a big money spinner for my madam, she still illtreats me. Yesterday I had a row with her, and the upshot was she set a sum of one thousand silver taels for me to buy my freedom. In any case I am sick of my sordid life, and want to find a kind and upright man to whom I could devote myself for the rest of my life. I can think of no one better than your good self, sir. If you can come up with a thousand taels, I will be your handmaiden to my dying day. I understand, sir, that you do not like to keep your savings in silver, in which case she would settle for two thousand strings of copper cash. The trouble is, yesterday a timber merchant heard about my body price; he has already returned to Tianjin to raise the money, and will be back here in about two weeks. I do not want to be tied to this vulgarian. If you can conclude the deal within ten days, I shall be eternally grateful."

The said rich man, whose name was Zhang, had long since been enchanted with this geisha, and he was delighted with this proposition. He hastened to open his grain store, and set the price low for a quick sale. Once the granary door was opened, buyers flooded in in such numbers that the door could not be shut again. So the whole stock was cleared out, and the price of rice largely reverted to normal levels.

When the cereals had all been sold off, the geisha sent a note of apology to the rich man, which went:

"My madam has taken good care of me for long years. We happened to have this blazing row, which led to the business of buying myself out. Now she regrets what she said, and wants me to stay. It would not be right to turn my back on her, so we will postpone what we agreed to a later day."

Their pact had been made in private, there was no middleman and no witness, and no money had changed hands as a betrothal present either, so in the end the rich man was helpless.

Since Li Luyuan also told me this story, it should be authentic. The geisha was said to be only sixteen years old. That she could carry this thing off shows she must have been a true heroine!

THE CHARGE OF THE GRANNY BRIGADE
RSWW IV 33

When a situation reaches a critical stage it can give rise to extraordinary deeds, and apparently unjust and heartless actions may have their own justification. Exploits that defy conventions may not be judged by the rule book.

For some unaccountable reason, an old lady in my home district led a horde of grannies in a sudden raid on a house in a neighbouring village, pushed her way in and abducted a daughter of the family. It could not have been to pursue a feud, because there had been no previous dealings between the two parties; it could not have been to capture a bride, because the old lady no longer had a son. The villagers were thrown into confusion, everyone completely baffled. The girl's family filed a suit with the magistrate, the magistrate issued a warrant for the old lady's arrest, but she had got clean away with the girl, and her escape route could not be traced. The other women in her gang had also scattered to the four winds.

With so many people being implicated, it took exhaustive investigation and questioning before one person came out with the facts. The witness stated:

"The old lady's only son was dying from consumption. As he lay on his sickbed, she soothed his brow, saying: 'Your early death was written in your fate. The pity is you leave behind no grandson for me, and without his offerings the ancestors will become hungry ghosts.' The son moaned, 'I cannot promise there will be a grandson for you, but in fact there is a chance of that. I have had relations with a certain girl, and she is eight months pregnant. I'm just afraid the baby will be killed on birth.' After the son died, the old lady mulled things over in her mind for a week or so before launching this coup. I suppose she snatched the girl in order to save the life of the child she was carrying."

The magistrate shrugged helplessly: "In that case there is no need to hunt her down. She will come back on her own in two or three months."

As predicted, after that time was up she turned herself in, the baby in her arms. The magistrate did not know what to do for the best: he simply determined that her crime was not a major one, and settled for having her flogged and fined.

This matter had brooked no delay, there was only a small window of chance: the old lady rose to the challenge, organized a lightning strike, and carried it out with amazing precision. An Jinghan explained:

"When she made off with the girl at night, she divided her force of women and maids between three carriages, and with her own making four, set off in all four directions, so throwing her pursuers off the scent. Nor did she keep to the high roads; instead she followed detours and byways where roads forked and forked again, making it impossible to work out where she was heading. On top of that, she stopped nowhere for more than one night. Not until the girl was brought to bed did she rent a house, so her route could not be traced by where she had stayed. From all this we can see her planning had left not the smallest detail out."

On the girl's return she was disowned by her parents, whereupon she stayed with the old lady to bring up her orphan child, and never married. Because of her youthful indiscretions she was not granted official recognition as a virtuous widow; for the same reason it would not be fitting for me to divulge her family name.

Decadence

GWTZ I 11

"Handfuls of grain" and "ears of corn" being left behind as "gleanings for widows": this scene is described in the *Book of Songs*, dating the custom back to the Zhou dynasty. When the corn in the fields ripens, bevies of women and children follow in the wake of the reapers, gathering the grains that have been passed over or spilled. The farmers are used to the custom, the reapers do not interfere, and so the ancient custom has continued.

However, standards decline, self-interest takes over, the profit motive reigns. When the gleanings from the harvest fall short, the stealing and snatching that goes on undermines the idea behind the custom. It has come to such a pass that in the fourth and fifth lunar month women camp out overnight all over the countryside so as to get first pickings.

In east Jinghai county a group of such women set out after dusk to travel in the cool of night time. They saw glimmerings of light in the distance, and headed for their source to beg a drink of water. They were faced with a stately hall, staffed by servants in smart livery. Lanterns blazed and music played, as if to entertain guests. The women could see three gentlemen inside, seated on couches and engaged in feasting. The women indicated their wish to put up for the night, and the gatekeeper passed on their request to his master, who gave his assent. Shortly afterwards the master called the gatekeeper back again, and seemed to whisper instructions in his ear. The gatekeeper came out to the women, drew aside an elderly one, and quietly told her:

"We are too far from the city to summon professional female company without notice. The master desires three good-looking women from among you to be selected to join their feast and share their beds. Each of these three women will be given a hundred taels of silver, and the other women will also be rewarded. For passing the word to the others, your reward will be double."

The woman assembled her companions and, keeping her voice down, put this proposal to them. Out of avarice they urged the younger women among them to agree, and three of them were led inside. There they were bathed, made up and attired, and went on to entertain the gentlemen guests. All the other women were assigned to another wing of the mansion, where they too were wined and dined. At midnight the three gentlemen embraced the woman of their choice and withdrew to the inner chambers. As all retired to bed, lights were doused over the whole mansion.

The women were exhausted after their long walk, and fell into so deep a slumber that they slept right through till the sun was high in the sky the next day. When they did wake up, the mansion and its occupants were no longer there, only an unbroken vista of heath land. They found the three young women lying naked in the grass, bereft of the fine clothes they had changed into; fortunately their old garments were strewn some paces from where they lay. The silver they had been given turned out to be paper ingots.

They suspected they had been deluded by a ghostly company, yet the food and drink had all been real, so it could have been fox spirits. On the other hand, they were close to the sea, so dragons or sea monsters were also a possibility. In the end, in return for giving way to greed at the expense of virtue, they only got a good meal. One can imagine that when these women looked at each other in bafflement and recalled the past night, it must have seemed to them like the "pillow dream" of the Tang dynasty tale, which taught that a life of luxury was the vanity of vanities.

My late brother Qinghu commented:

"The swirl of the skirt in dance, the flutter of the fan in song, the parade of pulchritude—those glories of the passing moment—all flow away like water in a stream. When lovers' revels come to an end, and one looks back through the mists of time, such things are drained of meaning. That awareness is no less an awakening from a dream than what those three women experienced when they found themselves lying naked in the grass. It is not only mirages that are transient illusions!"

RAPE

LYXXL I 7

In a village on the margin of the Wei River south of Cangzhou City there lived a ruffian called Fourth Brother Lü. His violence knew no limits, and people feared him like a wild beast. One day as dusk was falling he was taking the air outside the village with a bunch of young hooligans when a rumble of thunder was heard: a storm was fast approaching. In the far distance they caught a glimpse of a young woman going into an old temple on the river bank to escape the rain. "She's ripe for the taking," Lü told his mates. The time was already late, and the rain clouds made the sky black. Lü burst into the temple, and covered the woman's mouth with his hand. The whole crew of hooligans stripped her bare and gang-raped her. Then in a flash of lightning that lit up a window Lü saw that she resembled his wife. He hastily released her, and found out when he questioned her in the gloom that there was no mistake: she was indeed his wife. Lü dragged her to her feet in a fury, intending to throw her into the river, but she shrieked:

"Your idea was to rape someone else's woman, but what you

brought about was others raping me! Heaven has given you just what you deserved. Are you going to make it worse by killing me?"

Lü had no answer to that. He quickly looked around for his wife's clothes, but by this time they had been blown into the river. He fretted and fumed, but unable to come up with an alternative, was forced to carry his naked wife back home on his back. The clouds cleared and the moon came out: all the villagers roared with laughter at the spectacle and clamoured to know how that came about. Lü could offer no explanation; he ended up drowning himself in the river.

What had happened was this: His wife had gone back to her parents' home for a visit that was intended to last a month, but their house had burnt down, and having nowhere to stay, she returned ahead of time. Lü had not known of the change, which was his undoing. Some time afterwards, he appeared to his wife in a dream. He said:

"My sins were so grave that I should have been pitched into everlasting hell, but when the judges in the underworld examined my dossier and found that I had looked after my mother devotedly, they allowed me to be reborn as a snake. I am about to return to the world above. Your new husband will arrive shortly: serve his parents well, for unfiliality carries the stiffest penalty in the courts of the underworld. You don't want to volunteer to be plunged into a vat of boiling oil!"

On the day of her second marriage, a red-banded snake dangled down from a roof joist in her room, as if sorry to see her leave. Remembering her recent dream, the wife looked up and was on the point of questioning the snake when the wedding procession with its pipes and drums arrived at her door. The snake threshed about on its perch, then was gone like a shot.

A LIBERTINE REBUFFED

LYXXL I 16

A provincial graduate from Tianjin invited a number of friends to join him on a spring outing in the countryside. They were a lot of frisky and flighty young men. Seeing a young woman on a donkey pass under a stand of willows, the graduate decided to take advantage of the fact that she was on her own by getting his companions to pursue her and bait her with smutty talk. The woman simply ignored them and whipped up her donkey to put a distance between them. When a few of the young men caught her up, she unexpectedly dismounted and addressed them with undue familiarity, hinting she was willing to indulge in fun and games. The graduate soon arrived on the scene with the others, and now getting a close look at the woman, discovered she was none other than his wife. Yet his wife could not ride, neither had she any reason to be out in the countryside, so the sight confounded as well as angered him. He went up to her and upbraided her, but she merely carried on with her flirting. The graduate's anger reached boiling point, and he raised his hand to slap her face. His wife instantly leapt onto the donkey's back, and in an abrupt change of manner pointed her whip at him, delivering the reprimand:

"When you spot someone else's wife, you will plot and scheme to abuse her, yet in the case of your own wife you are driven to fury. You have studied the books of the sages, yet you don't even understand the first principle, 'Do as you would be done by'! How can you justify your place on the roll of elevated scholars?"

Having said her piece, she rode away without a backward glance. The graduate stood with ashen face by the roadside, as if rooted to the spot. He never found out what kind of spectre he had encountered.

A Fallen Woman of Upright Principle
HXZZ I 68

A provincial graduate from my home prefecture led a dissolute life in his youth, being a familiar sight in the brothel quarter. The prostitutes there all gave him the cold shoulder, with the exception of Pepper, as she was jokingly called in the sisterhood (her proper name having fallen out of use). She alone thought highly of him.

"This gent," she said, "is going to come up in the world, I'm betting on him!"

Besides often inviting him for cosy drinks she chipped in her night-time earnings to support his studies. When he was due to take his examinations, she fitted him out for his travelling and provided for his family while he was away. He was greatly touched. Taking her by the arm, he swore an oath: "If I achieve my ambition, I vow to take you to wife."

Pepper demurred: "The reason why I have backed you is that my sisters only have eyes for the big spenders. I wanted to prove that we aren't all just paint and powder: some of us can pick out a man of real promise. As for the "till death do us part" business, I'm not interested in that. I'm passionate and pleasure-loving by nature, there's no way I could be a respectable wife. If you set me up as the lady of the house but I still indulged my taste for romancing, you couldn't put up with that! From my point of view, to be shut up in a boudoir would be like being in prison, and I couldn't stand that either! Rather than start off in a love nest and end up in a broken marriage, it would be better to hold onto a lasting affection and pine for what might have been!"

When later on the graduate was appointed magistrate he frequently sent for her, but she did not respond. Though her clients drifted away after she lost her looks in middle age, she never appealed to him for help. One has to grant that she was a rare kind of woman. She knew better than General Han Xin, who helped Liu Bang to gain the throne, but afterwards bitterly regretted that he was then at Liu's mercy.

Shock and Horror

LYXXL III 11

Old Mrs Man was my younger brother's wet nurse. Her daughter Li married a farmhand from a nearby village. One day Li got word that her mother was ill; without waiting for her husband to accompany her, she dropped everything and hurried over to our house. Night had already fallen, and the waning moon afforded but little light. Sensing someone behind her, she looked back to see a man chasing after her, no doubt with evil intent. Out in the bare countryside, she was beyond the reach of help. She hid behind a poplar tree growing over an old grave mound, took off her hairpin and earrings, undid her waist sash and tied it round her neck, stuck out her tongue, and waited, staring straight in front of her with popping eyes. When the man drew near, she actually beckoned him to come and sit beside her. A close look at her convinced him she was the ghost of a woman who had hanged herself, and he fainted on the spot. Li lost no time in making her escape.

Li's disarray caused great alarm when she finally arrived on our doorstep. By stages we got her story out of her; naturally we were outraged, but also could not help seeing the funny side of it. The next day, while we were discussing how best to enquire in the neighbourhood as to the pursuer's identity, a hubbub erupted outside about a youth who had been bedevilled by a ghost who still had her hooks in him. The youth was already reduced to babbling like a madman. Subsequently his family tried all sorts of medication, and hired Taoist priests to paste up magical signs to cast out the evil spirit, all to no avail. He suffered from epileptic fits to the end of his days.

How do we account for his insanity? It might be that while he was in shock some prowling demon took its chance to possess him, one does not know. Or his illusions might have been wholly begotten by a fevered brain. Or a vigilant spirit might have punished him for his wicked intent by robbing him of his soul. Though there is no way of knowing the truth of the matter, each and any of those possibilities could serve as a warning to young rakes.

A Dangerous Woman
LYXL II 9

An idle son of the rich in my home district was obese of body, shambling of gait, and slovenly of appearance; his face he left unwashed for days on end. Nevertheless, he was a familiar figure in bawdy houses, and he would leer at any woman he passed.

One day this playboy was out walking on his own when he caught up with an extremely attractive young woman. The road was muddy after recent rain. He hurried forward and accosted her: "The ground is so slippery, young lady," he said flirtatiously, "would you like to take my arm?"

She rebuked him sternly: "Don't get stupid ideas, I am a fox maiden. I perfect myself by worshipping the moon, I've never gone in for seducing men to sap their virility and that sort of stuff. Who do you think you are, to be so impudent? You'd better look out, I'll make you sorry!"

With that she scooped up a handful of earth and threw it in his face. The playboy jumped back and fell into the roadside ditch. By the time he had struggled out, the woman was nowhere to be seen. For the next few days he started at his own shadow, but nothing untoward happened.

Then a friend invited him to a party where a new professional hostess was plying the guests with drinks. A close look at her told the playboy that she was the young woman he had previously encountered. That threw him off balance, causing him to doubt his own senses. Tentatively he hazarded a question:

"Did I see you the other day on your way to East Village, after the rain?"

The hostess replied nonchalantly: "On the day you mention, my elder sister did go to the East Village to visit our aunt, I didn't go myself. My sister is very like me in looks, would it have been her you saw?"

Confused by her noncommittal answer, the playboy could not decide if she was human or not, or if she was one person or two-in-one. He made an excuse to leave early.

When he was gone, the hostess told her story:

"Actually, I thought he was disgustingly ugly, and besides was afraid he would rape me, so I made up that story to bamboozle him in the hope of getting away. Luckily he took a fall, and I hid behind a stack of firewood on the threshing floor. I hadn't really thought he would believe me."

The whole company doubled up with mirth. But one of the guests pointed out:

"Since you have taken up the profession, you can't pick and choose who to entertain. This fellow will spend a fortune on any woman who takes his fancy. What do you say to me taking you along to pay a call on him?"

That was indeed what they did. To reassure the playboy that the woman was of humankind, the guest gave particulars of the names of her husband and parents-in-law. That dispelled his doubts. The woman herself apologized for her behaviour, saying she had known who the playboy was since she was a girl, and was delighted when he flirted with her. She had just put on an act out of playfulness, and had never dreamt it would end in upset, for which she was deeply sorry. To make amends she would be only too happy to share his bed.

She spoke in dulcet tones and displayed her charms to full advantage. The playboy was entranced, and detained her for a good many nights. Well satisfied, he summoned her husband and agreed monthly terms for her prostitution. After keeping her for a whole year, his flesh wasted away and he died from his dissipation.

My late brother Qinghu commented:

"Men are fearful of foxes impersonating women, their fear being that a relationship with them would sound a death knell. Yet when a woman impersonates a fox, men neither show fear of her nor think of dying. Is that because she can pass herself off as his kind? Remember, she did predict 'I'll make you sorry!' This playboy died at the hands of a prostitute, but you could still say it was at the hands of a fox."

A Delicate Flower

HXZZ III 60

Shen Shusun, granddaughter of the censor Shen Zhiguang, came from Suzhou in Jiangsu province. Because her father and uncles all died young, she was brought up by her grandmother. This grandmother, born Yang Fen, was the younger sister of Mr Yang Wenshu; she wrote good poetry and prose, but stood out as a painter of flowers. Shusun was likewise versed in the literary arts, and in her painting she conveyed mood and feeling particularly well. She was betrothed in girlhood to my nephew Rubei, but died before the marriage took place.

My mother paid Shusun a visit in her last illness. Old Mrs Shen called out to her, "Your grandmother-in-law has come to see you—you can get acquainted now." Though Shusun was sinking fast by then, she still opened her eyes wide to look at her visitor. Her eyelashes speckled with tears, she lifted a hand to pluck at my mother's gold bangle. My mother took it off and slid it over her wrist. Shusun smiled and passed peacefully away. Only then did the two old ladies realize that she wished to be buried with something belonging to the Ji family.

Already at the outset of her illness Shusun knew it would be fatal. She painted a picture, rolled it up, and sealed the scroll securely; thereafter she always kept it beside her pillow. When asked what she had painted, she gave no answer. Now they knew she meant to reserve it for my mother's eyes. When the scroll was unrolled, a painting of an orchid in rain was revealed. The inscription read:

> I sit quietly by myself and paint an orchid
> The picture done, only I look at it
> I feel for it alone in its deep valley
> It can't stand up to cold wind and rain

What no doubt lay behind the poem was the unmentionable matter within her family which put off her marriage.

My mother grieved over her, and wanted to buy a burial plot for her, but my father held that would be improper, so in the end her coffin was shipped back to Suzhou by barge. My mother actually dreamed of her weeping as she bowed in farewell.

23

HOMOSEXUALITY

Pretty Boy as Lure for a Tender Trap
LYXXL III 22

Bisexuality and homosexuality were common in the Qing dynasty; one region in the south-east was indeed known for adult males grooming juveniles, rather in the Greek style. What is significant about the following story is that the malefactor was able to assume that a high official of whom he had no personal knowledge would be susceptible to the charms of a boy prostitute. No clearer token of the wide spread of this practice could be forthcoming.

* * *

The story is told of a certain commissioner who was returning from an assignment in the provinces. He stopped over at a guest house provided by a local government. The chrysanthemums in the courtyard were in full bloom, and as he lingered in their midst he caught sight of a boy standing on the other side of a screen of bamboos. The boy was in his mid-teens, sedate and gentle in demeanour, and in appearance as appealing as a maiden dressed up in her best. Learning that this was the son of the guest house's owner, the commissioner called the boy over and engaged him in conversation. Well pleased by his bright mind and ready response, the commissioner presented him with his fan. The boy made sheep's eyes at him, to convey the promise of willing intimacy. On his part, the commissioner was smitten with the boy's grace and fluency, and dallied to talk fondly with him. At that point the commissioner had no one attending on him, and the boy knelt down, pulled at his sleeve, and said:

"At the risk of rejection, sir, I have a confession to make. My father languishes in gaol on a false charge. A word from you could save his life. If you were willing to reach out a helping hand, I would gladly place my body at your disposal."

Just as the boy was taking a copy of the indictment from his sleeve, a violent wind arose, blowing open all the window shutters of the guest house and exposing their situation to the eyes of the commissioner's escort. Realizing that this was something untoward, he hurriedly dismissed the boy, saying, "We can go into the matter at leisure this evening." Thereupon he quickly ordered his carriage and departed thence.

On later enquiring into the case, the commissioner discovered that a local despot had murdered someone, and was having difficulty in engineering acquittal, so he bribed a petty official to have the commissioner directed to stay in his own residence; at the same time he bought the services of a pretty boy to pretend to be his son. Then he bribed one of the commissioner's retinue to bring the boy into the commissioner's presence, so springing the tender trap. What he had not counted on was the uncanny intervention of the murdered man's vengeful ghost.

His Excellency Qiu Wenda commented: "The commissioner let himself be drawn into meddling with affairs that did not concern him, and came within an ace of falling for the ruse. Those in high authority must be circumspect in every word and deed. If at that time the commissioner's mien had been as forbidding as that of the incorruptible Judge Bao, the miscreant would have had no opening to exploit."

Catamites

HXZZ II 33

Ji Xiaolan's preamble to the piece that follows deals only with the earliest historical references to the practice of homosexuality. If he had wanted to he could have cited many plain allusions to it in the centuries that followed. For instance, the Zhan guo ce (Intrigues of the Warring States), put together in the third century BC, records classic cases of male favourites of the rulers of the states; the names of two of them later entered the language as eponyms for that sexual preference. Of those two, the better known one is Lord Longyang, favourite of a king of Wei state. When Longyang was out fishing with his patron, he threw back smaller fish on catching bigger ones; the thought then struck him that one day he might suffer a similar fate as the smaller fish, should a more handsome man than him come along and supplant him in the king's favour, and he fell to weeping. He need not have worried, because the king's response was to threaten death for anyone who made mention to him of handsome men. That anecdote secured immortality for Longyang.

* * *

Popular history reckons that the keeping of pretty boys began with the Yellow Emperor, but that attribution is unsound. Intimacy with boys is first referred to in the *Shang shu* [*Book of History*, earliest archival work in China], but only in the "Old Text" version forged by Mei Yi of the Eastern Jin dynasty, so that is also not reliable evidence. However, there is a sentence in the *Zhou shu* [*Book of Zhou*], compiled in the Warring States period, which says: "The beautiful man captivated his lord, estranging him from the trusty ministers", which may point to homosexuality.

The *Rites of Zhou* records an allegation of "unmanliness", which is glossed as being unable to have sexual congress with a woman, but throughout history there has been no instance of impotence being a ground for litigation. The classics are terse in their wording; I suspect that in fact it is homosexuality that is again implied here.

Now, wantonness in women derives from the natural instinct of sexual desire. In contrast, catamites have no such impulsion: they are all either initiated into the practice while still naïve, or induced to perform by threats or rewards.

The story is told of a certain grandee whose pleasure was to debauch young boys, but who was worried they might resist out of a sense of shame. So he bought a number of children under ten years of age, good-looking and clean of limb. When he indulged his nocturnal perversions with older boys, he had the younger boys attend on the sidelines with their lanterns, until by and by they became used to seeing the various obscene postures, and regarded them as natural and normal. After a few years, when they were somewhat more mature and could be slept with, they slipped easily into the role.

A priest in the grandee's service remonstrated with him thus:

"This practice is endemic in society, and you my patron cannot be forbidden to indulge, on condition that the boys should participate of their own free will. The sinfulness is lesser than that of consorting with prostitutes, but to deliberately and methodically undermine the purity of innocent children will, I fear, rouse the ire of the gods."

The grandee did not heed this warning, and later came to a sticky end. The Creator abhors gaining one's end through manipulation, all the more so in a case like this!

Incubus Debauches Boy

RSWW I 43

Liu Xiangwan contributed this.

Close to the sea in Cangzhou county there lived a shepherd boy aged fourteen who though from a peasant family was passing fair of complexion. One afternoon he woke from a nap on a grassy bank with the sense that something was on his back. But there was nothing visible to be seen, no substance to be felt, and no sound came in response to his question. He ran home in alarm to tell his parents, but they could not make sense of it. Days went by, and from the initial sensation of being embraced there followed the sensation of being fondled, then that of being battened on, and finally of being defiled. Thereafter these violations of the boy's person occurred at any time of day, yet as before his incubus betrayed no shape, no substance, and no sound. Sometimes presents of money and confectionery were left for the boy, though not in any great quantity. The local schoolteacher advised the boy's father:

"I fear this is a fox spirit. I suggest you hide a hunting hound away in your house, and when you hear the sounds of seduction taking place, throw the door open and set the hound loose on it."

The father did as instructed. The fox let out a howl, dived through the window, and danced about in fury on the roof, cursing the boy for deserting him. The schoolmaster raised his voice to address the fox:

"You have acquired supernatural powers, so you must be aware of what counts as normal in our world. Men and women enjoy each other because they are moved by mutual affection; nevertheless, it is all too common that they will vow in the morning to share the same grave, and when evening comes cross to another boat. The boy lover, for his part, falls even short of womankind, so when he joins you in bed, it is only sex for sale. When painted and perfumed he simpers and makes eyes at you, he is offered princely reward for his favours; as affectionate as a doting concubine, he then falls into your embrace. But when the moneybags bankrupts himself and the powerful man is stripped of his authority, the boy either waves blithe goodbye or stabs his patron in the back. They are as changeable as the weather, and have always been so.

"History records Xiao Shao's callous treatment of his patron Yu Xin, and Mu Rongchong's taking arms against his patron Fu Jian, those being only the most prominent examples. Great though the generosity of one side was, it was still matched by the scale of ingratitude of the other. So we see that to think of forming a bond with such people is like believing you can knead sand into a ball. Besides, the presents you have given are a drop in the ocean compared with the bounty those grandees bestowed, and yet you expect this lad's constancy to be as firm as a rock. Isn't that the height of idiocy?"

The schoolmaster's reproach was met with silence. After a

long wait, there came the sound of angry stamping of feet from the roof, and a voice uttered:

"Enough, enough, sir! I have only now come to my senses."

The fox spirit sighed loud and long, and was heard of no more.

Innocence

LYXXL VI 37

While making a journey by boat, Wang Lanzhou bought a houseboy on a quay. The boy was about twelve years old, very pleasing in countenance and modest in manner, and also able to read simple writing. He told Wang that his family had fallen on hard times when his father died. He had come north with his mother and elder brother to seek refuge with relatives, but they found no welcome, and were about to return south by boat. The money they had got from selling their belongings had run out, so their mother had to resort to selling him to raise their fare. Wang found on talking to the boy that his manner was bashful like a bride's, which already caused him some surprise.

Come bedtime, the boy stripped naked and sprawled out on the bed. Wang had actually bought the boy solely with the intention of employing him to do chores, but seeing him offer himself so compliantly, he could not restrain himself. Afterwards the boy buried his face in the pillow and wept quietly. Wang asked him, "Weren't you willing?" The boy answered, "No, I wasn't." So Wang asked him why he had taken the initiative. The boy replied:

"When my father was alive, he kept several houseboys, and slept with them all. If a new boy resisted out of shame, my father would whip him, saying: 'What do you think I bought you for? How could you be so gormless?' I took it that this was expected of a servant in serving his master, otherwise he was in for a thrashing. That is why I offered myself of my own accord."

Wang jumped up from the bed, exclaiming, "How frightful!" He made haste to bid his boatmen row with all their might, and overnight they caught up with the boy's mother and brother. He restored the boy to them, and presented them with fifty pieces of silver to boot. Still his mind was not at peace, and he went to the Temple of Compassion to genuflect to the Buddha and express his contrition. That night he dreamt of the guardian god of the temple telling him:

"You righted your wrong in no time, before the underworld recorder could enter it in his ledger. You need not worry about having profaned the Lord Buddha's name."

Revulsion
LYXXL III 14

A certain scholar bestowed his favour on a pretty boy; they were as devoted to one another as husband and wife. The boy fell ill, and on his deathbed heart-rendingly avowed his deep love. His hand still gripped the scholar's wrist after he breathed his last, so tightly that it had to be prised free. The scholar afterwards saw the boy in his dreams, then by lamplight and moonlight, and still later in broad daylight, but always some yards away from him. The boy did not respond when questioned, did not near when called, and retreated when approached. The constant frustration brought on brain sickness. A Taoist priest was called in, but his spells and incantations had no effect.

The scholar's father resorted to ordering a stay in a major Buddhist monastery, in the hope that the phantom would not venture onto holy ground, but the haunting persisted after the scholar moved in. An old monk said:

"The seeds of devilment—what we call mara—are many and varied, but they are all planted in the mind. Now, is this apparition truly the boy? If so, he is summoned up by your mind. Has the apparition just taken on the guise of the boy? Then it is a trick of your mind. You only have to empty your mind for that all to be obliterated."

Another old monk said:

"You are talking way above his head, my learned friend. Unless he learns how to strengthen his will, how will he be able to empty his mind? It is like describing the symptoms of a disease without administering the medicine."

He turned to address the scholar:

"Unclean thoughts tangle and spread like the roots of couch grass. The way to dispel them is similar to using a peg to unblock a hole: if the dimensions of the peg are equal to those of the hole, the foreign matter will surely all be cleared. You should think on these things:

"After the boy died, his corpse little by little stiffened, little by little bloated, little by little putrefied, little by little rotted away. By and by the corpse pullulated with maggots, the entrails burst, flesh and blood were reduced to a horribly discoloured gory mess. Imagine his features gradually changing, becoming unrecognizable, eventually turning as hideous as a raksha demon's. In this way the sense of horror will be engendered in you.

"Next consider this: If the boy had lived, he would have grown older by the day, his body become stout and stalwart, losing its maidenly charm. Little by little his face would sprout whiskers, little by little his beard would harden to sharp spikes, little by little his complexion would darken, his hair grow grey and his temples whiten; by and by his head would go bald, his teeth drop out, his back crook; he would wheeze and cough, have a runny nose and watery eyes, and end up so disgusting that you would not bear to be near him. In this way the sense of aversion will be engendered.

"A further thing to think on: Since the boy predeceased you, you survive to miss him. On the other hand, imagine yourself dying while he is still rosy-cheeked. There are sure to be those who will use inducements to entice him, or power to coerce him: there can be no certainty that he will remain chaste like a widow woman. Once he is lured away and shares another's bed, all that smutty talk, all that lewdness he indulged in for your benefit, will now be redirected to that other person to heighten his pleasure. The tender intimacies you once shared will have melted away like wispy clouds, leaving not a wrack behind. In this way the sense of wrath will be engendered.

"Yet another thing to consider: Suppose the boy were still alive, he might bank on your pampering of him to become domineering and hard to put up with. If you were to cross him, he would turn on you and curse you; if your funds ran low, insufficient to satisfy his demands, he would not hesitate to turn his back on you, and treat you with cold indifference; or he might be tempted by another man's wealth and status, desert you for him, and walk straight by you in the street. In this way the sense of resentment will be engendered.

"With these sundry thoughts seething in your mind, there will be no room to spare for anything else. It follows that the roots of love and desire will find no nutriment, and the devilment will abate of its own accord, without the need for exorcism."

The scholar followed these instructions, and for several days the apparition was sometimes seen, sometimes not. After several days more, it indeed disappeared without trace. When the scholar revisited the monastery after his recovery, neither monk was to be found. Some thought they had been a manifestation of a former Buddha, while others took the view that since the monastery offered open house to itinerant monks who came and went like floating clouds and flowing water, the two in question had taken wing to distant parts after this encounter.

24

IMPERSONATION

The dichotomy between the slighting of the actor's life as degraded and the enthusiasm for the theatrical production was unusually pronounced in traditional China: in fact the contempt for the acting profession was so strong that members of it were denied civil rights, while at the same time the ruling class showed as much devotion to the entertainment as the crowds for travelling shows. The Qianlong emperor himself was a great fan of the theatre. The precincts of his palace were supplied with numerous theatres, and his playhouse at the Summer Resort was equipped with extravagant mechanical contraptions like movable and storeyed stages. Spectacle was intrinsic to the Chinese theatre, all productions being operatic, and the plots no more realistic than those common to the opera as a genre, but the productions that Qianlong prescribed and occasionally himself devised were shorn of everything but spectacle, the contents being limited to glorifying loyalist virtues and castigating traitors and villains, much like the "model operas" masterminded by Madam Mao in the Cultural Revolution (1966–1976). Everything remotely subversive or immoral was banned from public performance, which meant that many of the stock items were erased from theatre bills, though just how far this writ ran in practice is an open question.

In the first of the following items the discussion of acting follows on from an explication of the Taoist formula for transcendence to a higher realm, which is fairly standard fare; the explanation of the actor's technique for making his performance lifelike, by contrast, shows rare understanding: it seems to anticipate the Stanislavsky Method. Nevertheless the concluding comment reflects the conventional view of the stage as a den of iniquity. The second item leads into interesting speculation on the source of dreams.

Transcendence

HXZZ II 35

The following was told me by Guo Shizhou.

Zhu Jingyuan made friends with a fox spirit while he was studying at the Imperial Academy. One day Zhu invited the fox to his house for a few drinks. The fox got dead drunk, and fell asleep amid the flower beds. When he woke up, Jingyuan asked him: "I have heard that when your esteemed kind get drunk, they resume their original form, so I covered you with a quilt and kept watch over you. In fact you did not change form. Why was that?"

"It all depends," the fox replied, "on the level of our spiritual attainment. At a superficial level of attainment we can transform our appearance only by creating an illusory persona, which is why we are liable to revert to our original form when drunk, or asleep, or in a panic. When we reach a profound level of attainment we can shed our original form in the same way that Taoist saints throw off their mortal coil. Once we have assimilated to the human sphere the human body becomes our proper form: there is no question of its changing."

Jingyuan expressed his desire to learn the fox's way to spiritual elevation. The fox answered:

"I am afraid that is not for you. It is easier for humans than for other creatures to cultivate the Way, because their vital constitution is pure, whereas that of other creatures is adulterated. Yet to *perfect* the Way it is easier for other creatures, because their mind is focused on the one goal, while men's minds run on other things. To refine one's outward form, one has first to refine one's internal constitution, and to do that one has first to purify the mind—isn't it said that the mind is the "commander of the aspirations"? When the mind is settled, the vital energies concentrate and the outer form consolidates. If on the other hand the mind fluctuates, then the vital energies are sapped and the form slackens. What the ancient immortal Guangchengzi told the Yellow Emperor was the true core of Taoism, not some fable that Zhuangzi put about. I can express it like this: Secluded in deep caves and dark ravines, eyes and ears shut to the external world, spirit rapt and breathing regulated, in harmony with Heaven and Earth, and with yin and yang, a hundred years passing like a single day. Now, is that something humans are capable of?"

Thereupon Jingyuan ceased to pursue the matter.

I was reminded of a certain imperial censor, who like me took his provincial degree in the twelfth year of the Qianlong reign [1747]. He put this question to an actor he was intimate with: "Given the large number of actors, how is it that you alone stand out?"

The actor replied: "For us actors to impersonate a woman, we have to *feel* like a woman; only then will our seductive charm come across to the audience and hold them spellbound. If we do not banish every last trace of the male mind, some hint of non-femininity will be betrayed. If that happens, how can we rival the allure of a real woman?

"When I step onto the stage in the role of a virtuous woman, I make my thoughts pure, so that even when I behave playfully I still preserve her virtue. If I portray a lewd woman, I make my heart dissolute, so though I may sit sedately I do not conceal her lewdness. If a highborn lady, my thoughts are noble and refined, so that even when wearing a plain dress her nobility is evident. If a lowborn woman, I am narrow-minded and repressed, so though dressed in finery her commonness will surface. If a dutiful wife, I soften my heart, so that though provoked to great anger she does not show vindictiveness. If a shrew, I make my thinking perverse, so that though she is clearly in the wrong her tone is not apologetic. All other passions and emotions, moods and attitudes, are likewise internalized, not taken as play-acting but as real, so that to onlookers it does indeed seem real life they are watching.

"Other actors try to behave like women without inhabiting

the female mind. They adopt women's postures but fail to master women's way of thinking. That is why I alone stand out."

Li Yudian commented: "Admittedly the background to this speech is disreputable, and the subject beneath our notice, yet it makes a vital point. Trivial in itself, it sheds light on great matters. No endeavour on earth can reach its acme unless the mind is wholly upon it, and conversely there is no enterprise that a dedicated mind cannot accomplish to perfection. When heart and mind are focused on a skill, that skill will be expert; when focused on a profession, success will be spectacular. Both in small things like Yi Liao's dexterity with the catapult and Lun Bian's crafting of the wheel, and in great things like the running of the empire by Yao and Shun's four chief ministers, the principle is the same. That concept and the notion of refining the vital constitution by first purifying the mind are mutually illuminating."

Beau Fang the Actor
RSWW III 6

The actor known as Beau Fang was top of the bill in his youth because of his looks and dramatic artistry, and was feted by the literati. In his old age he took up the trade of a pedlar in curios, and was often seen in the capital. He was known to have looked in the mirror and sighed dejectedly: "Alas that Beau Fang should look like this! Who would believe that I was once the talk of the town as I danced and sang with swirling skirt and fluttering fan!"

Ni Yujiang wrote a little poem about him:

Drifting about, down and out, his hair now thin,
He conducts himself in songs he sang of yore.
Where did the butterfly end up that Zhuangzi dreamed of?
Sad that only a sprig of faded blossom remains.

By his own account, Beau Fang came from a scholarly family. While a pupil at the local academy, at about thirteen years of age he had an extraordinary dream. He is hustled into a nuptial chamber lit by blazing candles, amid the blare of festive music. He finds he is wearing an embroidered dress and flowery cape, a headdress decorated with pearls; looking down he sees his shoes are tiny and bow-shaped: to all appearances he is a bride. He is bewildered and distraught, not knowing what is happening to him. His arms are held, and powerless to resist he is handed through the bed curtain and seated next to a man. Timid and ashamed, he breaks out into a sweat, which is when he wakes up.

He says that subsequently he fell into bad company, and forfeited his good name by entering the twilight world of the playhouse. He deduced then that his dream had portended a fate already determined. But Ni Yujiang told him:

"When in the old story Wei Jie asked Yue Guang about dreams, he replied that dreams were thoughts. You probably had this dream because you had long been thinking along those lines. Your fall from grace followed upon those thoughts and that dream. The consequence had its cause, and the cause was created in your mind. How can you attribute it to fate?"

In my view, the sinking of such people to degraded ways of life represents the outcome in this life of sins committed in a previous life; the element of predestination cannot be dismissed out of hand. What Ni Yujiang had in mind was only to point out that it is possible to reform oneself by an act of will. Later on Su Xingcun heard of this affair, and offered the following comment:

"Ji Xiaolan thought of cause and consequence in terms of past, present and future lives, warning of what might happen in the next life. Yujiang spoke of cause and consequence in terms of the power of thought, out of concern for the here and now. Though both views have something to say for them, I incline towards Yujiang's, because it puts a check on giving way to impulses."

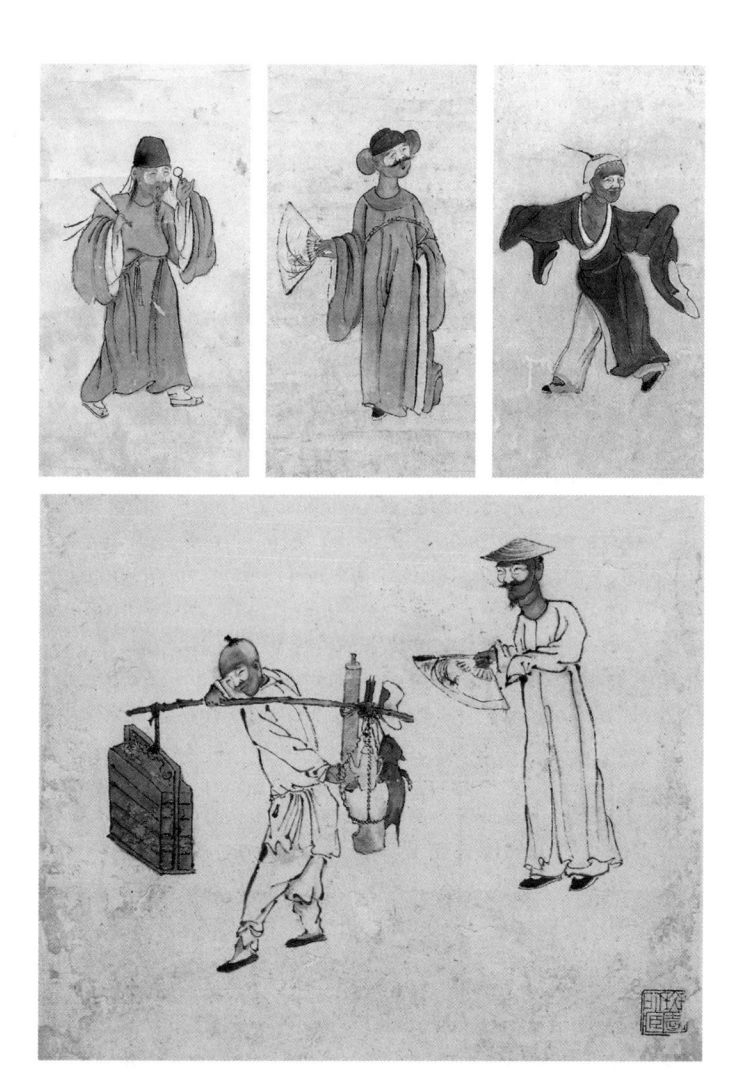

Figure 14. Stage performances as depicted by the famous Qing painter Ju Chao showing various actor's costumes. Reproduced by permission of the Art Museum of The Chinese University of Hong Kong from the collection of the Art Museum of The Chinese University of Hong Kong.

25

FRAUD

Hardly a day goes by nowadays when the media do not report some startling case of fraud, duplicity or counterfeiting in China. Since the abandonment of Communism as a creed, the new moral compass points only to making money, it would seem. From government and party officials demanding bribes and embezzling public funds right down to traders faking medicines, liquor, milk powder and even eggs, it looks as if there has been a return to old ways, ways that the following anecdotes illustrate in some specifics, but can also be inferred from the generalization that Ji Xiaolan makes elsewhere that it would be surprising to find even an honest ghost in the capital.

If an example for fraud had to be set, it was set at the highest level of provincial government and military command. It was practically routine for funds allocated to military campaigns to be filtered out on their way to the troops; instead we choose one civil case from the many that occurred in the Qianlong reign as an example. In 1775 Wang Danwang, the Treasurer for Gansu province, reported a prolonged drought, and proposed to the throne that an honorary degree be conferred on landowners who donated large amounts of grain to relieve the starving. In fact Wang took silver in place of grain, and the silver went into his own pocket and those of his subordinates who cooked the books for him. When in the following year inspectors from the capital were sent to check the district granaries, a layer of grain spread over raised platforms persuaded them that the promised deliveries had been made in full. Wang was promoted to be Governor of Zhejiang province in recognition of his compassionate measure. His fraud came to light six years later, by sheer chance; he was then executed and his possessions were confiscated. Along with him twenty-two officials complicit in the fraud were also put to death, and numerous subordinates transported to the hard frontiers.

The sequel to his case bordered on the farcical. From the list of articles Wang had previously offered as tribute to the throne, the emperor knew that he owned choice jade artefacts, and he ordered Wang's valuables to be shipped to the palace. Over a hundred prize objects listed by clerks at the time of confiscation were missing from the shipments: they turned out to have been appropriated by none other than Wang's superior, the Governor-General of Fujian and Zhejiang provinces! Compounding his felony, he also replaced gold bullion with silver. He was duly ordered to commit suicide.

Needless to say, Ji Xiaolan does not venture onto such dangerous ground here. He keeps to the workaday world.

Taking the Bait
GWTZ III 50

The deceitfulness of human nature is most blatant in our capital city. I once bought sixteen ink-slabs there, said to have come from the workshop of Luo Longwen, the best ink maker of the previous dynasty. The lacquer box they came in was dulled with age and well worn, seemingly a genuine antique. But when I came to grind the ink, it turned out to be moulded clay, dyed black; the frosting on the surface had been produced by keeping the slabs in a dark place. Similarly, in the twelfth year of the Qianlong reign [1747], when I sat my provincial level examination, I bought a candle in a small hostelry. It would not burn when I tried to light it: its core was dried mud, just coated with mutton fat.

My cousin bought a roast duck from a street vendor at a night stall. When he went to carve it, he found the skeleton intact, but the meat all gone. The skeleton had been plastered with clay and pasted over with a layer of paper dyed the colour of roast duck, and as a finishing touch brushed with oil. Only the feet and neck were genuine.

My house servant Zhao Ping paid 2,000 coppers for a pair of leather boots, of which he was very proud. One day there was a sudden downpour; he had gone out wearing his leather boots, but came back barefoot. It appeared that the boot legs were made of cartridge paper, crinkled and polished black, while the soles were made of cotton waste, glued together and bound in cloth.

Other fakes I could mention are of a similar kind, but they are of a trivial nature. Let me go on to tell of deceptions of a different order. An official up in the capital to await assignment to a post noticed a very comely and presentable lady living across the street from him. He found out that her husband was working in the provinces as a magistrate's private secretary; while he was away his wife lodged with her mother in the capital. Some months later, funerary white paper strips were stuck on this wife's door and the house was filled with weeping and wailing, for notice had reached them that her husband had died. The husband's spirit tablet was set up, offerings made, scriptures chanted, and prayers recited for his soul. A good number of mourners attended the ceremonies.

Soon this woman was selling off clothes, saying that the family was going hungry; she also let it be known that she was considering remarrying. The intendant official responded, was accepted, and moved in as son-in-law. After some more months passed, the husband suddenly came back: obviously his death had been reported in error. The husband raged, threatening to take the official to law. Mother and daughter begged and pleaded with him, and the matter was settled by the official being ejected and forfeiting his chests.

Six months or so later the official saw from documents in the office of the Metropolitan Police Superintendent that the same woman was currently on trial. It had transpired that the man who had turned up at the house was the wife's secret lover: the two of them had plotted to trap the official into surrendering his possessions. Their deceit was exposed only when the real husband did truly come back from the dead. You can see how the knavish trick of imposture gets more and more preposterous!

Another example concerns a mansion in the west city comprising some forty to fifty rooms that was let out at a monthly rent of twenty taels of silver. A certain person rented it for something like six months, always paying the rent in advance; hence the owner asked no questions. One day the tenant shut up and left without giving notice to the owner. When the owner went to inspect his property, there was rubble all over the place, and all the rafters had been removed; only the frontages onto the streets at front and back were left intact. It turned out that the mansion had both front and back gates; the tenant had set up a timber yard at the rear entrance where he sold material for house building. Secretly he dismantled the mansion's roof timbers, posts, doors and windows, and sold them off among the other materials. Since the back gate opened onto a different thoroughfare from the front gate, the demolition went unnoticed. That the whole framework of a house could have been carted away without detection was a feat that verges on the miraculous.

Looking at these half-dozen examples, the victims were either out to get something on the cheap or to cash in on a good thing. They swallowed the bait out of covetousness, so the blame cannot be laid entirely at the door of others. Qian Weicheng commented:

"If you can manage to protect your own interests in dealing with people in the capital, and not fall into their traps, you can count yourself lucky. Behind every apparent good bargain there is a snare. The city is full of masterly fraudsters and insatiable bloodsuckers, and there is no limit to what they will get up to. Easy pickings are not going to come to the likes of us."

A truer word was never spoken.

THE OLDEST PROFESSION

RSWW I 46

Qian the zither master contributed this.

Qian was a comical man, a real bag of tricks. Because he had purple patches on his skin, he was given the nickname "Flower Face Qian". He was hired to play the zither in the house of my tutor Qiu Wenda, and though I knew him for several years, I never found out where he came from or what his personal name was.

A gentleman up in the capital to wait for an appointment to office was staying in the guest house for his fellow provincials. He espied a woman standing in a gap in the back wall: she was very attractive, her clothes well worn but kept clean and tidy. He took a strong fancy to her. The manager of the guest house had a mother in her fifties who had formerly served in a grand house, and in speech and manners still observed a high degree of decorum. She frequently stood in for her son as receptionist. Judging her to be a woman of the world, this gentleman offered her a sweetener to arrange a rendezvous with the woman he had seen. She replied:

"I have never seen this lady, she may be new on the scene. I will try to make some enquiries, but don't set your hopes too high."

Ten days passed before she reported back:

"I have tracked her down now. She comes from a good family, and was only driven by poverty to overcome her shame and take up this profession. Because she is still fearful for her reputation, she will only come at dead of night and when the moon is hidden. She asks that you light no lamp, neither talk nor laugh, let neither servants nor fellow guests hear any noise, and do not detain her after the dawn bell has sounded. She would be satisfied with a present of two taels of silver for each night."

The intendant official complied with these conditions, and the affair went on for over a month. Then one night a fire broke out next door, causing the official to jump up in alarm. His servants rushed in to rescue his bags and trunks from the flames. One of them pulled open the bed curtain and dragged away the bedding. There came a howl and a naked woman tumbled out onto the floor. It was none other than the manager's mother! They all doubled up with laughter.

It should be told that the matchmakers in the capital are full of wiles and ruses. When an intendant official from the provinces makes it known that he wishes to take a concubine, their practice is to produce a good-looking girl for his inspection, but at the last minute surreptitiously swap her for an inferior girl, as is attested by the fact that matchmakers have been prosecuted when this has come to light. What happens is this: the girl is introduced with a shawl over her head, stands with her back to the lamplight, and conceals her face behind a fan, the deception being discovered only after the ritual of engagement is completed. In some cases the man so gulled reluctantly puts up with a bad job. The old woman in this story was familiar with these underhand local practices, and went to the length of playing the substitute herself.

Enquiries were later made of the neighbours on all sides, and they all denied seeing any sign of the young woman glimpsed in the gap of the wall. One person who heard Qian's story reckoned she must have been a sprite. My teacher Qiu Wenda's own opinion was that the old woman had hired a prostitute to turn the intendant official's head, as simple as that.

Monks Get up to Knavish Tricks
LYXXL III 13

South of Jing City there was a dilapidated temple, set apart from its neighbours, which had only one monk and his two disciples looking after its upkeep. To all appearances they were as slow-witted as any country bumpkin, and were entirely lacking in social graces; in fact they were as canny as they come. They bought pine resin on the quiet, ground it into powder, packed the powder in paper twists, and threw the lighted twists into the air at dead of night, so that their radiance could be seen far and wide. By the time people who had seen the glow arrived at the monastery, the monk and his disciples were sleeping soundly behind barred gates. They denied all knowledge of the manifestation.

Another trick of theirs was to secretly buy Buddhist stage

costumes, get themselves up as Bodhisattvas and Arhats, and on moonlit nights either stand on the temple roof or show glimpses of themselves under the trees by the temple gate. When this display similarly attracted attention, they claimed again that they had seen nothing.

On occasion someone would describe what he had seen, whereupon the monk would reverently bring his palms together and reply:

"The Buddha dwells in the Western Paradise—what would he be doing in this hole? Now that the government has put a ban on the White Lotus sect because they pretend to work miracles, you come along with your far-fetched stories to tar us with the same brush. What have we done to offend you?"

The result was to confirm people in the belief that what they had seen was a true manifestation of the heavenly host, and almsgiving grew by the day. All the while the fabric of the temple deteriorated also by the day, but not one broken tile or rotten rafter was replaced. The excuse the monk gave was:

"The people round here love nothing better than spreading idle gossip, making out there have been all sorts of weird goings on in this temple. If we did the temple up, it would only give the rumour-mongers more to go on."

Over the course of the next decade the monk and his disciples accumulated a handsome nest egg. Then out of the blue a band of robbers turned their attention to this temple, tortured the monk and his disciples to death, and made off with all their money. When the local officials investigated, they discovered in their trunks the pine resin, stage costumes and suchlike: only then did their deceptions come to light.

This took place in the last reign of the Ming dynasty. My great-great-grandfather commented: "These monks made a fine art of deluding people by pretending not to delude them, but the reward of their cleverness was their own demise. So you could also call their cunning schemes the height of stupidity!"

The Attraction of Buddha
GWTZ III 34

An itinerant monk set up a market stall in my home prefecture of Hejian to sell medicines. He placed a brass figurine of the Buddha on a table and filled a tray with different pills. The Buddha had one hand stretched out as if reaching for something.

When a customer came along, the monk first addressed a prayer to the Buddha, then presented the tray to the figurine. If the customer's illness could be cured, a pill leapt from the tray into the Buddha's hand; if none of his pills would work, they all stayed on the tray. The demonstration was totally convincing.

In time someone discovered that back in the monastery where he was lodging the monk was making iron filings. They deduced that half the pills in the tray must be packed with the filings, and half not, while the figurine's hand must be made of magnetite just coated with metal. On testing, that indeed proved to be the case, and the trickery was exposed.

[...]

MERCHANTS

According to basic Confucian doctrine, merchants come last in the four social classes, namely scholars, farmers, artisans and merchants. At the time the ideology was formulated that low grading was understandable: evidently, life could not go on without farmers and artisans, while the contribution of merchants was ancillary. Secondly, Confucian morality was diametrically opposed to the pursuit of self-interest, which most concretely meant making material gain or profit, and that denigration was extended to the livelihood which depended on making a profit out of barter. Disesteem and distrust of merchants by the intellectual class persisted down the ages, which goes to explain why as soon as merchants acquired enough wealth they educated their sons to become officials, and also why the central government both maintained a monopoly over the production and distribution of certain key commodities and regulated market prices for others (besides drawing revenue from the former). Foremost among the government monopolies was that of salt, which everyone needed for preserving foodstuffs; sale of licences for the distribution of salt was a big money-spinner for the authorities, as was the operation of the system for the merchants: "salt merchant" more or less became a byword for extreme wealth.

By the mid-Qing period, government control of commerce had been freed up: appointed brokers for market trading were largely abolished, and central government requisition of such things as grain and textiles could be replaced by cash payments. Urbanization led to more people being dependent on buying what they needed from merchants rather than producing the same for themselves. Hence trading networks expanded, and more and more goods were shipped over long distances, "shipped" being the operative word, for goods were mostly transported by water. Market operations also became more complex, with big operators speculating on rises and falls in the price of commodities.

Both the following items have to do with Shanxi merchants in particular. One of them concerns a prominent merchant intent on buying for himself a post in government, thus to exercise as opposed to being subservient to authority; the other is set in the milieu of rank-and-file traders whose success or failure was balanced on a knife-edge. Generally speaking, traders were organized in clans or confederacies based on cities or provinces, and had guildhalls and warehouses situated in transport hubs over wide areas. The merchants of Shanxi province operated the biggest network. It extended from the province's central geographical position westward into Turkestan, where Ji Xiaolan was exiled, and eastward to Peking-Tianjin where he lived, which is possibly why that and not some other group like the one based in Anhui featured in his writing. In addition to dominating the trade in goods, Shanxi merchants controlled commercial capital, operating banking houses which dealt in bills of exchange. Their merchant princes kept in with government by donating correspondingly princely sums to support major military and civil enterprises.

A Precarious Life

LYXL V 3

Shanxi merchants conduct their business far and wide. They are apprenticed to their trade in their teenage. Not until they have amassed a certain capital for themselves do they go back to take a wife, and after their marriage they resume their enterprise abroad. As a general rule they return home to see their family every two to three years. If the terms of trade are adverse, or they get caught up in some complicated affair, they sometimes have to stay away for as long as ten or twenty years. It is also not uncommon for their money to run out and their clothes turn to rags; ashamed then to go home, they drift from pillar to post, and are not heard from again.

A young merchant named Li, having found himself destitute in the Tianjin area, was adopted by a fellow provincial called Jin, whose name he took. His family back in Shanxi had lost track of him, and he was rumoured to be dead. Back home both his parents died, and his wife was left without support, so was taken in by an uncle on her mother's side. This uncle's home was in another county, and on top of that he took his whole family with him on trading expeditions which led him north and south along the waterways: the result was that from one year's end to another Li's wife had no settled abode.

Li, for his part, also thought his wife must have died, as he had had no letters from home. His adoptive father Jin proposed that he should remarry. Coincidentally his wife's uncle died on his travels, and his family ended up in Tianjin. Mrs Li's aunt thought she was too youthful to remain a widow, and planned to find a Shanxi man for her to marry, so that she could eventually return to her native place. Afraid that potential husbands might be put off if they knew her niece had no mother to fall back on, this aunt pretended that she was her own daughter.

Both parties secured the good offices of a matchmaker, and the matter was soon settled. The couple had their suspicions awakened when they drank together from the wedding cup, but having been separated for eight whole years, they could not be sure. It was not until they retired to the nuptial chamber that the truth came out. Li was angry that his spouse had been in a hurry to remarry before there was sure proof of his demise, and fell to cursing and striking her. The commotion roused the whole Jin household from their beds. Mr Jin called through the window:

"Did you have sure proof of your wife's death before you remarried yourself? Homeless and always on the move, she waited eight years for you before she married: surely you can understand she had no other choice?"

Li had no answer to that. The two were reconciled, and resumed their marital relationship.

We have read about "a broken mirror pieced together again" in ancient times, but never since books were written have I heard of a husband remarrying his original wife and a wife remarrying while preserving her virtue intact. My aunt's husband Wei Keting personally witnessed this happening.

A Welsher

LYXXL IV 14

A Shanxi merchant took rooms in the Probity Guest House in the capital. His dress, retinue and carriage were all resplendent. He gave out that he was intending to secure a government appointment by donating a large sum of money to the court, as countenanced by statute. One day a poor old man presented himself at the gate, but the merchant's servants declined to announce him. Only by refusing to go away did he obtain admission. The merchant received him ungraciously, and after the requisite cup of tea was served, did not engage him in civil conversation. When the old man hinted that he had come to seek assistance, the merchant scowled and said: "I haven't even sufficient funds at present to purchase office, how could I afford charity to you?"

The old man waxed indignant, and went on to relate for all to hear how in times gone by the merchant hadn't a penny to his name, and for ten long years had looked to the old man for his next meal; how the old man had lent him a hundred taels of silver to make a start in trade; and how he had built up his present wealth. Later on the old man had been dismissed from office and had taken to the road as a vagabond. Hearing now of the merchant's arrival in the capital, he had been delighted at the prospect of finding his feet again. He had no great expectations: he would be satisfied if he could get back the sum of money he had helped the merchant with in order to repay some of his debts and take his old self back to his native place to die.

The old man continued to weep after his recitation ended,

but the Shanxi merchant was unmoved. At this point a fellow lodger in the guest house intervened. Styling himself a Mr Yang from Jiangxi, he bowed to the merchant and asked: "Is what this old man said true?" The merchant reddened and replied: "I cannot deny it, but I regret my finances are insufficient to pay him back."

Yang said: "You, sir, will soon take office, and you will find it easy enough to borrow money to tide yourself over. If someone were now to offer you a loan of a hundred taels of silver, not to be repaid until a year hence, and without charging a farthing of interest, would you be willing to repay this person with it?"

The merchant grudgingly replied: "Of course."

Yang said: "In that case, just sign your promissory note. I have the silver here."

The merchant had no option but to bend to the general will and make out his note of hand. Yang accepted it, opened a battered suitcase, took out the stated amount of silver, and handed it to the merchant, who sullenly passed it on to the old man. Yang proceeded to order a celebration banquet for the old man and the Shanxi merchant to partake of. The old man was in high spirits, while the merchant only moodily sat the meal out. The old man departed with his thanks, and some days later Yang moved on elsewhere, not to be heard of again. Subsequently the merchant discovered that one hundred taels of silver were missing from his trunk, though the locks had not been tampered with and the sealing strips were still intact, making it impossible to accuse anyone of stealing the money. A fox fur jerkin was also missing; in its place was a pawn ticket to the value of two thousand coppers, roughly equivalent to the sum Yang had paid for the banquet. The merchant then realized he had been taken for a ride by a magician. His fellow guests were quietly amused at his expense. Having been put to shame, he gave up his lodgings. Where he went was anybody's guess.

BANDITS, BRIGANDS AND ROBBERS

England had its highwaymen, America had its outlaws, Australia its bushrangers, in Germany Schiller had the material to write a big play called "The Brigands", and so on. Doubtless all of those were feared and abominated in real life, but in legend some were elevated to the status of heroes. So it was in China. The biggest legend of all was that of the 108 honest and upright men and women whose being forced into banditry spawned the long novel Shuihu zhuan (variously translated as All Men Are Brothers, The Marshes of Mount Liang, Outlaws of the Marsh, etc.) and many operas. We learn from Ji Xiaolan that in his time some local bandit chiefs were also credited with having a code of honour, though we also gather that they were very exceptional. The battlements built on top of residences in the north which he mentions somewhere show that bandits were a real and present danger.

The particular reasons for banditry being rife then were (a) bands formed from the remnants of defeated Ming dynasty army units and (b) the precarious livelihood of working people. Members of the British mission headed by Lord Macartney in 1793, seeing China with fresh eyes, observed that economic resources were stretched to the limit: no patch of land left unsown, no fields left fallow, no opportunity for business neglected. They were struck by the huge disparity between the luxury of the corpulent elite and the penury of the emaciated masses, whom they saw whipped into line, and were especially shocked at the sight of the corpses of abandoned babies in rivers and at the roadside. The poverty was no fault of the Qianlong emperor, who had shown great generosity in relieving famine and had had notable success in *increasing agricultural production, but ironically the resultant growth in population largely offset those gains.* Overpopulation became a matter of serious concern to certain Chinese scholars, who foresaw, like Malthus, dire consequences. In 1793 even the emperor was moved to issue a "Proclamation of Concern" expressing alarm at the enormous growth in population since the census taken in his grandfather's time, and the consequent swallowing up of farmland: now "the producers of food are few, and the eaters of food are multitude," he wrote, and concluded, "I am extremely disturbed!"

The White Lotus rebellion broke out in 1796, before Ji Xiaolan published the last volume in his collection. Uniting the disaffected and desperate under the banner of a messianic cult, this rebellion spread so widely as to shake the pillars of the state; corrupt generalship of the imperial armies delayed suppression for seven years. The verdict of the new Jiaqing emperor was: "the people were forced to rebel by the oppression of the authorities."

Robbers Get Their Own Back
GWTZ I 39

Mencius said, "Confucius taught that we should never go to extremes." By that he did not simply mean that we should not go overboard in correcting faults—no, the sage's concerns were more far-reaching.

Laozi said, "The common people do not fear death, so what is the point of trying to frighten them with the threat of death?" The fact is not that the common people do not fear death, it is that when they know death is inevitable they cease to be afraid. And when that point is reached, there is nothing they will shrink from.

When I was young I heard tell of a grandee whose house was burglarized. He posted a reward for the capture of the perpetrators. Well within a year the robbers were rounded up, and they all confessed their guilt. Yet the grandee's animus against them was so virulent that he liberally bribed their gaolers to torture them in every possible way while they were awaiting sentence: they were strung up off the ground, deprived of sleep, so tightly shackled that they could not go to the lavatory, with the result that vermin infested their trousers and gnawed at their groin. The only thing not done to them was to starve them, to cheat them of a quick death.

The robbers conceived an undying hatred of the grandee. They conferred among themselves along these lines: the penalty for robbery was beheading for all those involved; likewise the penalty for gang rape was beheading for leaders and accomplices alike. The sentence for both crimes being prescribed, there was no possibility of upgrading the punishment to dismemberment. So when they were brought before the judge they voluntarily confessed to having violated all the women in the household. The clerks did not enter that into the court record, but since all the culprits were vocal in making this confession, and everyone in attendance heard it, knowledge of their claim could not be suppressed.

People hostile to the grandee supplied elaboration, saying that the sentence of death was adequate retribution for robbery, and the reason why his venom for the robbers was so profound as to cause him to lay out a lot of money to have them tortured into the bargain was precisely because of the other crime of rape. The affair created a hubbub, and the grandee having no means of quelling such suspicions, his family's reputation was ruined, and regret came too late.

The robbers could not blame the grandee for being executed for their crime; neither could they blame him for being flogged to extract a confession or being chained up in gaol: that treatment is condoned under the law. What they could not put up with was the illegal cruelty inflicted upon them. If you throw a stone too hard against a wall, it will bounce back and hit you. To incur ineradicable ignominy for the sake of temporary gratification, was that not due to going to extremes? Evidently the sage's concerns were indeed far-reaching.

Grave Robbers
GWTZ I 50

When my maternal grandfather An passed away his family was still very well off, and my uncles determined to bury quantities of gold and jewels along with him. They were warned that ostentatious wealth invites unwelcome attention, but took no notice. As a safeguard they constructed sentry boxes outside the boundary walls of the graveyard, and had sturdy watchmen patrol the perimeter. The sound of their clappers and bells responding to each other was heard all night long. It was pointed out that this was "planting a flag to summon robbers", but they still took no notice. It was not long before the grave was robbed.

What had happened was, the robbers had waited till the watchmen went to sleep in the daytime, draped themselves in capes made of plaited grass as camouflage, scaled the boundary wall and concealed themselves in the shrubbery. Hence their entry was not detected. After night fell they drilled into the coffin with an auger: when the clappers were struck twice, they bored twice; when the clappers were struck thrice, they bored thrice. So ironically it was because of striking the watch that the sound of boring could not be heard. The robbers lay low until dawn broke and the sound of clappers and bells ceased, at which point they scaled the wall and made off. So their exit was not detected either.

The first news my grandfather's family got of the robbery was that the robbers had broken the corpse's jaw to get at the pearl as big as the pit of a longan fruit in his mouth. They reported the robbery to the authorities, and extensive searches were made, without result. My uncles all had the same dream of my grandfather telling them:

"In my previous life I owed these three men money. They have now claimed compensation, and they will not be caught. Still, I never hacked them to pieces, while they desecrated my corpse and cut open my jaws. For that the perpetrator should get his deserts. I have been granted redress in the courts of the dead."

A month or so later, one of the robbers was arrested, and indeed it was he who had prised out the pearl. The pearl had been corroded by the reek of the corpse, and was so discoloured as to be worthless. The names of the two others came to light, but despite a reward of 1,000 taels being offered for their arrest, they evaded justice. That shows that my grandfather's dream message was correct.

Outlaws' Exploits
RSWW II 41

As the concluding remark indicates, outlaws were credited with phenomenal physical feats that link them with the tradition of the swordsmen and "knights errant" celebrated in early fiction. Here we are introduced to two kinds: the first gentlemanly in manner and presumably honourable in his exploits, the second callous and degenerate in his deeds.

* * *

My grand-uncle Zhang Xuetang contributed this.

"When I was about seventeen years old I held a midnight feast with a few friends. It being autumn, the crabs were plump and fatty, the fresh wine was ready for drinking, and we were all in a merry mood, when suddenly we looked up to see a man standing before us in the moonlight. He wore a conical straw hat on his head, was clad in a stone-blue gown, and shod in shoes embroidered with a cloud design. He clasped his hands in salutation, and said: 'Though I am a mean and uncouth person, I have a passion for good wine and fine crabs. I beg you to grant me the lowest seat at your table.'

"We were all nonplussed, and not knowing how to react otherwise, invited him to be seated. When we asked his name, he simply smiled. Neither did he utter a word as he tucked into his food and quaffed his wine. Having drunk and eaten his fill he abruptly rose to his feet, saying: 'That I should have the pleasure of your company today was written in our fate. There is no telling when our paths will cross again, or whether I shall be able to return your generous hospitality.'

"Thereupon he launched himself into the air. Where he landed was a mystery, for no sound came from the roof tiles. A bright object was left behind on his chair, which turned out to be a silver ingot, whose value roughly matched what the feast had cost. Some said he was a wizard, while others guessed that he was a master thief."

I myself incline to the latter view. When I was small I saw the likes of Li Jinliang [see next item], and his physical feats were of that order. I also heard tell of the legendary Du Erdong's band (he was a major brigand in my county of Xian). They were known to sneak into someone's house at night, wait until the womenfolk had gone to bed, threaten them with a knife to stop them crying out, then roll them up in their bedding and carry them under their arm over the rooftops. Just before the dawn bell rang they would roll the women up again and return them by the same route. To the abducted women it was like an unbelievable dream.

One night the master of a house where the wife had gone missing planted some men in her bedroom. When the brigand returned, they broke cover and attacked him. The brigand fended them off with his sword while he dumped the woman back on her bed. He moved with dazzling speed, and vanished before anyone could look round.

We might see such brigands as an offshoot of the daring soldiers of fortune we read about in the Tang dynasty tales.

Honour among Thieves
RSWW III 18

In my home county of Xian the brothers Li Jinliang and Li Jinzhu were famous robbers. One night Li Jinliang dreamt of his late father addressing him thus:

"You must know that some robbers come to a bad end and

others do not. Taking the possessions of corrupt officials gained by duress or threats; of big crooks and swindlers got by seizure or trickery; of family members appropriated by deceit and by the backstairs; of friends and relations through pressure and cajolery; of wily servants and cunning bailiffs acquired by graft and rake-off; of big merchants and plutocrats amassed by exploitation and charging killing interest; and of each and every person who profits from other people's misery—all those ill-gotten gains are fair game for the robber. Even killing the most monstrous miscreants brings no harm, because in any case they are abominated by Heaven. But as for basically good people, whose possessions are honestly acquired, they enjoy Heaven's protection: if you prey upon them you offend against Heaven, and those who do that come to a bad end. You two brothers have robbed a chaste widow, causing mother and child to rail at the injustice, and incensing the gods. If you do not make amends, calamity will tread on your heels."

Indeed, a year or so later both brothers were captured and condemned to death. Li Jinliang, knowing that he was doomed, told this story to Shi Zhenru, who was his prison overseer. Zhenru is from my home county, and he relayed it to my father to support his contention that there is honour among thieves. He also passed on the words of the robber chief Li Zhihong:

"I spent thirty years in the saddle as a highwayman. I acquired a lot of booty that way, and saw plenty of others do the same. At a guess, some two or three out of ten of them were caught, which meant the majority were not. As for those who violated women, though, I can't think of even one who got away with it." So he habitually held that up as a warning to his followers, and incidentally confirmed our belief that Heaven does not let the crime of ravishment go unpunished.

BANDITS DESTROY BANDITS

LYXL IV 2

In Urumqi farmers mostly irrigate their fields from nearby streams, and build their dwellings next to their fields; hence they do not form communal settlements. As a rule, people throw up a house in an isolated spot, like the "one family village" that Du Fu refers to in a poem. Since they are not subject to corvee labour, nor is their land surveyed, as long as they pay the standard tax on thirty mu [ca. five acres] they can in fact farm land ten times that area. That state of affairs is common in the back country.

A party of soldiers from Jimusa set out into the hills to hunt. They came across a house where the doors and windows were tightly shut, but there seemed to be rather a lot of horses milling about in the yard, all saddled up. The soldiers guessed that the house had been taken over by bandits, so they surrounded it and shouted for them to come out. Seeing that the soldiers were there in strength, the bandits abandoned their gear, broke through the cordon and fled. Since the bandits would be desperate enough to fight to the death, the soldiers did not pursue them. When they entered the compound they found it strewn with human remains; there were no signs of life. The only sound was a kind of whimpering, which on investigation turned out to come from a boy about thirteen who was suspended, completely naked, over a window frame inside. After they freed him from his bonds he told them:

"The bandits came four days ago. My father and elder brothers fought them, but were overpowered, and all of us were trussed up. Each day they took two of our family to the stream, washed them clean, dragged them back, sliced off their flesh and roasted and ate it. Seven or eight of us, men and women both, were finished off that way. Today they prepared to move on. Having washed me, they were on the point of eating me on the spot when one of them raised his hand to stop them. I don't understand their Eleut dialect, but judging by their gestures it seemed they decided to dismember me, and give each member a portion to eat as jerky while they were on the move. Luckily you soldiers turned up and they left me alone. That's how I'm alive today."

The boy rambled on and on, weeping copiously. The soldiers felt sorry for him, took him back to camp with them, and employed him on sundry chores. In time the boy revealed that there were still things buried in the cellar of his farmhouse. The camp commander had him point out the place, and a large hoard of silver coins and clothes was unearthed. It emerged from close questioning of the boy that his father and brothers were all highway robbers. The places where they carried out their robberies had to be where the post road skirted a hilly area. When they saw one or two wagons travelling without escort, and no help was at hand for miles around, they broke from cover and killed the drivers, loaded the corpses on the wagons and drove deep into the hills. When the wagons could go no further, they smashed them up with axes and tipped the pieces along with the corpses, bundles and bedding into a deep gully, loading the merchandise onto the horses. Pressing on until the horses in turn could go no further, they threw their harnesses into another gully, and turned the horses loose to run wild. Then they divided the merchants' goods up and humped them back home along untrodden ways. The place where the robbery was committed could well have been a hundred miles from their base.

Having stored their booty in their cellar for one or two years, some of them masqueraded as hawkers and went round towns selling the goods in markets. Consequently their crimes went undetected for many years. What they had not foreseen was that one day their whole family would be wiped out by Mongol bandits. The boy was exonerated on account of his youth, but later died from a fall off a cliff while herding horses, hence the family line came to an end.

I dealt with this case when I was aide to the commanding general, and judged it not worth pursuing in view of the fact that the robbers were already dead. Looking back on it now, it seems that considering how skilfully they covered their tracks, there was no immediate prospect of arresting that band of robbers. The advent of the Mongolian bandits was in retribution for the bloody murders they committed. Though the bandits' appetite for human flesh was insatiable, a boy was left to tell the reason why his family brought about their self-destruction. It seems that divine and natural justice were at work here, not mere accidence. I have forgotten the family name of the robbers, but when the boy fell from the cliff, the official report on his death gave his personal name as Qiu-er.

ADDENDUM: Ji Xiaolan's letter to his younger cousin Xiulan (*Family Letters*, FLP edition, p. 158)

Our local brigand chief, Lu Hunan, has now been hunted down, his hideout razed, and our folks can henceforth sleep easy in their beds. Zhili being the neighbouring province to the imperial capital, it was insufferable that such brigands should dare to flout law and order and pile crime on crime. The governor-general was justifiably enraged, and swore not to rest till he had exterminated them. However, a brigand chief will have many henchmen; since only the leaders have been captured, one has to guard against those henchmen retaliating. Seeing that the militia you organized were bold enough to back up the county force in capturing the said brigand chief, there must be many good fighting men in their ranks. You should keep up their spirits with speeches on bounden duty, and encourage them to step up their training so as to be in readiness for reprisals by those outlaws.

In response to the magistrate's call for support, on this occasion you did not hesitate to order your militia to draw their swords to rid the vicinity of this scourge, showing admirable zeal for the public good. But after all, you are not a military man, and would do well to avoid provoking the ire of desperadoes. Their like are not afraid of any punishment the law might mete out, and words cannot describe how vicious they can be.

Our uncle Mei'an told me about a brigand chief in Fujian province called Pockmarked Cao. His band's stock-in-trade was killing and plundering. Though there was a government price on his head, such was his reputation for brutality that no one dared go after him. However, a certain scholar named Sun, who lived in a village close to the brigand's lair, secretly laid a plot with his fellow villagers: they would ask Cao to the Spring Festival banquet, make him drunk, tie him up, and deliver him to the county yamen; the reward would be shared all round. All the villagers signed up to the plan. So in the first month of the new year they invited Pockmarked Cao to the banquet as their special guest. He fell for their trick and was duly taken captive. The full complement of able-bodied men from the village escorted him by boat to the yamen.

The outlaw band waited up until dawn for their leader, but when he had not returned by then they knew that something had gone wrong. It did not take them long to find out that he had been brought down by Sun, and they conceived an implacable hatred for him. That same night they stole into his village with explosives and set the place ablaze. All the thirty houses were burnt to the ground. Sun himself escaped from the flames, but still fell into the brigands' clutches: they tied him up and threw him back into the fire. No more than two or three out of ten in that village survived. A truly frightening thing!

When in future you take on something for the public good, you should be careful not to overreach yourself. You would be well advised to avoid actions likely to bring repercussions.

28

PHYSICAL PROWESS

The kind of physical prowess Ji credited to outlaws is celebrated on a broader canvas in Chinese folklore and fiction, not to mention the modern cinema. Some feats described are not far from the truth. Here Ji Xiaolan personally attests to the authenticity of one seemingly miraculous ability.

Professional skills, here represented by those of the tiger hunter, really did reach amazing levels, as the Macartney mission witnessed, but in legend and fable they inevitably reached ineffable heights. The god of carpenters Lu Ban, for instance, was said in one legend to have made a model kite that stayed aloft for three days, but that must have been child's play for him, because in another story he constructed a model carriage complete with horses and coachman to please his mother, so lifelike that it started into motion when his mother was seated therein. The snag was it never stopped going, so his mother was forever lost to him.

The cook Ding occupied a more classical setting, featuring in the book of the Taoist luminary Zhuangzi. His skills in butchery had been honed to the point of becoming unconscious: when he dismembered an ox carcase his blade was guided not by sight but intuition, finding by itself the divisions between muscles and joints so accurately that it met with no resistance. He boasted that after cutting up thousands of oxen his blade was still as sharp as when it was first lifted from the grindstone.

Our author's informant is more modest in his claims for the tiger hunter, though his account of the hunter's delivery of the coup de grace takes some swallowing. As for the wolf trapper, few would want to test the credibility of his exploits.

A Remarkable Athlete
LYXL IV 20

In my home district there was a man named Ding Yishi. He had great strength and agility, and practised unarmed combat and leaping as well. A high jump of twenty or thirty feet was child's play to him, and he could manage long jumps of similar distance.

I had the good fortune to know him when I was a boy, and once prevailed upon him to demonstrate his prowess. He had me stand in the middle of the passage way through a gate lodge. When I faced the front entrance, he stood outside looking at me; when I turned to face the back entrance, there he was standing outside looking at me again. He repeated that feat seven or eight times: each time he must have cleared the ridge of the roof in one jump.

Some years later, Ding Yishi was passing through the town of Dulin in the south of the province when he fell in with a friend, who invited him for a drink in a tavern next to the bridge, and they both got tipsy. Standing on the river bank, the friend said, "Can you jump to the other side?" Straightaway Yishi launched himself in the air and landed on the opposite bank. The friend beckoned him to come back, and without hesitating Yishi jumped back again. What had not been foreseen was that the bank was on the point of giving way: Yishi had not noticed that cracks had opened up on its brow at the water's edge, and when his feet landed on it, it crumbled into the river with the impact, taking him with it. Being unable to swim, he was carried downstream with the current. His leaps took him some feet above the surface, but only straight upwards: they brought him no closer the bank. When his strength was exhausted, he drowned.

The greatest hazard in life is overconfidence. Those who put their trust in wealth perish through wealth; for those who trust to power, power will be their downfall; reliance on native wits or physical strength will have the same result. The reason is, confidence in an asset encourages you to take risks. My venerable colleague Tian Songyan addressed a poem to a fine walking stick he bought in the imperial summer hill resort; it ran:

> You are with me on morning strolls and moonlight jaunts
> For even on level ground I fear to trip and fall
> If through relying on you I threw caution to the wind
> I might tackle rugged climbs and bite the dust!

That is the voice of experience: it should be taken as one's constant guide.

The Tiger Hunter

HXZZ I 56

When my cousin Ji Zhonghan was Magistrate of Jingde county in south-east Anhui province, a marauding tiger in the environs of the county town wounded several hunters, while evading capture itself. The local people petitioned: "This menace will never be removed unless Hunter Tang from Huizhou is appointed to the task." (The erudite Dai Zhen, from Anhui himself, notes that in the Ming dynasty a certain Tang was killed by a tiger soon after he married. His wife later bore his child, and she swore to him: "If you can't kill tigers, you are not my son; if your own sons can't kill tigers, they are not my grandsons." Hence generation after generation of Tangs were expert tiger catchers.)

Ji Zhonghan thereupon dispatched an assistant to Huizhou with a commissioning fee. His emissary returned to report that the Tang family were sending two of their most expert men, who were already on their way. When they arrived at the yamen, Ji saw that one was an old man with a snowy white beard who had a hacking cough. The other was a teenager. Ji was greatly disappointed, but as a holding action ordered refreshments for them. The old man discerned from Zhonghan's expression that he was put out; he went down on one knee and announced:

"I hear the tiger is holed up only a few miles from the town. The meal can wait till we have gone and disposed of it."

Zhonghan then ordered a yamen runner to lead the way. The runner would not go further than the mouth of the valley. The old man scoffed: "Don't tell me you are scared with me around!" Halfway down the valley the old man said to the youngster: "The brute is still asleep. Give it a shout to wake it up." The youngster imitated the tiger's roar. True to form, the tiger emerged from the trees and charged straight at the old man. He had a short-handled axe in his hand, about eight or nine inches in length and half that measure in depth. He raised his arm and stood stock still in the tiger's path. When the tiger leapt at him, he bent his head to dodge it. Having sailed over its target, the tiger lay lifeless on the ground, streaming with blood. Inspection showed that it had been split open from jaw to tail.

Zhonghan rewarded the hunters generously on their return. The old man explained that he had taken ten years to strengthen his arm and another ten years to perfect his eyesight. His eyes did not blink even when brushed with a feather duster, and a strong man could suspend his whole weight from his raised arm without budging it.

As Zhuangzi said, "It is practice that builds up superhuman prowess; native dexterity is only a start." Indeed, I have witnessed the courtier Shi Sibiao write a long strip of characters in the dark, absolutely identical to the same written in the light. I have also heard that Li Duna, Vice-President of the Board of Punishments, would cut up a sheet of thin paper into 100 one-inch squares, write the same character on each square, overlay the squares and hold them up to the sunlight: not one brush stroke varied by a hairbreadth. These feats come from practice, nothing else; there is no trickery or sleight of hand involved.

Wolf Trappers

HXZZ IV 35

A strip of foreshore near Cangzhou given over to salt boiling extends north-south for some hundred miles. The soil is so saline that crops cannot be grown there. Weeds stretch as far as the eye can see, as in the wastelands beyond the frontiers. Hence wolves favour it as a place to make their lairs.

The wolf trappers dig out a pit several feet deep and three to four feet wide, and cover the pit with a board. Holes as big as a large cup are bored in the board, somewhat like the holes for the neck and hands in the wooden cangue prisoners wear. The trapper takes with him a puppy or piglet, crouches in the pit, and pricks the animal to make it howl or squeal as the case may be. Any wolf which is lured by the sound is sure to thrust its paws through the holes to get at the decoy. The trapper then grabs the paws, stands up and carries the board with the wolf on it back home. Being unable to use its teeth or claws because of the barrier of the board, the wolf is helpless.

The danger for the trapper is that he could be set upon by a pack of wolves, in which case he might be killed and eaten. If a lone wolf spied him, it would press its snout to the ground and howl; the whole pack would then be drawn to the spot as if by command. That is also an ever present hazard for ordinary travellers.

[…]

29

JESUITS IN CHINA

The Society of Jesus had the mission to spread the gospel worldwide. It turned its attention to China in the late sixteenth century. Being aware that Chinese society was at least as civilized as their own, the Jesuits adopted the strategy of overcoming initial resistance by demonstrating kinds of knowledge that their hosts did not have, particularly in science and technology. To that end, the Society dispatched as missionaries polymaths of extremely high intellectual calibre. Chief among them was the sagely Matteo Ricci (1552–1610). Not the least of his means of securing the recommendation of scholar-officials in Guangdong for his admission to the capital was to display a map of the world which showed continents that they did not even know existed. Once permitted to set up in Peking, Ricci and his learned colleagues and successors were able to prove to the intellectual elite the validity of Euclidean pure and applied mathematics, and— crucially—the superiority of European astronomical calculations, which were vital to correcting the agricultural Chinese calendar. Imperial approval was given in 1629 for them to equip and direct a Western Observatory, which they continued to do for two centuries.

Over the course of the first four reigns of the succeeding Qing dynasty, Jesuit priests amply proved their worth in such practical fields of cartography, surveying, architecture, instrument making (including clocks, telescopes, crystal-lensed spectacles), and even in the design and manufacture of artillery. Emperors also employed them as personal physicians and court painters. Giuseppe Castiglione (1688–1766) stands out in the latter respect: he served as court painter to three emperors, making numerous portraits of them and their entourage, and illustrations of Manchu military victories, both of which kinds used the novel technique of perspective. In that role he enjoyed a close relationship with his royal masters, a privilege shared by a select few of his predecessors and contemporaries. Physical monuments to the Jesuit endeavour remain in the form of the observatory, and more romantically the ruins of the European-style stone palace complex built in the grounds of the Yuanmingyuan imperial park by Michel Benoist from 1751 to 1783. The Catholic Southern Church mentioned below, one of the three big churches built in Peking, still stands, though transformed by rebuilding.

Given all these contributions, it would seem that the Catholic mission should have basked in imperial favour. Indeed, the Kangxi emperor in particular was tolerant of its religious activities, which the Jesuits and other orders that joined them pursued as actively as circumstances allowed. Since Buddhism and Islam already enjoyed that freedom, despite having also been imported to China, there seemed no objection to Roman Catholicism being treated likewise. But that toleration was not to last. It had been facilitated by the accommodation of the Jesuits to Chinese rites, and their stress on the correspondences between Christian and Confucian ethics. However, on the insistence of the Franciscans and Dominicans that such rites as the veneration of the Chinese emperor as "Son of Heaven" and ancestor worship, to give but two examples, were heretical, the Pope in Rome sent delegations to Peking to require the precedence of sacred over temporal authority. Kangxi understandably took that as an insult, and responded in 1717 by proscribing missionary activity and sending obdurate priests packing. His successor Yongzheng, a devout Buddhist, enforced more drastic measures. Thereafter Jesuit priests were allowed to stay on at court only as foreign experts. Following these signs of disapproval from on high, the Christian religion was widely and openly denigrated, and even "Western Learning" fell into disrepute. Since in any case the Chinese belief in their superiority in all things had led the literati to argue that Western science had merely capitalized on knowledge that had originated in China and filtered through to the West in ancient times, they would have noted with approval the thesis of Antoine Gaubil (1689–1759), also in China, that the basis of European astronomy was a system perfected in Zhou dynasty China in the first millennium BC. It is little wonder that Western Learning had to start all over again in the nineteenth century, when entry was made by force of arms.

Now we can come to the question of what Ji Xiaolan made of all that. As general editor of the catalogue for the Compendium, he either wrote himself or closely scrutinized and approved the entries therein. Some thirty publications mainly of a scientific nature by Jesuits or their baptized Chinese collaborators are reviewed. Tribute is paid to the excellence of European scientific methodology: the thoroughness of experiments, the high standard of proof required, the continuous refinement of theory (all absent from Chinese practice). At the same time, the suspicion is raised that because the primary aim of the priests was spreading their gospel rather than altruistically imparting scientific knowledge, they held back key elements in order to keep power in their own hands. That was to impute to the Jesuits the Chinese custom of "liu yi shou" (keeping a trick up the sleeve), by which the master of a craft made sure he would not be outdone by his apprentice. In fact the Jesuits seem to have passed on their knowledge without reservation when allowed to do so by papal doctrine, as when they introduced the Copernican theory of the earth revolving round the sun as soon as the papal ban was lifted.

More negatively, the reviews castigate and ridicule the Christian religion, dismissing it as derivative of Buddhism, presumably because it shared with authentic Buddhism the principle of universal compassion and with popular Buddhism the notion of paradise and hell. The reviews also reiterate the view that Western science originated in ancient Chinese science, which was more or less obligatory, since both the Kangxi and Yongzheng emperors had declared as much. One example given was the use of a gnomon to make accurate astronomical calculations, as set out in a work attributed to the eleventh century BC.

So we have to conclude that Ji Xiaolan's impression of the foreign experts at court differed little if at all from that conventional for those in his position and of his time, that is to say, a generally dim one. Since he obviously had easy access to them, it is disappointing that he does not tell us more about them, but his primary purpose is to tell of the uncanny, and uncanniness was not what the foreigners were about.

Jesuits Deluded
RSWW IV 37

My tutor Qiu Wenda heard this from Shi Dongcun.

A police lieutenant who enjoyed reading and had a lively curiosity was on duty one night over the capital's Xuanwu Gate. He took a walk along the battlements to enjoy the cool air, and when he got to the east side of the gate tower he saw two men leaning over the parapet, engaged in conversation. He knew instinctively that they were fox spirits. Holding his breath, he kept them under observation.

One of them pointed to the north, saying:

"In the Ming dynasty that was the site of the Paramount Academy; now the Westerners' Catholic church stands there. Those Westerners truly cannot be matched for their know-how in calculating the movements of heavenly bodies and their ingenuity in manufacturing machines, but their religion is no more than a variation of the Buddhist scriptures, dressed up with some Confucian principles. I once went to eavesdrop on their services. Whenever discussion turns to things they can't account for, they evoke the mysterious ways of God as a way out. So their gospel has made little or no headway. At the same time, when we look at their practices, we realize their designs are extremely devious."

The other said:

"You speak of their deviousness, while I would rather criticize them for their stupidity. They crossed the oceans at the bidding of their ruler with the express object of converting China to their religion. Any true measure of our society would show that was nothing but a pipe dream! Yet in the wake of Matteo Ricci, they have come in an unending stream, and will never stop until they realize their ambitions. Isn't this a madcap idea?"

The first one continued:

"It is not only they who are stupid, those who established the Paramount Academy were also extremely stupid. The traitorous eunuchs had taken power at court, and were just on the lookout for gaps in the defences of upright officials so that they could impeach and expel them. Yet those selfsame officials gathered in the academy to engage in free and open debate, so giving the eunuchs the handle against them of forming political factions. They were all rounded up in one fell swoop. Who did they have to blame but themselves?

"Looking back on our history, Confucius alone was worthy to have a following of three thousand disciples. Mencius admitted he was inferior to Confucius, which is why he had only a handful of disciples, people like Gongsun Chou and Wan Zhang. The Song dynasty Neo-Confucians lacked the moral standing of Confucius, yet they still gathered hundreds and thousands of followers to themselves, bringing birds of different feathers together. The consequence was that they split into separate factions who warred among themselves, leading to the fall of the dynasty. Then in the late Ming dynasty, the scholars who formed the Donglin School ignored the lessons of history, and through their pursuit of illusory fame invited real disaster. When we now mournfully look out on the site of the academy they founded, can we refrain from blaming those worthies?"

They were just turning to face each other to share a sigh when they caught sight of someone behind them, and they melted into thin air.

Shi Dongcun commented: "While we all flock to embrace current trends of thought, detached fox spirits privately decry them. Are we wrong, or the foxes wrong?"

Figure 15. Rebuilt after a fire in 1775 with a gift of 10,000 taels of silver from Emperor Qianlong, the Catholic Southern Church in Peking was located within a short walk of Ji Xiaolan's house. Photograph by Eva Hung. The photograph below shows the façade of the church around 1990.

The Super Weapon
LYXL I 13

In the Song dynasty they had something called the Super Bow, actually a giant crossbow. Its string was cocked by resting the stock on the ground and depressing the lever with the foot, and its bolt could penetrate steel armour at three hundred paces. Another name for it was the Conquering Bow, as used by Hong Mai of the Southern Song dynasty in the title for an examination essay he set, namely "An Inscription for the Conquering Bow". The Southern Song armies were able to resist the Jin invaders largely thanks to this superior weapon. Military law decreed that every bow must be accounted for: if any could not be carried away by retreating troops, it had to be broken into little pieces on the spot, so as to prevent the enemy gaining knowledge of its mechanism and reproducing it. When Kublai Khan destroyed the Southern Song, he obtained the design and used the bow in his victorious campaigns. But by the time of the following Ming dynasty the knowledge of the bow's manufacture was lost: there only remained an illustrated manual reprinted in the *Yongle Encyclopedia*. The trouble was, this manual supplied a separate drawing for each component part of the bow, just giving length and breadth measurements and the pattern of tenon and mortise joints, without any illustration of the whole assembly. I spent entire days together with Zou Yixiao, Vice-President of the Board of Works, trying to work out how it fitted together, but got nowhere.

I intended to make a copy of the designs and hand it to the Westerners at court to work out, but my late teacher Liu Wenzhong said:

"The purposes of the Westerners are inscrutable. Take for instance the 'borrowing root' system of mathematics: this was originally a Chinese system that was transmitted to the West, which is why it was called 'oriental reckoning' in those countries. But now when we want to learn their own mathematics, they perversely refuse to fully disclose their methodology. Since this crossbow is a superior weapon of our unique invention, how do we know they won't steal its design, and stall us by pretending they don't understand how to make it work? Since the Hanlin Academy holds a copy of the *Yongle Encyclopedia*, it is quite possible that in time to come one of our own experts will solve the problem. Why do we have to seek help from foreigners?"

So I and Zou Yixiao desisted. It says in the *Book of Songs*, "It takes a wise old pair of eyes to see farther than the horizon." My teacher was truly a man of great discernment!

Superior Firearms

LYXL I 12

Mr Dai Suitang and my late father graduated together in the fifty-second year of the Kangxi reign [1713]. After Mr Dai was dismissed from his post as magistrate in Shandong province, he was employed as our family tutor. He said his father was very clever and inventive, and enjoyed pitting his wits against the Westerners. While serving at the Imperial Observatory he clashed with Nan Huairen (the Westerner in charge of the Observatory) and was demoted to a post in Tieling, Liaoning province, where he settled, hence my tutor's native place is given as Tieling.

Mr Dai said that when he was young he saw his father design and make a type of musket: it was shaped like a mandolin; the powder and shot was all packed in the breech, which was opened and closed with a wheel device; the firing mechanism consisted of two interlocking levers. When the trigger was pressed, one lever deposited powder and shot in the barrel, and the second lever struck a flint which ignited a spark and fired the gun. After the gun had been fired twenty-eight times, the powder and shot was used up, and it had to be reloaded.

Mr Dai senior planned to make a gift of his invention to the military, but he dreamt of a man taking him to task:

"The Lord of Heaven cherishes life. If you release the design of this weapon and it comes into general use, none of your descendants will survive."

Mr Dai's father took fright and abandoned that idea.

At this point in his discourse my tutor looked aside at his nephew Binyan and asked:

"Do you still have that gun at home? You should go and fetch it, so we can all get a look at it."

His nephew replied:

"When I was studying at the Board of Revenue, the son of fifth brother stole and pawned it. It can't be traced now."

Whether it is truly lost or is hoarded away as a prized possession, it is impossible to say. In any event, we can all agree that this was a remarkable weapon.

The Manchu duke A-Gui took up the theme. He told how in the campaign to crush the Mohammedan revolt in Ush [1765], his forces formed up in two wings at a distance of roughly six hundred yards from the enemy stronghold. Whenever his two field commanders rode across from one wing to the other, bullets fell around them, luckily without hitting them. They estimated the range of the enemy musketry at no more than sixty yards, which meant they should have been well clear. The fire must therefore have come from snipers concealed in nearby gullies, they assumed, but their scouts found none, which was perplexing. It was only after the stronghold fell and prisoners were interrogated that they learned the Mohammedans possessed two muskets whose range was over a third of a mile. These two weapons were found and tested, and the claim was proved right. Both commanders were given one of them. One commander later died on campaign in Burma, and his musket was lost without trace. The second musket is still kept in the other commander's home. Its design remains a secret to this day.

* * *

The Westerner named here as Nan Huairen was the Belgian Jesuit Ferdinand Verbiest (1623–1688). After he and Adam Schall (1591–1666) just survived the attacks of rabid Chinese xenophobes, Verbiest succeeded to Schall's post as chief astronomer, in which connection his clash with Dai's father must have occurred. Verbiest's skill in making astronomical instruments was extended on the emperor's order to designing artillery needed to put down the warlord Wu Sangui's rebellion. His light and heavy field guns, first tested in 1675, were instrumental in securing Kangxi's victory. Dai's father's invention of a revolutionary kind of firearm seems to have been undertaken to rival Verbiest in weaponry. European armies were still using single-shot flintlock muskets with an accurate range of only about 100 yards well into the nineteenth century, so old Mr Dai must have been a genius if the description of his invention was at all accurate.

The point of more general interest, however, is what became of the firearms discussed: we learn that they all found their way to the cupboards of individual collectors, from where they never emerged. The lack of technical progress in Chinese weaponry which the Macartney mission noted is thus partially accounted for. More broadly, it was in any case deliberate state policy to suppress advances in weapons technology so that rebel forces had no chance of being better armed than imperial troops. Come to that, very little of the scientific and technical knowledge introduced by the Jesuits went beyond court circles. Independent advances in the physical sciences would also have been severely impeded by the total ban on learned men forming groups or societies to pursue joint interests, for fear of dissidence arising: so no equivalent in China to the institutes of engineers and scientists which were by then flourishing in the West.